White Liberal Identity, Literary Pedagogy, and Classic American Realism

White Liberal Identity, Literary Pedagogy, and Classic American Realism

PHILLIP BARRISH

The Ohio State University Press
Columbus

Library of Congress Cataloging-in-Publication Data
Barrish, Phillip.
White liberal identity, literary pedagogy, and classic American realism
/ Phillip Barrish.
p. cm.
Includes bibliographical references and index.
ISBN 0–8142–1010–4 (alk. paper)—ISBN 0–8142–5145–5 (pbk. :
alk. paper)—ISBN 0–8142–9088–4 (cd-rom)
1. American fiction—White authors—History and criticism. 2.
Liberalism in literature. 3. Didactic fiction, American—History and crit-
icism. 4. Ethnic relations in literature. 5. Race relations in literature. 6.
Group identity in literature. 7. Sex role in literature. 8. Realism in literature. 9. Race in literature. I. Title.
PS374.L42B37 2005
810.9'358—dc22
2005015171

Cover design by Design Smith.
Type set in Adobe Garamond
Printed by Thomson-Shore, Inc.

9 8 7 6 5 4 3 2 1

For Sabrina and Eli

CONTENTS

Acknowledgments

I could not have written *White Liberal Identity, Literary Pedagogy, and Classic American Realism* without the help and support of many people. Beginning the book during a difficult time in my professional life, I relied on the keen minds and generous hearts of the following colleagues at the University of Texas at Austin more heavily than even they probably realized: Sabrina Barton, Joanna Brooks, Evan Carton, Ann Cvetkovich, Alan Friedman, Kurt Heinzelman, Susan Sage Heinzelman, and Lisa Moore.

Others at UT-Austin and elsewhere who made important contributions to the project include Nancy Bentley, Jeffrey Berman, Brian Bremen, Douglas Bruster, Scott Derrick, Wai Chee Dimock, Alyssa Harad, Martin Kevorkian, Dominick LaCapra, Caroline Levander, Susan Lurie, Laura Mandell, Helena Michie, Donald Pease, Peter L. Rudnytsky, and Jeffrey Williams. Todd Onderdonk's research assistance was prompt and helpful.

Dominick LaCapra and Cornell University's Society for the Humanities provided an ideal working environment. I want to thank the other 2002–2003 fellows at the Society for offering intellectual stimulation and friendly collegiality. I also want to thank the staff at the A.D. White House: Mary Ahl, Linda Allen, and Lisa Patti. James Garrison, Chair of the English department at UT-Austin, and Richard Lariviere, Dean of the College of Liberal Arts, each arranged for additional funding to help make my year at Cornell possible. At The Ohio State University Press, Heather Lee Miller was an entusiastic early supporter of the project and Eugene O'Connor expertly oversaw production of the actual book. A version of chapter 2 appeared in *American Imago: Studies in Psychoanalysis and Culture*. Permission to reprint is gratefully acknowledged.

It would be an understatement to call Sabrina Barton's contributions to the project invaluable. She read, commented on, and talked with me at length about every chapter. The book's more successful portions are really her work as much as mine. She is my closest colleague. This book is dedicated to her and to our son, Elijah Barton Barrish.

Introduction

White Liberal Identity, Literary Pedagogy, and Classic American Realism brings literary works from the turn of the twentieth century face to face with dilemmas and paradoxes that currently define white liberal identity in the United States. More specifically, it uses close analysis of works by canonical American realists such as Henry James, Edith Wharton, Mark Twain, and Kate Chopin to "read" white liberal identity in contemporary contexts that range from an affirmative action court case, to the liberal arts classroom, to debates about our nation's role in the world. In this book, I offer fresh critical and classroom approaches to realist texts at the same time as I strive to develop new analytic and pedagogical tools for probing contemporary liberalism.

The project originated several years ago in my attempt to resolve a classroom dilemma, one whose structure may sound familiar to others even if the details are specific to my own university. In 1996, the Fifth Circuit Court of Appeals issued its decision in an important affirmative-action case, *Hopwood v. Texas.* As interpreted by the Texas attorney general, the ruling effectively banned any use of race-based affirmative action in the state's public universities. Although the *Hopwood* ruling would be superseded in 2003, when the U.S. Supreme Court would reinstate a limited use of affirmative action, at the time the case had an extremely high profile at the University of Texas at Austin. Like many other teachers on campus, I had discussed the case and its implications more than once with my students. After the appeals court ruling became known, a faculty/student group to which I belonged sent out an email suggesting a specific day during the following week for us to hold new classroom discussions on the latest *Hopwood* developments and on the importance of affirmative action.

One of the classes I was teaching at the time was an upper-division course on Henry James and Edith Wharton. James and Wharton are two writers about whose work I care passionately, although in truth I have always felt a bit uncomfortable about my investment in figures who are today so associated with elitism. At the time that I received the faculty/student group's suggestion to devote class time to the appeals court's decision and to the attorney general's interpretation of it, I was already behind on my syllabus. Moreover, I did not want to eliminate or ignore reading that I had been exhorting my students to keep up with. On the day in question, we were scheduled to discuss several short stories by Wharton, including "Souls Belated, "Roman Fever," and "*Autre Temps . . . ,*" works that I had grouped together with an idea of teasing out something about Wharton's way of intertwining representations of travel, sexuality, and national identity. As inclined as I usually would have been to join in a concerted effort by teachers (and friends) across campus to focus on a topic that I did see as urgently important, and which was poised to have an immediate impact on campus, I nonetheless felt reluctant to abandon those stories.

Upon rereading "*Autre Temps . . . ,*" however, something unexpected happened. I began to see that the story spoke with force and complexity to certain aspects of the campus and courtroom controversy around *Hopwood* that many white students, in particular, seemed to find especially difficult to grasp. Or rather, *I saw that I could actively enable* the story to so speak, given the discursive climate of the campus at that time.

Perhaps, in typical left-liberal fashion, I was trying to have it both ways, trying to satisfy two contingents within the discipline that were also mirrored in my own conflicting impulses to continue investigating the canonical aesthetic objects on which the course was "supposed" to be focused, but simultaneously to use my classroom as a space for immediate social and political critique. In any case, rereading "*Autre Temps . . .*"before class, I was struck anew by Wharton's depiction of the ambiguous social exclusion of the returned divorcée Mrs. Lidcote, even though the supposedly "freer" and more tolerant upper-class New York world to which she comes back, after having been gone for twenty years, now explicitly disavows its former practice of marginalizing divorced women. As chapter 1 will explore in more detail, Mrs. Lidcote's continued sense of social exclusion appears irrational within the terms by which her society had come to understand itself; it is also impossible to attribute her sense of exclusion to anyone's conscious intentions. When students read "*Autre Temps . . . ,*" they often express frustration that the happy marriage and reunification with her daughter and friends that seem sincerely proffered to Mrs. Lidcote remain unconsummated. Students tend to blame the unsatisfying ending on Mrs. Lidcote's own self-destructive unwillingness to move on from the past, or else they say, more sympathetically, that she has been too "damaged" by prior decades of shunning to do so.

Many white undergraduates at UT-Austin have a hard time grasping how, or even that, racism and racial exclusion could still have powerful effects on campus, for several reasons, including how much they hear about the university's commitment to diversity. I asked students in the seminar to concentrate on unraveling the factors that interfere with the happy, redemptive ending for which Wharton's story seems to be preparing us—most of all the paradox by which Mrs. Lidcote continued to be "cut" or excluded by a society that believed itself to be allowing her free entry—while also keeping in mind issues presented by the recent *Hopwood* decision. I hoped that focusing our interpretative process on the problematic ending of "*Autre Temps . . .*" might assist all students in the class, whatever their racial identities, in moving toward new cognitive, linguistic, and affective tools for grasping how racial exclusion could possibly still be a structuring facet of our university, despite the presumably good intentions of nearly everyone involved. We had an unusually successful class session, during which every student in the room spoke. In their end-of-the-term evaluations several students singled that session out as the most thought-provoking of the semester. We had achieved, I felt, something along the lines of Kenneth Burke's "perspective by incongruity."[1]

White Liberal Identity, Literary Pedagogy, and Classic American Realism seeks to expand upon the critical and pedagogical strategy (it cannot be called a methodology) that germinated in that 1996 class session. But if I wish to probe liberal identity in such contemporary contexts as affirmative-action court cases, the liberal arts classroom, the war on drugs, and national discourses of guilt and innocence, then why appeal to literary works from one hundred years ago? Further, in the case of a juxtaposition such as that between Wharton's short story and the legal case *Hopwood v. Texas*, do the important differences in genre (fictional and non-fictional) and—even more glaring—in subject matter not compound the problem of anachronism? After all, Wharton's "*Autre Temps . . .*" focuses on a well-off middle-aged white woman whose marginalization within New York high society links to historically specific, as well as region- and class-specific, sexual mores. If my goal is a fuller and more nuanced perspective on tensions surrounding race-based affirmative action at a twenty-first-century public university, then why read *this* story, which turns on changing attitudes toward divorce and divorced women among wealthy WASPs of the early twentieth century? Would there not be other texts—whether literary or nonliterary—with more obvious pertinence to issues raised by *Hopwood v. Texas?*

The question is a crucial one for each of this book's chapters, and each chapter tries to respond in the context of the specific juxtapositions there elaborated. Let me be clear from the start, however, that the particular works by Wharton, James, Twain, and Chopin selected here—and, for that matter, American realism as such—by no means constitute *the* crucial or necessary literary texts to explore if we wish to improve our grasp of present-day white liberalism. Others who wish to explore American liberalism in conjunction with literary materials would make (and have made) their own selections. First and foremost, I chose the literary texts treated here for the reason that each one seemed to me, as an individual reader and as a teacher, interestingly and unexpectedly productive for the patch of contemporary terrain upon which (or next to which) I wished to set it. That said, I will briefly sketch here three justifications—which might be broadly defined as historical, literary/rhetorical, and pedagogical—for using works from the heyday of literary realism to deepen our understanding of contemporary modes of liberal identity.

Literary criticism that seeks some underlying deep structure to American liberalism almost always gives primacy to literary works of the mid-nineteenth century.[2] There are analytic consequences, however, to centering one's consideration of American liberalism on New England's Renaissance writing. First among these is that individualism (whether celebrated or subverted) necessarily becomes the center of attention. I do not argue with the presumption that, if one wishes to speak about American liberalism over several centuries, the unifying idea must be individualism, or rather individualism and its discontents. Moreover, the American Renaissance does remain our most canonical literary period, and it is difficult to overestimate the influence of its brilliant writers—Ralph Waldo Emerson, in particular, but also, for example, Walt Whitman—on the development of American liberal thought and identity. Nonetheless, I will attempt to show in what follows that foregrounding literary works of the realist period, rather than of the mid-nineteenth century, can provide valuable alternative perspectives specifically on challenges and inner conflicts confronted by left-thinking people today. One neither can nor should separate individualism as a concept, experience, or desire from the aspects of contemporary liberal subjectivity that I will examine, but a difference in emphasis can yield fresh insights.

Although detailed historicization—whether of literary realism or of contemporary white liberalism—is not my primary project here, if one were seeking to construct a historical genealogy for the antagonisms within present-day liberal subjectivity to be investigated below, then the late nineteenth and early twentieth centuries would mark a crucial period of emergence. Middle-class professionalism rose to prominence around the turn of the twentieth century, and that professionalism found itself confronted by large urban slums, which were inhabited by what many began to see as a permanent underclass. The United States became both a global and an imperial power. Private and public research universities took shape. Modern academic disciplines formed. Several factors around the turn of the twentieth century complicated the tenets of classic American liberalism—that is, freedom and individualism—both as concepts and as plausible possibilities. The frontier, as Frederick Jackson Turner famously announced in 1893, was "closed." The Jeffersonian yeoman farmer, as agrarian populists recognized (and as the realist fiction of Hamlin Garland rendered vivid), could decisively be viewed as more myth than actuality, a change due to the radically shifted economic and technological environments in which farming occurred (railroad monopolies, for instance). Indeed, more and more people worked for increasingly rationalized and ever-larger corporate and government entities, living what Martha Banta has called "Taylored lives." The expanding advertising industry took as its project the shaping of human desire. Moreover, if, as Toni Morrison has demonstrated, the idea and existence of racial slavery were essential to white American understandings of freedom and individualism, then without slavery as an ever-present contrast the notion of "liberty" itself became less clear-cut.[3]

One might aptly consider the century lying between the literary and nonliterary materials addressed by *White Liberal Identity, Literary Pedagogy, and Classic American Realism* as constituting a long historical moment. One might describe a trajectory from, say, William Dean Howells's to Richard Rorty's liberalism, moving through the Progressive movement into the New Deal, flirting with communism but then becoming solidly anticommunist (the Cold War liberalism whose high point was the nineteen fifties), and so on. One could plausibly situate Howells and Rorty as marking two points of a long moment in white American liberalism, with the realist writer near the beginning of this historical moment and the contemporary philosopher and political writer near (possibly) its end.[4] Moreover, certain rough but striking sociohistorical parallels between the turns of the twentieth and twenty-first centuries add extra resonance and suggestiveness to juxtapositions of materials from then and from now. Such rough parallels include, for example, the end of Reconstruction with its great strides and even greater promises and, almost exactly one hundred years later, the effective end of the Civil Rights era, with *its* great strides and even greater promises. In addition, at the turn of the twentieth century, the mass immigration of what were regarded as racial and ethnic "others" from eastern and southern Europe challenged and complicated the overlapping identity categories of "white" and "American," as is also happening today in the United States with its unprecedented levels of Latin American and Asian immigration. Finally, the previously unimagined scale and role of national corporations in the

American economy in the early twentieth century anticipated the power of international corporations and global business today.

The possibility of situating all of this book's often incongruous material within a plausible historical account helps to provide grounding for arguments derived via closely read juxtapositions of what often appear to be (and in important senses *are*) quite divergent texts and events. In addition, that these diverse materials might be viewed as part of one extended historical moment should help counter any impression that my juxtaposition of canonical literary works with recent nonliterary materials is simply another way of claiming the universal human significance of great works of literature. Indeed, new historicist readings have taught us that shared cultural logics may often be traced in places where one would least expect to find them, including in seemingly disjunctive spheres of discourse—for example, in economic and literary discourses.

Nevertheless, this study does not itself engage in drawing historically based connections, analogies, or trajectories between now and an earlier nodal point in white liberal identity. It will be clear throughout that I remain indebted to those who perform the critical and scholarly work of historiography, but in themselves the chapters to follow have little or nothing to offer about the turn of the twentieth century *as* a historical locus, whether to point out its close continuities with or its marked differences from our own. I do not offer contextualizing information for the literary works analyzed here regarding the specific "'historical situation' in which they were produced" or initially received, despite the fact that doing so is expected under the disciplinary protocols currently prevailing in literary studies.[5] As Stephen Knapp has observed, it has become virtually an article of doxa within left-oriented criticism, including "a range of feminist, Marxist, and New Historicist treatments of canonical texts," that "foregrounding the actual circumstances from which a certain work emerged has a necessary or intrinsic relevance to ethical and political action in the present."[6]

Yet *White Liberal Identity, Literary Pedagogy, and Classic American Realism* emphatically does aim for "relevance to ethical or political action in the present." Rather than foregrounding the social and historical circumstances within which literary realism emerged, however, this project strives to achieve such relevance through taking instrumental advantage of the dense complexity these literary texts present. Literary works by such artists as James and Wharton are famous for how they artistically trace and circumscribe the densely overcrossing lines and cracks of social and emotional "relations," while still preserving those relations' multidimensional intricacies. Henry James commented that, "really, universally, relations stop nowhere, and the exquisite problem of the artist is eternally but to draw, by a geometry of his own, the circle within which they shall happily *appear* to do so."[7] I suggest that we can heuristically use the complicated "geometry" of the circles such artists draw to help us reframe and thus reread certain facets of contemporary liberal identity that are otherwise hard to bring into focus. Indeed, we might think of the dense textual circles classic realist literature provides not merely as frames but as *refractive lenses*—lenses bulging (like those of the classic bookworm's glasses) with the thickness both of what James called "the art of fiction" and "the air of reality." These literarily "thick" lenses can, as it were, break up the light differently, revealing different angles, surfaces, and contiguities of our social present than are usually apparent. Wharton's portrayal in "*Autre Temps . . .*" of a social exclusion that remains counterrational and unspoken (indeed unspeakable), but nonetheless effective, refocuses for us the hazy, murky terrain of "liberal" racial exclusion in the post–Civil Rights era.

Pedagogically, juxtapositions such as those explored here can, I believe, help empower students and teachers to view the work of analyzing literature as offering the possibility of an unexpectedly proximate social and political payoff. The approach that this book develops offers a new answer to that perennial student question, which is often posed most forcefully by intelligent, motivated students committed to progressive political agendas: the question, that is, of why so much valuable time should be devoted to detailed analyses of canonical American literature, especially by elitists such as James and Wharton. One of the more radical implications of the New Critical pedagogy, particularly as it evolved during the period of the G.I. Bill, was to democratize the study of literary aesthetics beyond those with detailed knowledge of philology and literary history. The literature-liberalism juxtapositions presented here aspire to the same democratizing impulse, although directed not toward aesthetic evaluation but toward what has become the defining problematic of American literary studies since the 1970s—that is, the relationships among literature, identity, and politics. In this book, I wish through demonstration to remind students and teachers that closely reading literature—even literature that may seem anachronistic or "irrelevant"—can sometimes improve our leverage over contemporary modalities of identity and power without our needing first to elaborate historical genealogies. The same attentive, complex, and creative readings of literary texts that we develop in our classrooms and writing assignments may, at least in some cases, be self-consciously turned or "troped" to shed new light on even the most intricate dimensions of the social world that permeates our classrooms and our selves.

In *The Other Henry James,* John Carlos Rowe has argued for using "Henry James in the classroom to offer students more nuanced accounts of the social conflicts shaping modern societies."[8] His strong readings reveal

Henry James's sometimes surprising engagement with social, cultural, and political critique. For Rowe, there is a "critical dimension" in James's writing that effectively challenges many of the same "modern Euramerican attitudes toward gender, sexuality, race, and ethnicity that have been so profoundly criticized by contemporary cultural critics" of our own day.[9] In contrast to Rowe's book, *White Liberal Identity, Literary Pedagogy, and Classic American Realism* does not seek to situate James or other American literary realists as anticipating our own progressive insights about the evils of racism, sexism, and homophobia. Rather than finding moments in which realist writers of another century seem in accord with us regarding society's injustices, my interest lies above all in how the intricate geometry of social and psychological relations delineated in their texts can improve our apperception of certain *crises* that beset contemporary liberal identity, particularly internal or structural crises. Such crises include those everyday junctures at which the white liberal is forced to encounter his or her own contradictions.

Several different threads of this study, for instance, tug at a split in the liberal white subject that is "constitutive of contemporary white racial formation": the split between a strong identification *against* openly racist modes of inhabiting whiteness and a continuing, albeit disavowed, participation in and benefit from white privilege and white power.[10] As George Lipsitz observes in analyzing what he terms "the possessive investment in whiteness," "Despite intense and frequent disavowals that whiteness means anything at all to those so designated, recent surveys have shown repeatedly that nearly every social choice that white people make about where they live, what schools their children attend, what careers they pursue, and what policies they endorse is shaped by considerations involving race."[11]

Consider the nexus of personal and structural difficulties, which may ultimately be insuperable, involved in relinquishing white privilege even for individuals or institutions who are deeply critical of it. For example, as chapter 2 explores, white antiracist secondary-school and college teachers may strive in their classrooms to undercut or to reduce the "cake" of white privilege. But they—I—eat it too. We keep eating it because, despite our moral disgust at white privilege, most of the time it both feels natural and tastes good. Moreover, the cake is already in our mouths and there is a strong sense in which we literally *can't* spit it out, even if we think that we want to: white privilege continues to work in, on, and for us, supporting and structuring our socioprofessional identities as well as our inner selves. Indeed, it now seems to me immensely complicated for whites opposed to racism even to *want* to lessen our own white privilege; such a desire, or professed desire, is one of the things about which, I believe, white antiracist writing and teaching must learn to be more self-reflexive. A white desire to undercut white privilege faces individual will with internal and external constraints. It confronts feelings about guilt and innocence, justice and injustice, with the narcissistic self and its possible forms of relation to otherness. It intertwines matters of social, professional, and institutional identity with figurations of history and the "present." Motivating the current book is my conviction that, if we wish to grasp the full complexity of such a desire, as well as its possible impact on others, then we do well to appeal to the sinuous, multidimensional ambivalences compressed into works of literature.

Chapters 1 and 2 employ literary realist texts to help probe the University of Texas at Austin's self-understanding as a nonracist institution, focusing in particular on the temporal relationship between the institution's openly racist past and its "progress" to a present of purportedly antiracist aims and practices. My own university is chosen not for its uniqueness but because I know it best.[12] Insights generated in relation to it apply to other schools, as well as beyond the academic sphere. In chapter 1, the temporality of Wharton's *"Autre Temps . . ."*—recall, twenty years later, Mrs. Lidcote's status in New York as a marked woman simultaneously had, and had not, changed—offers a surprisingly apt rhetoric, as well as a set of figurations, for a subtler and more complex understanding of what the *Hopwood* court decision simplistically referred to as "the present effects of past discrimination." More specifically, the story helps us both to envision and to articulate the possibility that, for the University of Texas at the turn of the twenty-first century, the racial "real" consists of that which stubbornly, repulsively, perversely, and sometimes pleasurably rasps against the institution's present-day identity. Chapter 1 also considers further the methodological question of what it means to juxtapose such genuinely different sorts of material as *Hopwood v. Texas* and Wharton's almost century-earlier short story.

If chapter 1 uses *"Autre Temps . . ."* as a prism through which to refract *Hopwood v. Texas,* chapter 2 takes a different juxtapositional tack. The second chapter is anomalous within the book in that, unlike each of the other sections, it does not develop an extended interpretation of a literary text from the realist period. Instead, the chapter seeks to read the uncanny temporal force within the liberal arts classroom itself, as well as in liberal spaces outside the university, of one word that appears over two hundred times in Mark Twain's *Adventures of Huckleberry Finn,* and which teachers and students cannot help ritualistically reciting when they study Twain's novel: "nigger." Citations of the word performatively render visible the pervasive, recalcitrant *presentness* of a post-Reconstruction American racial order that liberal settings today would like to think they left behind long ago.

In Part Two, chapters titled "Awakened White Femininity and a Shaping Mexicanist Presence" (chapter 3) and "Trafficking in Liberal Masculinities" (chapter 4) shift our focus from the temporality of white liberal identity to what might be construed as a problem of spatiality. Working from and between Kate Chopin's 1899 novel *The Awakening* and Steven Soderbergh's movie *Traffic* (2000), a culturally influential film about the so-called war on drugs, the two chapters map a complex geometry (recurring to Henry James's word) among "real or imagined" Mexican, African-American, and white identities, the latter including both liberal and supremacist modes of whiteness. ("Real or imagined" is a crucial term in Toni Morrison's *Playing in the Dark*.) Ultimately, I contend that the lines and angles of racialized identifications that become visible in these texts help demonstrate two things about liberal identity: First, that what Robyn Wiegman refers to as the "contemporary reconfiguration of white power and privilege" is intertwined with the rise to prominence of "new" gender identities, identities freer from sex-role orthodoxy.[13] Second, that these "new" white gender identities need to be understood as constructed not only in relation to a subordinated blackness but also within a white-dominated multiculturalism, one in which Latinos play prominent roles. Chapters 3 and 4 thus reflect critically on a still-powerful tendency within literary and cultural whiteness studies to translate U.S. racial dynamics into a pure black/white binary.

Part Three, "White Innocence vs. Liberal Guilt," concentrates on the dynamics of innocence and guilt that churn in and around white liberal identity. Juxtaposing Henry James's *The American* (1877) with an uncomfortably prescient speech about America's essential goodness delivered by then-Senator Jesse Helms to the United Nations Security Council in January 2000, chapter 5, "A Good Fellow Wronged," expands the purview of *White Liberal Identity, Literary Pedagogy, and Classic American Realism* toward an international context, as well as toward a more "conservative" constellation of liberal identity. The chapter analyzes the structure of feeling immanent in the performance on an international stage, by Helms and by James's protagonist Christopher Newman, of an unyielding presumption of American innocence. Such innocence, which is reflexively shared by many Americans, including those who view themselves as significantly further to the left than Jesse Helms, presumes the United States' purity of motive, transparency of character, and utter forbearance from any actions perceivable, by reasonable people, as morally wrong.

Chapter 5's investigation of mainstream American presumptions of national innocence prepares for chapter 6, "Liberal Guilt and *The Age of Innocence*," which responds to a potent juncture in contemporary leftist identity: liberal guilt. Liberal guilt is dialectically generated and regenerated by, among other things, leftists' continual demystification of American innocence. In its bleakest versions—which this book's often severe (self-)critique of white liberal identity might be experienced as ratifying—liberal guilt intersects with what Wendy Brown calls "left melancholy." For Brown, "left melancholy" characterizes "a Left that has become more attached to its impossibility than to its potential fruitfulness."[14] Suffering from liberal guilt or left melancholy, one feels hopelessly implicated in mechanisms of violence, injustice, and exploitation. Returning to Edith Wharton, I take her 1920 historical novel *The Age of Innocence* as a thick lens through which to refract the problem of liberal guilt. Through most of Wharton's novel, Newland Archer simultaneously recognizes Old New York's social structures as arbitrary, unfair, and often cruel, yet also, to his own self-disgust, continues to live in alignment with them. At the same time, Newland recurrently imagines that he is just one step away from escaping to some "new land" with Ellen Olenska, a land apart from the social world that he has spent the novel theorizing and critiquing, where he will at last be exempt from its, and his own, guilty hypocrisies. During the novel's much-discussed coda, however, he comes to see his long-held fantasy of finding a discrete space for personal and social innocence explicitly *as* a fantasy, but he also sees this fantasy of innocence as worth holding on to. When read next to contemporary writings on liberal guilt by Lauren Berlant, Richard Rorty, and others, Wharton's conclusion evokes possibilities for renegotiating, or at least loosening the bonds of, our own relationships with left melancholy, with political self-disgust—and with the illusory dream of leaving these facets of American liberal identity behind.

Before concluding this introduction, some words about the term "white liberal identity" are in order. The white liberal identity to which my title refers is not intended as a totalizing description of any contemporary white person who calls him or herself "liberal." For that matter, of course, American liberals constitute a racially and ethnically diverse population. This book is centrally concerned, however, with the investments in whiteness that still play a key role in shaping American liberalism and its discourses. Moreover, I do not mean for the term "liberal" to suggest a predetermined set of policy preferences or a single mode of political behavior. As Alan Ryan has recently noted, "As a concept, liberalism is so amorphous that it may be embraced by people holding quite different political views, all of whom rightly consider themselves liberals."[15]

My notion of white liberal identity is indebted to Raymond Williams's concept, "structure of feeling." As Williams explains, "The term is difficult, but 'feeling' is chosen to emphasize a distinction from more formal concepts of 'world-view' or 'ideology.' . . . [W]e are concerned with meanings and values as they are actively lived and felt, and the relations between these and formal or systematic beliefs are in practice variable."[16] Instead of invoking firm definitions of contemporary American liberalism, I hope instead to evoke something along the lines of what Christopher Newfield calls "political subjectivity," which he defines as "feelings about the forms of one's social being."[17] Below, I explore various instances of white liberal identity as *constellations* of shifting elements. These elements include political beliefs, as well as racial, class, and gender markers, but they also include emotional patterns, psychological frameworks, and tacit as well as unconscious senses about oneself, others near or distant, various group contexts, and one's own possibilities for affecting the world.

The explicitly political views associated with the different liberal identities at issue in different chapters will range from the "centrist" policy positions of the so-called moderate wing of the Democratic party (and, in chapter 5, positions still more to the right), to views held by those significantly further to the left, who challenge important facets of global capitalism and who regard antiracism, anticolonialism, and the subversion of heteronormativity as crucial continuing struggles. While the differences between "liberal" and more "radical" political/cultural views certainly do matter in certain contexts, I have come to believe that "feelings about the forms of one's social being" are shaped at least as much by the other elements listed. Within institutional academe, for instance, where the differences between "liberal" and "radical" commitments sometimes seem to loom large, shared professional investments and practices (teaching, research, or inclusion within a bureaucracy, for example) usually loom at least as large, if not larger. Indeed, white liberal identity in the sense that I will use it may be embodied not only in individuals but in institutions or even in "society" as such.

PART ONE

Liberal Time vs. Literary Time

Liberalism is a perspective that posits the intrinsic reasonableness of human beings and that views progress as proceeding from the exercise of reason.

Ruth H. Bloch, "Utopianism, Sentimentalism, and Liberal Culture in America."

Thirty years ago, with the passage of the great civil rights laws, one could have reasonably expected—as I did—that all would be set right by now.

Nathan Glazer, *We Are All Multiculturalists Now.*

O n April 1, 2003, a lawyer defending the University of Michigan before the Unites States Supreme Court was pressed by the justices to answer a single question. The case, *Gratz v. Bollinger*, concerned the university's use of affirmative action when reviewing student applications. Supreme Court transcripts do not identify by name the individual justices who ask questions during oral arguments.

QUESTION: "Mr. Payton, let me ask Justice O'Connor's question, when does all of this come to an end?"

"End" can be taken here to mean not only finishing point but also goal. Versions of the very same question have been posed in every case I have read involving affirmative action at universities. Assuming (for now) that affirmative action is allowed to continue, when will it stop? When will it have achieved its goal and hence no longer be necessary? Despite its obviously unedited nature, I provide lawyer John Payton's response in full. Its inner conflict on the issue of temporal progress points to the following two chapters' main areas of concern.

I think that we all certainly expect it to come to an end. I think we're all quite surprised, if we looked back at *Bakke*, in 1978, I think all of us would be quite surprised from that vantage point to realize that

14

today in Michigan students live in such segregated circumstances
growing up. It's really quite unbelievable. We could not have foreseen
that. I think people thought that we were coming together in a way
and that hasn't occurred. That's created some educational challenges
and opportunities. The test score gap, I think is narrowing—we put
that in our brief. I think we're all quite optimistic about how this is
going to progress. There is progress. I think the pool is increasing.
But I can't give you how long is it going to last. I think we're all quite
confident that it's only going to last for X number of finite years, I
just can't answer with any precision that question either.[1]

Payton's response to the judges' repeated question has two main elements, but the elements do not fit together very well. Both his opening
line and the second half of his answer insist on "progress," which he uses
as verb and noun in quick succession. These portions of Payton's answer
claim an optimistic confidence that "we" all share regarding racial circumstances in Michigan and at its university. Yet he also admits to amazement,
even bafflement—"it's really quite unbelievable"—at what he sees as a *lack*
of progress in moving toward racial equity over the last twenty-five years
in Michigan and by extension, the United States. Like Nathan Glazer, a
prominent ex-liberal who for decades opposed affirmative action but who
recently changed his mind and now supports it (see second epigraph,
above), lawyer John Payton here finds himself divided between two seemingly irreconcilable understandings of the relationship between temporality and racial justice in the United States.

Liberal common sense, or as Glazer puts it, what it is reasonable to
expect, suggests that race relations and racial justice must be progressing
along a model of positive change, in the same way that history itself is presumed to do, from the past (concerning racial injustice a dire past) to the
present (with its substantial improvements) to the future (when, one reasonably expects, racial injustice will finally be "set right").[2] Yet history
somehow refuses, or is unable, to move past the "segregated circumstances"
that Payton references or the "undeniable reality" of "radical disparities"
between blacks and whites in higher education that, Nathan Glazer is
forced to admit, still persist. Though this second sort of observation may
be "undeniable," it can nonetheless also be called "unbelievable" because,
for both Payton and Glazer, it runs contrary to reason itself. Occurring
outside of "what one could have reasonably expected," given the adoption
of "the great civil rights laws" of the 1960s and more than three decades of
affirmative action—such stasis defies the temporal relationship of cause
and effect integral to liberal visions of human progress. When it comes to
race matters in the United States, the reasonable predictions of reasonable

people appear useless. "I think people thought that we were coming together in a way and that hasn't occurred," Payton says: "We could not have foreseen that."

Now, as an individual, John Payton (who happens himself to be African American) might well be prepared to offer any number of cogent remarks regarding the apparent lack of progress in resolving the deeply rooted inequities that were supposed to be "set right" by a modest, after all, and narrowly tailored affirmative-action program, especially in the context of a nationally eroding commitment to social justice. Civil rights activists, historians, and critical theorists have, for several decades now, been exploring and exposing myriad facets of the permeating deep structure of white privilege in U.S. society. But as a lawyer defending the University of Michigan's affirmative-action program—and hence representing the university's "liberal identity"—John Payton is in a bind. On the one hand, he cannot help but cite intransigence in Michigan's racial "circumstances" in answer to why, after more than a quarter century of vigorous operation, affirmative action has not yet achieved its own "end." But he needs to move quickly past—even to cancel out—his mention of this intransigence in order to assure the justices that affirmative action *is* effecting steady progress toward its end. He must assure them, that is, that the affront affirmative action ("racial preferences") presents to the Constitution's requirement for color-blind treatment will, beyond doubt, cease after "X number of finite years" because there will no longer be any need for it.

At the turn of the twenty-first century, it is not only lawyers defending affirmative action in court who seem to oscillate between an optimistic view of racial injustice in the United States as slowly but nonetheless surely lessening, thanks to all the affirmative efforts made by individuals, institutions, and society as a whole, and a contrasting feeling, however intermittent or even involuntary, that "progress" in this area is somehow stuck. Nor is lawyer John Payton alone in eliding any serious attempt to reconcile these two contrasting views, or even to explain their propinquity in his own discourse. Contradictory takes on the temporality of racial progress and an embarrassed awkwardness (at the minimum) around that contradiction characterize many white Americans today, particularly, I believe, those who would identify themselves as liberal regarding matters of race and racism.

The most common way in which liberals seek to resolve this tension is through what Paul de Man would call "the rhetoric of temporality."[3] Seemingly immovable racial injustices and inequalities are aligned with the past—for most liberals a past that is almost, if not quite yet, entirely behind us—while progressive improvement is aligned with the present, or at the very least with a presumptive future. Consider the University of

Texas, which was founded during the 1880s, when segregation and racial violence were at a high point in the southern United States, and which vigorously defended its white supremacist practices into the 1950s. Over the past several decades, the university has striven to embody the "liberal whiteness" that, for Robyn Wiegman, "is characterized by its disaffiliation from segregationist forms of white identity and identification."[4] Mason Stokes observes that when whiteness defines itself *against* white supremacy (as it does for white students, faculty, and administrators at UT-Austin today), "white supremacy makes whiteness possible because it allows whiteness the space of moderation and normality that it needs to survive. White supremacy, so often imagined as extreme, allows whiteness once again its status as the nonthreatening, as the good."[5] In other words, white supremacy and "segregationist forms of white identity" allow liberal whiteness to stand as normative. In the rhetoric of temporality prevalent at the University of Texas, and formally articulated by its lawyers in *Hopwood v. Texas*, segregationist forms of white identity are aligned with the past. That past is clearly distinct from our nonracist present, except for certain localized and ever-lessening residues that affirmative action can help to clean up.

Regarding race, white liberal identity is intellectually, emotionally, and structurally invested in the idea of a developing history and an oncoming future of substantive, positive change. By practicing a version of what Wai Chee Dimock has called "offbeat reading," reading that is temporally "at odds with the chronological progression of the nation," the purposefully anachronistic juxtapositions of Part One strive to produce new angles of vision on how the past can and does uncannily and unpredictably pervade the intimate present of our selves, our institutions, and our nation.[6]

CHAPTER ONE

What Edith Wharton Teaches about the Defense of Affirmative Action

Critical Presentism

Edith Wharton's fiction illuminates campus and legal struggles over affirmative action in higher education—despite, and in part *because of,* the discontinuities in time and subject matter involved. Today, such conflicts center primarily on how to interpret subtly nuanced dynamics of institutional inclusion and exclusion: what Robert Charles Smith has called the "now you see it, now you don't" character of racial discrimination in the "post–Civil Rights era."[1] Wharton's fiction provides American literature's most sustained and most canny exploration of the overlapping mechanisms by which inclusion, exclusion, and marginalization function in relation to a range of different social institutions. Moreover, she sets much of this fiction within the context of struggles over the liberalization of long-standing social mores. Finally, her fiction probes into how socioinstitutional mechanisms of inclusion and exclusion *feel* to those involved.

In what follows, I juxtapose Edith Wharton's 1911 short story *"Autre Temps . . ."* with key documents from a Fifth Circuit Court case, which in 1996 rendered illegal all state-sponsored affirmative action programs in Texas higher education.[2] The *Hopwood* case constituted the first successful attack on a university's practice of affirmative action sponsored by the privately funded Center for Individual Rights in Washington, D.C. It set many patterns followed later in the 1990s and in the first few years of the twenty-first century by similar cases in Georgia, Michigan, and elsewhere, where plaintiffs also relied on the Center for Individual Rights.[3] I argue here that, despite the obvious disjunctions, Wharton's story can serve as a penetrating examination, albeit *avant le mot,* of some of the *Hopwood* trial's most central and difficult aspects. Above all, in improving our understanding of the University of Texas's inability to mount a successful argument in support of its own affirmative action programs, reading

"*Autre Temps . . .*" next to *Hopwood* helps illuminate the curious relation-ship among racism, liberalism, and temporality in the United States.[4]

Wharton's fiction portrays the dynamics of inclusion and exclusion, however, in the context of late-nineteenth- and early-twentieth-century New York's fashionable high society, and she portrays such dynamics most-ly in relation to changing conventions surrounding sexuality, marriage, and wealth, not race. In seeking detailed connections between Wharton's earli-er fiction of "manners" and our own conflicts over race-based affirmative action, I purposefully engage in a strategy that might be thought of as "critical presentism." Under literary studies' current "regime of histori-cism,"[5] to convict a piece of literary criticism as "presentist" is to imply that it is glib, underresearched, textually forced, and, above all, insensitive to pertinent historical context. Used pejoratively, "presentist" refers to criti-cism perceived as blithely and unselfconsciously projecting a critic's own political or social concerns onto the literature of an earlier period. The impulse toward "critical presentism" that motivates this essay, however, seeks new ways of reading specific literature of the past not only *in* but *with* the social present—and of doing so self-consciously and also produc-tively. I believe that in certain cases we can gain unique interpretative and pedagogical leverage over both "present" matters and "past" literary works by locating unexpected, even uncanny, points of contact between them.

Historian Dominick LaCapra defines what he calls presentism—but what I would call blithe or *uncritical* presentism—as "the dream of total liberation from the 'burden' of history."[6] But there is also a version of his-toricism—one duly acknowledging the pastness of the past—that seeks a similar liberation from history's burden. In his "Theses on the Philosophy of History," Walter Benjamin associates "objective" historiography with Leopold von Ranke and his influential promotion of "scientific" history-writing. Regarding the past, such history-writing seeks to "recognize it 'the way it really was.'" Yet this "objective" historiography implicitly treats the past as having existed "once upon a time," a time now passed, which is a corollary of the liberal vision of progress as "boundless" and "irresistible."[7] The historicism that Benjamin critiques presumes, in Russell Berman's paraphrase, our own "objectified separation from the historical period."[8]

Perhaps few professional historians today would subscribe to the tenets of scientific historiography in the Rankean sense. Exactly this way of understanding history is at work, however, in what Barbara Flagg identi-fies as the United States' "popular white story about progress in race rela-tions": "The central theme of this story is that our society has an unfortu-nate history of race discrimination that is largely behind us. In the past, the story goes, some unenlightened individuals practiced slavery and other forms of overt oppression of black people, but the belief in the inferiority of blacks upon which these practices were premised has almost entirely disappeared today."[9] The same "objective" historicism leads white undergraduates, who may have studied slavery and the Civil Rights movement in high school, to assert that racial oppression (or, for another example, sexism) *used* to be a problem, "back then."

Yet if liberal or mainstream white identity in the United States relies on a historicism that views the past as unproblematically *passed,* it also clings to an uncritical form of presentism by resisting the idea that normative whiteness itself even *has* a history. Scholars have begun to render visible American whiteness's often hidden past by uncovering, for instance, the mechanisms by which various immigrant groups initially counting as non-white (such as the Irish and Eastern European Jews) achieved white identities and, thereby, the economic, social, and political benefits that whiteness confers.[10] Critical presentist reading can function to probe and to subvert liberal whiteness's double status as antihistorical (forever pushing away its own overlapping histories) yet also "objectively" historicist in the Rankean sense (conceiving slavery and segregation as nothing but history, clearly distinct from our own national "now").

Political Metaphor

One might draw encouragement for a self-consciously "presentist" reading of this particular Edith Wharton short story from its title, *"Autre Temps . . ."* ("Other Times . . ."), which Wharton puts in italics and follows with open-ended ellipses. For further support, I would appeal to the distinguished, if still sometimes controversial, theatrical tradition in which directors devise purposefully anachronistic stagings of plays to comment politically on the directors' own times and places. Defending this presentist practice, Jonathan Miller (himself responsible for several such productions in theater and opera) asserts that every dramatic work "must necessarily undergo change with the passage of time, and that this change is best inflicted upon the work deliberately rather than, as it were, by default."[11] In his book *After Dickens: Reading, Adaptation, and Performance,* John Glavin goes so far as to propose that not only theatrical staging but any literary reading, or at least any reading that "problematizes" its own processes, should be seen as a performative "adaptation" of a text, a text regarding which, in any case, a reading or performance can only ever be "after" ("after" in the sense, for instance, that the paintings of an art-historical school are considered "after" the style of their master). Using Jerzy Grotowki's Poor Theater techniques as a model, Glavin and a group of performers adapted the novel *Little Dorrit* for a Dickens conference in

Santa Cruz, California. Glavin comments that, "Through Poor Theater, we can *update* the Dickens we are *after,* to perform him belatedly as 'present.' We thereby re-make his fictions into something 'comprehensible, usable and relevant to our own interests' (Orgel 1996: 64), understanding our 'interests' as simultaneously theoretical and pragmatic, intellectual and emotional, the community's and our own."[12]

Shakespeare's plays, more than the work of any other writer, have a history of having been staged specifically so as to produce what director John Elsom calls "political metaphor." For instance, "at a time when the rigours of Stalinist censorship could be felt through Eastern Europe, Shakespearean productions became a way of commenting on political events without running the risk of banning or imprisonment."[13] The possibility for political metaphor has motivated directors even in contexts not heavily burdened by state censorship. Discussing his staging of *Henry IV* and *Henry V* in 1988, British director Michael Bogdanov observed, "When Prince John of Lancaster meets the Archbishop on neutral ground, and tricks the rebels into laying down their arms, I think of Reagan and Gorbachev in Reykjavik."[14] I too wish to undertake "political metaphor" in my reading of Wharton's short story, but not in Bogdanov's sense of finding one-to-one correspondences between given actors or events. Bogdanov conceives the political metaphors that directing Shakespeare makes available to him as based on parallels or analogies: "I look for the ways in which the political circumstances were handled then, and find inspirational parallels in what is happening now. We governed disgustingly in the fourteenth century, and we are still governing disgustingly today."[15] When "political metaphor" is understood as Bogdanov seems to, that is, as a way to underline parallels between two sets of "political circumstances," the metaphor presumes a certain transparency, an easy readability, for both sets of circumstances. Even before juxtaposing them, the director can already *see*—he already *knows*—the underlying essence of each political moment. This prior grasp of each political moment's central truth ("we" govern disgustingly) inspires the director to emphasize what he sees as preexisting analogies, parallels simply there in the material itself and needing only to be made more obvious for an audience.

Presuming that we already grasp in full each side of a comparison, metaphor as analogy indeed can obscure crucial dimensions of difference between "then" and "now," or between an older text and its presentist adaptation. Moreover, as several critics have recently argued, thinking that we see preexisting or "natural" analogies between racial and gender discrimination can be particularly hazardous. In order for them to be rendered parallel, each side of the racism/sexism analogy tends to be reductively simplified.[16] Wharton's "*Autre Temps . . .*" depicts the effects of discrimination based on gender, marital status, and sexual behavior, all within an elite upper-class context; by contrast, *Hopwood v. Texas*'s central focus is racial discrimination at a large public university. The differences between these two subjects are significant and multidimensional. It is not my intent to gloss over such differences by claiming that the 1911 short story and the 1996 court case are in fact "parallels" of each other. Nor do I suggest that "*Autre Temps . . .*" and *Hopwood* each offer different surface manifestations of some underlying, transhistoric structure called "discrimination." Rather, I seek actively to locate various sorts of contingent, heuristic points of contact or resonance between the two—to locate such points not only in the sense of "find the location of" but also in the word's other, more creative sense of "establish in a certain place." Because of the compressed imaginative force of its literary art, "*Autre Temps . . .*" offers figuration, concepts, and even language for dimensions of *Hopwood* that are otherwise difficult to recognize and articulate.

Present Effects of Past Discrimination

I first became interested in a "presentist" reading of "*Autre Temps . . .*" next to *Hopwood v. Texas* because both the story and the court case center on a problem of historicity: that is, how to conceive what the *Hopwood* decision referred to as "the present effects of past discrimination."[17] Indeed, the University of Texas's defeat in *Hopwood* permanently removed from the legal arena the argument that affirmative action could help repair past or continuing wrongs—although similar arguments remain at the center of, for example, the debate over slavery reparations. The 2003 Supreme Court decision supporting affirmative action at the University of Michigan (*Grutter v. Bollinger*) was made exclusively on the grounds of the "diversity rationale," which holds that the quality of education for all students, white and nonwhite, depends upon the student body maintaining certain levels of racial and ethnic diversity.[18] (Ironically, in *Hopwood,* the diversity rationale was rejected by the courts at a relatively early stage; see chapter 2.) Despite the diversity rationale's later success at the Supreme Court, the question of racial temporality with which *Hopwood* leaves us still remains. Why is it so hard, in mainstream or even "liberal" arenas, to represent a continuing history of racial injustice?

Here is the conundrum that Edith Wharton's story presents: Mrs. Lidcote has been effectively banished from upper-class New York City society for almost eighteen years because she divorced her husband for another man, and thus she has spent most of her adult life in Florence, Italy. Braving a return to New York as the story opens, however, Mrs.

Lidcote discovers that "times have changed."[19] "Things are different now—altogether easier" (241). Under the "new dispensation," as a cousin explains to her, it has become widely agreed upon that "every woman ha[s] a right to happiness," which means that leaving one man for another is no longer grounds for social ostracism (271, 246). Indeed, Mrs. Lidcote is shown much concrete evidence that divorced women are no longer subject, as they were in her own youth, to what the *Hopwood* court might call "overt officially sanctioned discrimination." Yet, nonetheless, she finds herself mysteriously unable to enter into the new opportunities that people insist have now become open to her—including a supposed circle of waiting friends, an admirer who wishes to marry her, and a publicly acknowledged role as her daughter's mother. At story's end, and without any clear explanation, Mrs. Lidcote returns to her separate life abroad.

In asking us to grapple with the complex of factors that prevents Mrs. Lidcote from taking advantage of her supposed new opportunities to participate in New York's elite circles, *"Autre Temps . . ."* focuses our attention on three questions integral both to itself and to the circuit court decision in the *Hopwood* case:

> How does one think about the *temporal* relation of past and present when trying to describe "the present effects of past discrimination"?
>
> How does one understand the *agency* of continuing discriminatory effects that are seen as an unfortunate "legacy" of the past?
>
> When can past discrimination be considered as sufficiently *compensated or remedied*?

Regarding the *Hopwood* case, these three questions all depend upon the presumption shared by the white plaintiffs (Hopwood, et al), by the defendants (University of Texas et al.) and by the court itself that UT's Law School does not currently have any official policies that openly discriminate by race. Below, I have more to say about this shared presumption.

The circuit court's anxiety about the third question—When can past discrimination be considered as sufficiently remedied?—kept bringing the court back to versions of the first two questions. If UT's Law School itself no longer actively and officially discriminates, and if, at least in the court's view, "the vast majority of the faculty, staff, and students" currently at the Law School "had absolutely nothing to do with any discrimination that the Law School practiced in the past," then to what extent can the Law School as an institution still be held responsible? Held responsible, for instance, for its "alleged *current* lingering reputation in the minority community" as having a racially biased environment? The court decided that "mere knowledge of historical fact is not the kind of present effect that can justify a race-exclusive remedy. If it were otherwise, as long as there are people who have access to history books, there will be programs such as this." In other words, if a potential minority candidate hesitates to apply to UT's Law School today because she knows that the Law School *used to* refuse categorically to consider any minority applications, that could not be counted as a reason to continue affirmative action programs.

The court's insistence that history books should be regarded as mere repositories of fact with no illocutionary force in the present is simplistic, to say the least, but for comparison with "*Autre Temps . . .*" I want to underline the court's fear of a temporal collapse. If *past* acts of discrimination could continue to count as justification for *present* affirmative action remedies, what would that mean about the future? The court envisioned being asked to approve "remedies that are ageless in their reach into the past, and timeless in their ability to affect the future." If affirmative action could be allowed to find its own continuing necessity in a past of official discrimination, the court worried, then affirmative action might continue forever, into a "boundless" tomorrow. The *Hopwood* court seemed to fear ratifying a borderless spatialization of time, where past, present, and future would exist on the same simultaneous plane, where history books and outdated statutes would operate on the same level as today's, and even tomorrow's, newspaper.

At the start of "*Autre Temps . . . ,*" Mrs. Lidcote seems almost literally to embody the unending, all-consuming fixation on past social ostracism that the *Hopwood* court feared affirmative action might encourage. On the steamer taking Mrs. Lidcote back to New York City, "It was always the past that occupied her. . . . [I]t would always be there, huge, obstructing, encumbering, bigger and more dominant than anything the future could ever conjure up." The past "looked out at her from the face of every acquaintance, it appeared suddenly in the eyes of strangers" (235). However, even before the steamer docks, Mrs. Lidcote starts to perceive that the rigid sexual and social mores of her day have undergone remarkable loosening since the time, eighteen years earlier, when she was forced to leave the city. Everybody has divorced friends. Mrs. Lidcote's own daughter has left one husband and married another without seeming to pay any social penalty. What Mrs. Lidcote calls the "clan" constituted by her husband's family, which had united in expelling her eighteen years earlier, seems (not unlike today's "Klan") to have dissipated and lost much of its relevance. She starts to think that perhaps her own painful past can now, finally, cease to matter. In light of the "general readjustment" of society, with its "new tolerances and indifferences and accommodations," "was not she herself released?" (252).

Unfortunately, a series of social encounters convinces Mrs. Lidcote that it cannot be so simple. While staying at her daughter and new son-in-law's luxurious country home—in their large house, which strikes her as an "'establishment' . . . something solid, avowed, founded on sacraments and precedents and principles" (as a university is)—Mrs. Lidcote finds herself unable to recall "having ever had so strange a sense of being out alone, under the night, in a wind-beaten plain" (253, 263). Everyone avoids any mention of her divorce. Nor does anyone ask her where she has been, or what she has been doing, during the twenty intervening years. In *The Mother's Recompense*, a 1925 novel that draws heavily on "*Autre Temps . . . ,*" a divorced mother who has similarly returned to New York after many years of European exile reflects on society's "kind" avoidance of her own scandalous past: "Well, that was what people called 'starting with a clean slate,' she supposed; would no one ever again scribble anything unguardedly on hers? She felt indescribably alone."[20] So, too, the concerted social effort to guard Mrs. Lidcote's "slate" from any embarrassing or wounding references gives her the impression that no one speaks casually or naturally to her. She comes to feel that virtually all of her conversations occur through a "painted gauze let down between herself and the real facts of life" (274).

Still more disturbing, Mrs. Lidcote finds herself unable to ignore that several of the other guests at her daughter's new house, including many of the very same people who now claim easily to accept divorce—and who, in most instances, indeed do accept it—nonetheless still continue, although more subtly than in the past, to "cut" *her* socially, to avoid recognizing her presence. Her friends and allies deny it: "'Then you don't think Margaret Wynn meant to cut me?' 'I think your ideas are absurd,'" exclaims her admirer Franklin Ides. But Mrs. Lidcote concludes, "Oh, I saw she did, though she never moved an eyelid" (268). Here is the explanation that Mrs. Lidcote finally arrives at for these instances of cutting: "*My* case has been passed on and classified: I'm the woman who has been cut for nearly twenty years. The older people have half forgotten why, and the younger ones have never really known: it's simply become a tradition to cut me. And traditions that have lost their meaning are the hardest of all to destroy" (272). What does it mean for Mrs. Lidcote to say that the tradition of cutting her continues, even though, or in some sense *because,* it has lost its meaning? This is the dilemma at the heart both of "*Autre Temps . . .*" and, I contend, of the *Hopwood* case. While on the steamer taking her back to the States, Mrs. Lidcote had envisioned her past as a massive physical object—"a great concrete fact in her path that she had to walk around every time she moved in any direction" (235). Now, however, we might say that she sees it as something more like a sentence (both the linguistic and the penal senses of "sentence" are pertinent here), but a sentence in a no-longer spoken language: "Traditions that have lost their meaning are the hardest of all to destroy."

In part, the people surrounding Mrs. Lidcote, especially her daughter Leila and her admirer Franklin Ides, avoid putting into words Mrs. Lidcote's continuing status as "the woman who has been cut" because they wish to create a present space "in which she could think and feel and behave like any other woman" (239). In a society that prides itself on its "new tolerances and indifferences," they wish, as it were, to enact indifference for her—and thereby to make it true that her past need no longer mark her as different, that it has become an indifferent or non-signifying detail about her self. Using the same logic, the *Hopwood* court ruled that to strike down affirmative action would be to move significantly closer to realizing the ideal of a race-neutral society, insofar as we all now recognize that "the use of race, in and of itself, to choose students. . . . is no more rational on its own terms than would be choice based upon the physical size or blood type of applicants." It is only commonsense fairness, the court implied, that today's admissions and financial aid offices should be indifferent to all such irrelevant factors. Wharton's story makes visible, however, how a new and supposedly liberalizing "indifference" to some previously all-determining characteristic can nonetheless mask a continued "cutting" along the same line as before, however disavowed by common sense the cutting may now be, and however jagged or uneven.

The court's raising the question of the present *rationality* of the race-based preferences that affirmative action involves pushes us to think further about the implications of Wharton's saying that the tradition of cutting Mrs. Lidcote still continued even though it had lost its meaning. Twenty years earlier, what mainstream society thought it meant by cutting Mrs. Lidcote was manifest—she was a fallen woman who deserved to be shunned. But, in "the new order of things," continuing to cut her no longer makes any sense, which explains why the characters in Wharton's story find that cutting almost literally unspeakable. Given society's changed sexual mores, the cutting of Mrs. Lidcote can only transpire somewhere, as it were, outside her society's own self-understanding, which is why nobody except her is able to put it into words. So, too, what if in the post–Civil Rights era at the University of Texas the traditions of racial exclusion that affirmative action responds to have indeed lost whatever inner rationale or coherence they might once, at least on their own terms, have possessed? Although now incoherent and inexplicable even to themselves, what if those traditions of racial exclusion nonetheless persist at the university—and persist with a structuring force?

Throughout the course of Wharton's story, no one ever articulates Mrs. Lidcote's irrationally-continued exclusion. In fact, both her daughter Leila and her admirer Franklin Ides spend much of the story trying to convince Mrs. Lidcote and, in a way, themselves that it is *she* who is irrational, that she exaggerates or even imagines slights. They seek to "cure" her of her "delusions": "You don't *know* that any of the acts you describe are due to the causes you suppose," Franklin says to her (268, 270). "Don't you see what all these complications of feeling mean? Simply that you were too nervous at the moment to let things happen naturally, just as you're too nervous now to judge them rationally. . . . Give yourself a little more time" (273). What cannot be allowed for verbally, however, is acknowledged involuntarily by the bodies of Franklin and, even more so, Leila, in a pair of remarkable blushes.[21] Wharton figures these blushes as invasive eruptions, in each case triggered by Mrs. Lidcote's announcing that she intends to insert herself into a social situation (a dinner party, an evening visit) from which her daughter or her admirer has delicately tried to steer her away. Here is how Wharton describes the more spectacular of the blushes, which is Leila's:

> Leila stopped short, her lips half parted to reply. As she paused, the colour stole over her bare neck, swept up to her throat, and burst into flame in her cheeks. Thence it sent its devastating crimson up to her very temples, to the lobes of her ears, to the edges of her eye-lids, beating all over her in fiery waves, as if fanned by some imperceptible wind. Mrs. Lidcote silently watched the conflagration. (264–65)

The eruptive blush displaces what Leila had parted her lips to say. The blush marks the limit of what can be said in words that make sense under the "new dispensation" of Mrs. Lidcote's society. Yet although what the blush acknowledges is something that disrupts sense itself—it is indeed now "preposterous," as Franklin says, to think that Mrs. Lidcote would still be cut for having done twenty years ago what is today commonly accepted—that preposterousness does not render the cut less forceful (271).

In the *Hopwood* decision, the circuit court insisted that it would, in effect, be nonsense to find the university's Law School guilty of the sort of continuing racial exclusions that legally imply the need for redress by affirmative action. As the court emphasized, since the late 1960s the University of Texas and its Law School have officially welcomed diversity and have, moreover, devoted what the court considered "a significant amount of scholarship money" to minority recruitment and retention programs.

Given its apparently active and proactive recent history around diversity, the university was unable to articulate to the court's satisfaction how it could still be a racially exclusionary institution. "*Autre Temps . . . ,*" however, faces us with the challenge of learning how better to *represent* (in both the legal and the literary senses of the word "represent") a persisting reality of exclusion. We must learn how to give effective language and figure to a reality of exclusion that persists irrationally and unspeakably, but persists nonetheless, even within an institution that genuinely wishes to see itself as having already moved past such exclusions.

The Past as Past?

I return to Leila's eruptive blush at the beginning of the next chapter. First, however, I want to note that during the *Hopwood* trial the University of Texas did actively participate, although perhaps more indirectly than directly, in rendering unsayable one aspect of its own exclusionary reality: the discriminatory impact of LSAT scores on the admissions process. To grasp this crucial dimension of the university's actions, it is important to realize that, in turning down the university's appeal, the Fifth Circuit judges declared that any state agency wishing to continue using affirmative action first had to demonstrate that it still *required* affirmative action to counter its *own* continuing legacy of institutional racism. This specific demonstration would be necessary in order to overcome the constitutional obligation of color-blindness on the part of all government entities, as set out in the "equal protection" clause of the Reconstruction-era Fourteenth Amendment. The court stringently insisted that the university should not, and legally *could* not, use "racial preferences" (affirmative action) to compensate for general "societal discrimination" against minorities—not even for discrimination by other "state actors," such as public school systems. A state Law School such as that at UT could deploy affirmative action's "system of racial preferences" only if such an action were "narrowly tailored" to "remediate" an equivalent or worse form of discrimination practiced by the Law School itself (*Hopwood* 5th Cir). As Texas Attorney General Daniel Morales later put it, the Law School was the only "relevant putative discriminator."[22] This narrow guideline rendered irrelevant any attempts to show that minority applicants to UT's Law School continue to find themselves at a disadvantage because of manifold forms of past or even present discrimination by other arms of the government. For example, one university argument declared irrelevant by the court involved the effects on current minority applicants of Texas's recent history of legally segregated and vastly unequal public school systems, which strongly affected the educational possibilities and attainments of many applicants' parents. For that matter, largely segregated schools with unequal resources remain more or less the status quo in many parts of the state.

Anticipating and responding to this legal impasse, however, two university organizations representing black students had tried to gain official status as "interveners" since the case's early months in 1994: the undergraduate Black Pre-Law Association and the Law School's Thurgood Marshall Legal Society. The would-be interveners wished "to present evidence which showed that admissions practices currently in use had a discriminatory impact on African-American students." Specifically, the two student organizations wished to introduce research studies and expert witnesses to establish that the LSAT is a poor guide to how individual African-American students will actually perform in law school. The LSAT's "differential predictive validity" means that it tends to measure academic potential more accurately for white than for black applicants. Being allowed to demonstrate the LSAT's "racially discriminatory impact," the prospective interveners argued, would "establish the need for the Law School to take race into account . . . in order to mitigate" the LSAT's prejudicial effects on its admissions process. In effect, the interveners wished to demonstrate that, through its heavy reliance on the LSATs, the Law School as an entity not only did once but still *does* practice officially sanctioned discrimination against minorities. This demonstration would meet the court's stringent requirement for allowing an affirmative action program to continue.[23]

However, from 1994 to 1998 petition after petition to intervene was denied, first by the district court, then on appeal by the Fifth Circuit panel, and finally by the Supreme Court (which declined to get involved in the case at all). Of course, the *Hopwood* plaintiffs consistently opposed the petitions. More significantly, however, the university's lawyers' response to the proposed intervention wavered between discouraging, neutral, and, at best, ambiguously supportive. In fact, although the two African American student groups supplied university lawyers with the relevant studies about the LSATs and offered to provide expert witnesses to interpret them, university and state lawyers chose to use none of this evidence in their defense of the Law School's affirmative action policy.[24]

Why not? The African American student groups argued in a later brief that "It was in neither plaintiffs' interest nor defendants' to advance the argument regarding the invalidity of the Texas Index for the selection of African-American students." University officials probably worried, the students' brief suggested, that the court might indeed validate an argument that use of the LSATs gives white applicants an unfair advantage. At that point, the university might find itself exposed to potential lawsuits by

minority applicants who had been previously rejected because of low
LSAT scores—rejected, that is, because of what would now be legally
established as racially discriminatory criteria.[25]

Beyond opening themselves to the possibility of new lawsuits, for the
University of Texas and its Law School to have accepted that the LSATs are,
in effect, rigged to favor white applicants would have been for the institution radically to challenge its own ways of defining itself. Higher education,
the legal system, and ideologies of professionalism in the United States (all
of which were at issue in the *Hopwood* case) construe their most central values in close relation to Enlightenment ideals of reason, neutral expertise, and
the unbiased recognition of "merit." Although institutional self-envisioning
may allow for certain necessary deviations from these Enlightenment values,
they have always remained absolutely central as defining ideals. A key
insight of recent work in critical race theory has been that these same
Enlightenment ideals have historically been developed and interpreted within contexts that also accepted white supremacy as common sense. Might not
current versions of such supposedly neutral Enlightenment ideals still be, as
Gary Peller puts it, "a manifestation of group power, of politics"? Regarding
American higher education, Peller asks "whether 'standards,' definitions of
'merit,' and the other myriad features of the day-to-day aspects of institutional life constructed or maintained during [legal] segregation might have
reflected deeper aspects of a culture within which the explicit exclusion of
blacks seemed uncontroversial."[26]

As just one possible example, we should recall that the techniques for
measuring "scholastic aptitude" widely promulgated by the Educational
Testing Service (ETS) after World War II (the SAT, LSAT, and so on) were
themselves closely modeled on early-twentieth-century IQ tests. However,
the very idea of IQ as a measurable quantity was popularized in the United
States around the turn of the twentieth century by eugenicists explicitly
seeking a scientific basis for maintaining and extending racial hierarchies.
IQ "data" from the first mass testing, performed on inductees during the
First World War, served as an important justification for restrictive immigration quotas and other forms of ethnic and racial discrimination.[27] Of
course, this history does not necessarily equate the current ETS system of
exams with the racist purposes and uses of the earlier IQ tests on which
the exams were based, but it does suggest that Peller is right to wonder
about unrecognized ways in which "day-to-day aspects of institutional
life" may still "reflect" the past.

In the *Hopwood* case, not allowing the black student groups to participate as interveners served also to exclude their evidence about the racially
biased results of admissions decisions that rely on LSAT scores. This exclusion functioned to avoid any legal or official consideration of ways in

which the university's core values of merit, fairness, and reason might themselves remain hopelessly entangled with the relentlessly racializing, segregative culture of late-nineteenth- and early-twentieth-century America.[28] The University of Texas was founded in 1883. More generally, this was the period during which the competitive research-and-teaching university as we know it was envisioned and first developed in the United States. What if "deeper aspects" (in Peller's phrase) of that older, openly racist time still constitute an inassimilable real, a real carried within the identities of competitive colleges and universities nationwide? As recently as June 2000, the dean of UT's Law School at the time of *Hopwood*—a dean who worked hard to defend affirmative action policies during and after the trial—insisted that he could not imagine processing Law School admissions without relying on LSAT scores: "The [LSAT] is the one unifying examination and measurement. . . . I don't think that we or any law school that I know of is going to give up giving some weight to the LSAT."[29] The same institution going to court in vigorous defense of its well-meaning recent attempts to adjust for leftover racial imbalances still finds itself relying, for its continuing coherence *as* a distinctive institution, on certain concepts and technologies of "merit" shaped within and quite possibly *by* an actively white-supremacist culture.[30]

To confront such powerfully disturbing possibilities as a primal, perhaps inescapable connection between the supposedly "other days" (*autre temps . . .*) of eugenicism and racial segregation and its own current day-to-day modes of interpreting "standards" and "merit" would indeed be difficult for the university. Officially recognizing the LSATs—and above all the still-current understanding of "merit" for which they are a metonym—as potentially inextricable from white supremacy would have unforeseeable but traumatic implications for university self-conceptions, university practices and, not least, university personnel. If the university's quite possibly hard-wired commitment to racially biased hierarchy were to be authentically and fully interrogated, the resulting implications would surely reach far beyond the use or non-use of standardized admissions exams. "We" who comprise the predominantly white liberal university understandably resist grappling with the full range of such possibilities and implications, which might affect our professional status, our self-respect, and, indeed, our employment. We resist, consciously and unconsciously, at sites ranging from the courtroom and administrative office to the classroom and faculty office.

Achieving a more genuine understanding of the current university's relationship with its past requires a disjunctive act of historical recognition. We must learn to recognize how an anachronistic, seemingly disconnected moment of the past might best capture, uncannily—as in a window that turns out to be a mirror—the university's, and our, "present." By contrast,

to respect the otherness of the past—"the past *as* past"—as we are urged
to do by those who use "presentist" as a term of automatic condemnation,
would in this case be to correlate, first, with the *Hopwood* plaintiffs' argument that affirmative action may once have been necessary but is no
longer needed. At bottom, moreover, a similar emphasis on the essential
difference of past and present, then and now, also underlies the university's
"liberal" defense of affirmative action: the past is *almost* and will soon *be*
past, but not quite yet. Franklin Ides's advice to Mrs. Lidgate encapsulates
the liberal university's deployment of the idea of change as at once defin-
itively achieved but also still moving forward along its proper path. Even
as Franklin vigorously concurs with everyone around that "the times have
changed," he urges Mrs. Lidgate to give herself just "a little more time" in
order to feel fully reintegrated into New York society. The liberal view that
the bad past is *almost* past allows the university still to conceive itself within a narrative of progress, of improvement. The university can defend its
need for a limited affirmative-action program to help finish off the *virtually* completed past, yet it can do so without putting into question its currently most cherished tenets of identity.[31]

Working from Edith Wharton's *"Autre Temps . . . ,"* I have attempted here
to provide one example of how "past" literature may serve as a special kind
of "political metaphor," with the potential to open new ways of viewing current impasses in our culture or society. Seemingly disconnected literature of
the past can uncannily re-"present" our own present to us, including unexpected, idiosyncratic, or obscured facets of our present. Using a somewhat
different version of critical presentism, chapter 2 again explores the juxtaposition of a classic text of American literary realism with events at the
University of Texas. The juxtaposition again allows us to investigate questions that extend well beyond UT's campus. The text treated in chapter 2,
Mark Twain's *Adventures of Huckleberry Finn* (1884), is today the most
famous, most frequently taught, most widely read, and most written-about
example of American literary realism. Rather than mounting a new interpretative reading of Twain's novel in itself, I seek to understand the strange temporality, the foldings and unfoldings, of America's blatantly racist past and
of its liberal, integrationist present that ensue when *Huck Finn* is taught in
a predominantly white, middle-class college classroom.

Coda

On February 18, 2001, Richard C. Atkinson, president of the University
of California system, delivered a remarkable speech about the SAT examination to a largely surprised audience of college presidents and other

higher education officials. In light of the foregoing chapter, I believe that Atkinson's speech constituted then and, three years later, still does constitute, a moment of genuine possibility. Addressing members of the American Council on Education in Washington, D.C., he announced that he submitted a recommendation to his faculty that the University of California should stop requiring prospective undergraduates to take the SAT. Atkinson asserted that the test measures only "undefined notions of 'aptitude' or 'intelligence,'" and argued that its widespread use has had a pernicious influence on how "we . . . allocate educational opportunity" to all students, but "especially low-income and minority students."[32]

It is still too soon to assess the full implications of Atkinson's initiative, even within the University of California system. Nonetheless, given the size and prominence of the University of California, Atkinson's proposal has already begun (as put by the *New York Times*'s front-page story on the proposal) to "echo throughout the world of higher education."[33] My own discussion of *Hopwood v. Texas* has asked whether an "*Autre Temps . . .*" of openly racist exclusions might be inseparable from notions of standards and merit that are still centrally involved in the identities and the day-to-day operations of The University of Texas and other competitive research universities. The use of standardized "aptitude" tests for admissions (the LSATs) served in the current chapter as a synecdoche for this larger question. Nonetheless, one cannot predict how abandoning use of the SAT might affect notions of quality and merit beyond undergraduate admissions. (I should also mention that, as the Law School dean in Texas predicted, no major law school, at least to my knowledge, has yet indicated plans to abandon use of the LSAT.) For that matter, even within undergraduate admissions, I do not think that we can be certain what effect the absence of SAT scores would have on an uncannily ever-present "*Autre Temps . . .*" of open racial exclusion. If the SAT has indeed continued to play a role in excluding minorities, then removing it from the admissions equation should, by all logic, constitute a major step toward genuinely fairer and more equal educational access. Yet, if Edith Wharton's short story shows anything, it is that the persistence of exclusionary "other times" occurs most powerfully at the very limits of rational calculation or prediction.

It is precisely these radical uncertainties about the future that make Atkinson's bold initiative so exciting. To return to Wharton's short story, Mrs. Lidcote comes to conceive of her past as something like a sentence, but a sentence handed down in a no-longer spoken language: "Traditions that have lost their meaning are the hardest of all to destroy." One significant part of Atkinson's speech was devoted to chewing over the *meaning* of SAT. The initials used to stand for Scholastic Aptitude Test. But because "aptitude test" reeked too strongly of the increasingly controversial notion of IQ testing, in 1990, ETS said SAT would henceforth stand for Scholastic Assessment Test. Finally, in 1996, as Atkinson explained, ETS dropped a semantically recognizable name altogether for the exam and, in what Atkinson calls "a rhetorical sleight of hand," "said that the 'SAT' was the 'SAT' and that the initials no longer stood for anything." Again, "traditions that have lost their meaning are the hardest of all to destroy." But Atkinson's speech worked to *recover* or *translate* some of the unacknowledged but nonetheless effectual meanings of SAT. To many minority parents and others, he suggested, SAT means a past and present lack of fairness and transparency in determining educational opportunity. With the policy recommendation that it carries, Atkinson's speech may end up helping to re-speak, and thus perhaps to alter, some very persistent sentences.

CHAPTER TWO

Mark Twain and the Secret Joys of Antiracist Pedagogy

Combating racism in the hearts of politically and socially progressive white people is, in fact, one of the last great obstacles to dismantling institutional racism at all levels in the United States.
—M. Garlinda Burton, *Never Say Nigger Again! An Antiracism Guide for White Liberals.*

Before change is possible, that is, we need to recognize how we get our enjoyment.
—Dennis Foster, *Sublime Enjoyment: On the Perverse Motive in American Literature.*

Mark Twain's *Adventures of Huckleberry Finn* is a brilliant and seminal American novel in which the word "nigger" appears over two hundred times. Focusing on the oft-recognized dilemmas involved in teaching the novel, this chapter explores what I believe is an unavoidable paradox encountered by white liberal college teachers who set out to practice antiracist pedagogy in largely white classrooms. The paradox derives from the inevitability of the teachers and their students citing and thus in a sense performing the blatantly racist past—most emblematically the racist past compressed within the word "nigger"—even while trying to move beyond its influence. This performative citing of the past occurs within a purportedly nonracist psychic and socioinstitutional "present," but one that retains its coherent identity *as* nonracist by continuously turning away from its own dependence upon racialized hierarchies and exclusions.

I investigate here several implications of a rupture between the non-racist liberal arts space usually presumed within *Huck Finn* classrooms, on the one hand, and, on the other hand, racist realities that both undergird and permeate that educational space. At moments, this break comes

perilously close to dissolving presumed reasons for the existence of a liberal arts classroom in the first place. I suggest that the moments in which
such a dissolution most immediately impends—often when the word
"nigger" is spoken by a white person—may in some cases also produce an
inarticulate, even unconscious excitement, at least for the professor who
is supposed to guarantee the meaning and validity of the educational
process. Drawing on the Lacanian concept of *jouissance,* I argue that this
excitement can be experienced by the psyche as overwhelming and
unmanageable. In the latter portions of this chapter, I analyze some of my
own "symptomatic" experiences teaching *Huck Finn,* as well as other evidence from outside the classroom, to suggest that one way in which at
least a white liberal male may channel this overwhelming excitement is
through unconsciously inserting himself within fantasized scenarios of
domination and victimization.

Impossible Antiracism

A brief consideration of M. Garlinda Burton's 1995 paperback book *Never
Say Nigger Again! An Antiracism Guide for White Liberals* offers a useful
starting point. Burton, who is regional director of the United Methodist
News Service, identifies herself as an African American working in a very
liberal but predominantly white environment. Characterizing her text as a
"handbook, a question-and-answer book, a guidebook," Burton addresses
an audience of "white people who think they don't need a book on racism"
(2). She offers many cogent insights about liberal white racism, but I focus
here on her title as well as the genre of her work.

First, how is Burton's title, with its exclamation point, to be understood? Should it be heard as a strict, emphatic injunction?—*Never* say nigger again! Or should it, rather, be taken as an excited and enticing self-help
promise? Buy this book, follow its guided steps, and you will never say
nigger again—*guaranteed!* The latter reading of the title would cast the act
of speaking the racial slur as something of an unfortunate addiction or
compulsion, parallel to, say, overeating or entering relationships with
unsuitable partners. In this therapeutic paradigm, the addictive practices
in question may provide sharp enjoyment in response to a deeply felt need
in the short term, but, of course, overeating, entering self-destructive relationships, and—by extension—using the racial epithet can never lead to
satisfaction. An understanding of the title's main phrase as a Franklin-
esque promise of the specified self-improvement to be achieved (if you
have the self-discipline to follow the step-by-step method herein proffered) is supported not only by the book's self-description as a "guide" but

also by the many bulleted and numbered lists Burton includes. These lists provide questions to ask yourself, local do's and don'ts, and strategies for various situations: how to handle a loved older relative who uses racial slurs, for instance.

But the discursive passage inside the book from which, as it turns out, the title phrase is drawn supports the other possible interpretation—that is, as a "thou shalt not" commandment, which firmly, even angrily, underlines that never means *never*, no matter what. The title phrase appears, in bold type, as number four on a list of rules Burton asks white people to remember, "When You're Talking about *Us*":

> **4 Never say "nigger" again.** *Never* have I heard this word spoken by a white person—or a black one, for that matter—without feeling terribly angry and uncomfortable. Too much history and hostility are conjured up by this word. . . . I don't care how you use it. I don't care if you're quoting some horrible white racist you abhor—*do not say it,* and confront those white people who do. Say "the n-word" or "a racial slur" if you have to; it may sound silly or stilted, but you may save a relationship with an African American friend or colleague. If a black friend says she doesn't mind you saying it, she's lying. (33–34; emphasis in original)

Although it may seem an overly easy deconstructive point, it is important to recognize that Burton's very articulation of this rule entails breaking her own prohibition. Despite her insistence that no one, white or black, should *ever* say "this word," Burton's book repeats it at least five times. "Nigger" appears as the boldface heading of the quoted paragraph, in the table of contents, on the title page, on the back cover, and in a large, prominent typeface on the front cover.

Indeed, any potential purchaser or reader must voice the word at least to him- or herself when encountering the book. I had to request the book through interlibrary loan and thus had to cite its title in a form filled out for the librarian; if I had wanted to obtain the book on the very same day as I first came across a reference to it, I would have had to call around to area bookstores, a situation which would have required me to speak the word into the phone. Whether one takes the title as a self-help promise or as a strict commandment, its own existence makes the commandment or promise impossible to fulfill.

This double bind—one should never say the n-word, yet articulating this "never" involves citing and reciting the word both to oneself and to others—may appear something of a cheap paradox, a word game.[1] Yet the word in question is, as Burton asserts, more than a word. Like an evil incantation that always works, no matter where, how, or by whom it is spoken, it performatively "conjure[s] up" a "history and hostility" that are "too much," overwhelming any and all particular contexts. Moreover, Burton herself is sufficiently concerned about the citation paradox to try to head it off when she italicizes "*do not say it*" even if you are quoting "some horrible white racist" with abhorrence. Yet, as we have seen, she finds it impossible not to repeat the word herself, and her book's very presence, whether on a shelf or in a catalogue or a bibliography, requires her target audience—white liberals—to repeat it as well.

Certainly, one might make a similar point about other attempts to identify and restrict what has come to be known as "hate speech."[2] Because of America's racial history, however, the double bind seems uniquely tight in the case of "nigger." Consider Harvard law professor Randall Kennedy's well-publicized book, *Nigger: The Strange Career of a Troublesome Word* (2002). Pointing out that the word is sometimes used with other than pejorative meanings among African Americans, Kennedy's book develops a seemingly reasonable argument about white uses of the word: "There is nothing necessarily wrong with a white person saying 'nigger,' just as there is nothing necessarily wrong with a black person saying it. What should matter is the context in which the word is spoken—the speaker's aims, effects, alternatives" (51). Yet this attempt to "tame" (as Kennedy puts it) the word by emphasizing the context in which a white person speaks it presumes that context itself is tamable by individual human agency—that it can ever be cleanly delimited or decisively grasped. The "strange career" of Kennedy's own book shows otherwise. Among the mostly negative reviews that it received from black and nonblack writers alike, Patricia Williams told of a "friend" who was "sitting on the bus and this [white] man across the aisle starts waving a copy of law professor Randall Kennedy's new book *Nigger* . . . flashing it at black people." The friend resolves to start carrying a copy of Michael Moore's *Stupid White Men* to "flash" in return. In a more serious vein, Williams asserts, "Nigger, The Book, is an appeal to pure sensation. . . . What's selling this book is the ongoing liveliness of [the title's] negativity: It hits in the gut, catches the eye, knots the stomach, jerks the knee, grabs the arm. Kennedy milks this phenomenon only to ask with an entirely straight face: 'So what's the big deal?'" The *New York Times* reported that many of the mainly white staff at the book's publisher, Pantheon, refused even to say the name of the book they were supposed to be packaging and promoting.[3]

Even when trying to promote or to teach a book (whether Kennedy's or Twain's) that seeks to defuse the word's hateful power, the necessity of citing it inserts the white liberal into what can feel like a kind of verbal impossibility. In experiencing this paradox, I suggest, the white liberal toes the breaking point of a fundamental fracture. The fracture inheres in the relation (or, rather, the induced and unstable nonrelation) of white liberal spaces, psychic as well as socio-institutional, which nurture a notion of progress in American race relations, with the pervasive racial realities that still inform and even help shape those spaces. The sense of progress liberals nurture holds that America's racial problems are not yet fully resolved, but that they have historically gotten better and will continue to do so, even if movement is sometimes halting or uneven. In this view, despite the continuing inequalities of today, race relations at the turn of the twenty-first century are much closer to American ideals of democracy and justice than they were a century earlier, when systemic lynchings, Jim Crow segregation, and myriad other blatant forms of economic and political oppression were directed against African Americans.

It is difficult to argue against this commonsense feeling regarding progress—a feeling I usually share. But it is nonetheless the case that this sense of progress must strive to exclude—even though it is constitutively unable to do so—certain psychic and material realities in which it is enveloped. Moreover, to walk the knife-edge of this irresolvable tension can yield a vertiginous enjoyment, or *jouissance,* to white liberals (related, perhaps, to that "pure sensation" to which Williams ascribes the appeal of Kennedy's book). To develop the latter contention, I must first take a few detours before returning to the *Huck Finn* classroom. First, a brief reconsideration of the remarkable blush displayed by Mrs. Lidcote's daughter Leila in Edith Wharton's short story *"Autre Temps . . ."* (first discussed in chapter 1, above).

Leila's Blush, *Jouissance,* and the Real

Why does being forced to confirm, albeit without words, the unspeakable, irrational persistence of Mrs. Lidcote's social exclusion provoke such an intense bodily response on the part of two of her own most sympathetic supporters? Of course Leila's and Franklin Ides's blushes indicate, first, their strong embarrassment at suddenly finding themselves compelled—if not directly to admit the truth of Mrs. Lidcote's continuing exclusion—at least to cease their argumentative denials of it. Mrs. Lidcote has, so to speak, cornered them in the very place that reveals the hole—what we might think of as the unending "cut"—at the center of everything they have told her throughout the story. Yet, at the same time that it registers their humiliation at being revealed as liars, the rush of blood no doubt also points to Leila's and Franklin's strong sympathy for Mrs. Lidcote, their empathic identification with the rush of pain that they imagine she will feel at receiving confirmation of the truth she merely suspected: that is, even after so many genuine social changes, numerous people and contexts still withhold full recognition from her.

There is something in Wharton's description of these blushes, however, especially Leila's, that suggests more: a sort of sexual ecstasy, illicit but unstoppable. Compare Wharton's words about Leila's blush with the climax of the now famous "unpublishable fragment," labeled as such and kept by Wharton among her private papers until her death. Written in conjunction with the plot outline for a father-daughter incest story she never finished (Wharton had intended to publish the story in a collection with the planned title "Powers of Darkness"), the two-page fragment details the sexual consummation of Beatrice Palmato's incestuous relationship with her father. It is by far the most explicitly sexual writing by Wharton known to exist.

> As his hand stole higher she felt the secret bud of her body swelling, yearning, quivering hotly to burst into bloom. Ah, here was his subtle fore-finger pressing it, forcing its tight petals softly apart, and laying on their sensitive edges a circular touch so soft and yet so fiery that already lightnings of heat shot from that palpitating centre all over her surrendered body, to the tips of her fingers, and the ends of her loosened hair.[4]

For convenience, I repeat the description of Leila's blush in "*Autre Temps* . . .":

> Leila stopped short, her lips half parted to reply. As she paused, the colour stole over her bare neck, swept up to her throat, and burst into flame in her cheeks. Thence it sent its devastating crimson up to her very temples, to the lobes of her ears, to the edges of her eye-lids, beating all over her in fiery waves, as if fanned by some imperceptible wind. Mrs. Lidcote silently watched the conflagration. (264–65)

In both passages, parted lips are the epicenter of palpitating waves of "fiery" heat. Feeding on the illicit aura that, again in both passages, the term "stole" connotes, the flames penetrate to the extreme tips and ends of the body. The consuming force of the fiery experiences is suggested in the two passages by such terms as "devastating," "burst," and "all over her surrendered body." (Franklin's blush arrives with somewhat less of an explosive rush than do Leila's and Beatrice's fiery responses, but it demonstrates the same irresistibly spreading heat, and Wharton describes it as the "same blush" that Mrs. Lidcote had already seen on Leila's face [275].)

What are we to make of the orgasmic language with which Wharton describes Leila's blush? Although sometimes associated with sexual ecstasy, the elusive Lacanian term *jouissance* has been suggestively explicated by Joan Copjec as "a pleasure in the real."[5] In Lacanian theory, the "real" is that which cannot be assimilated within, but also can never fully be denied or excluded by, a given system of "reality," a structured "symbolic order." Although the real cannot fit within our symbolic (articulable) reality, neither does it have a freestanding existence outside of or beyond the order of reality. Rather, the real marks the *internal* limit of a system of reality. It is what prevents a given reality from ever achieving full consistency and transparency.

As a "pleasure in the real," *jouissance* differs from the joy of discovering or comprehending some aspect of reality, which is the form of joy that we usually hope to achieve in the classroom. Rather than marking knowledge or understanding, *jouissance* for Copjec arises "precisely there where we do *not* know. . . . Jouissance is a kind of 'secondary gain' obtained where knowledge fails" (emphasis in original).[6] The intensity of *jouissance* is stimulated when a not quite comprehensible or assimilable "real" and the normal reality that we *can* comprehend and symbolize are in immediate contradiction and rub directly against each other. The sensation of *jouissance* registers that we have reached an internal seam of language and of understanding, where both seem to fail us. Dennis Foster differentiates *jouissance* from garden-variety pleasures: "I use the term to distinguish an experience of intensity, of a loss of ego control and boundaries (which may be felt as horror or delight), from those 'pleasures' of satisfaction, of ego gratification."[7]

Certainly, at some level, Leila does realize that her mother will continue to be socially "cut," but she has no way to frame this fact, even to herself, because it makes no sense to her. Therefore, when Mrs. Lidcote's continued questioning of her daughter forces this incomprehensible, unacceptable real to the surface, it rasps against the liberal commonsense values with which Leila and those around her have come to identify. The intensity of the resultant friction—a friction between current common sense and the violating, against-the-grain, actuality of Mrs. Lidcote's continued cutting—ignites into the ecstatic fires of Leila's blush. It is important to my discussion of teaching *Adventures of Huckleberry Finn* to recognize also that the heated redness of Leila's blush carries both sadistic and masochistic tinges. Sadism always hovers in the air when one approaches some widely known "open secret" about one's interlocutor that would humiliate that person, especially if the interlocutor already suspects the humiliating truth but now begs at least for the certainty of having it confirmed. However, masochism also informs Leila's response. Note the eroticized language of passivity, even helplessness, in Wharton's descriptions both of Leila's intense blush and of Beatrice Palmato's orgasmic ecstasy. Beatrice's vaginal lips are "forc[ed]" softly apart, lightnings of heat shoot all over her "surrendered" body. Caught with "her lips half parted," flame sweeps up Leila's throat and sends its "devastating" crimson to her temples, earlobes, eyelids, until, finally, it is "beating all over her in fiery waves." Leila's forced encounter with her mother's unchanged status—her mother continues to be "cut"—produces an arousing, destabilizing, momentarily all-consuming sensation of punishment, of exciting devastation "beating all over her." Leila's masochistic investment may in part be motivated by a sense of guilt for her mother's situation, guilt deserving of punishment, but it may be motivated also by a desire to experience extremes of helplessness, of powerlessness, so that Leila cannot possibly be responsible for the dreadful, unreasonable position in which her mother finds herself.

"Diversity" Events

Two recent news events, one local to the University of Texas at Austin and the other a story that received national coverage, serve to illustrate my contention that within the symbolic reality of white liberalism the word "nigger" often functions as a trigger for sensations of "intensity" similar to those displayed by Leila. Together, the two events suggest that within white liberal culture the word acts as a sort of do-not-touch button that nonetheless keeps getting somehow pressed. Its activation releases a rush of indistinguishable "horror or delight" at what seems a loss of control and breaking of bounds. Moreover, the *jouissance* provoked by white liberal speakings of "nigger" is quickly repackaged by the media into a more readily consumable masochistic scene of fantasized white male suffering.

During the "diversity" portion of a new-employee orientation in 1999, UT-Austin's white director of Housing and Food Services commented, "When I worked up North, I heard 'nigger' as often or more than I do down here." An assistant later explained that her boss had used the word as an "example." Several offended employees at the orientation, however, took the word to have been uttered in not-so-subtle retaliation against an African American cook whom, just moments before, the administrator had noticed reading a newspaper while he was speaking. The majority of lower-ranking housing and food-service workers at the university are African American or Latino. The administrator apologized the next day for any unintended offense caused by his having spoken the word, emphasizing his personal and professional stand against racism as shown by a "10-Point Organizational Diversity Plan" implemented under his supervision. He conceded in somewhat frustrated disappointment that, in future, "I won't be as strong with my message."[8]

Barely a week before the above incident, the District of Columbia's African American mayor made national headlines by accepting the pressured resignation of a white city official who had used the word "niggardly" during a budget discussion with a black aide. This white official, the director of the Office of Public Advocate, had very strong liberal credentials and was the only openly gay official in the mayor's administration. He was later rehired. Here, the incident did not revolve around whether a racial slur had been spoken with hostile intent, as at the University of Texas event. Instead, the conflict was over whether a racial slur had been spoken at all. As commentators hastened to point out, the Old English derivation of "niggardly" appears to be entirely separate from the etymology of the racial slur, which goes back to the Latin "niger," or black. If the two words are unrelated both etymologically and semantically, can the very sound of "niggardly" nonetheless function as a performative speaking of the racial slur?

At this distance, we cannot judge what conscious or unconscious intentions may have motivated the white aide's choice of words in Washington, D.C., just as we cannot know whether the white administrator at UT intended his use of the word "nigger" to serve antiracist or racially aggressive purposes. (And of course there is also the possibility that he "intended" both at the same time, the former intention being more conscious than the latter.) In both of these incidents, however, a white speaker was at some level missing, not grasping, that the liberal space in which he presumably *thought* he was using a particular word was itself surrounded and permeated by a "real" that rendered that space incoherent. At the University of Texas's "diversity" event, the white administrator—by articulating his ten-point organizational plan, by sponsoring the session at which he spoke, and perhaps even by choosing the "example" that he did—was operating conscientiously within a commitment to moving forward on racial matters. Those African American employees who were offended by his use of the word no doubt also recognized the progressive intentions that certainly played some role in shaping the event during which the administrator made his statement. Yet the offended listeners also attended to another structure traversing, even propping up, the diversity event's progressive framework: that is, the historically familiar scene of a white boss disciplining workers of color (and here disciplining an African American male for *reading*, no less). The administrator's utterance of the word "nigger" marked the moment for the offended listeners at which they became unable or unwilling tacitly to cooperate in overlooking the disjunction between, on the one hand, the official progressive context and, on the other hand, that context's "other" racial structure. Racialized patterns of employment in the Division of Housing and Food Services (and at UT-Austin more generally) meant that, whatever the administrator's own racial attitudes or intentions may in fact have been, he would still remain a white boss saying "nigger" to a group of minority workers.

This underlying "real" ensured that, at least to some listeners, the word performatively "meant" racist insult. We might urge that the white administrator could and perhaps even should have been more sensitive to the racialized asymmetries of power that would complicate (to say the least) his intentions to symbolize and enact the Division of Housing and Food Service's opposition to racism. Yet strictly speaking, no matter how hard he tried, it would not have been possible for this white speaker to take the permeating racial real fully into account—to fit its stark asymmetries successfully into his liberal vision of how we must all work together to overcome the evil of racism.

The incidents at the University of Texas and in the District of Columbia together underscore the almost uncanny inescapability in white liberal discourse of the word "nigger" and all that it conjures up. In a further definition of the "real," Dennis Foster says, "the real names some stain, an obscurity in every representation. . . . It is what can be neither understood nor ignored and therefore is never a source of satisfaction."[9] America's continuing history of violent racial hierarchies and injustices constitutes an ever-present real.[10] At unpredictable moments, this real will "stain," clog, or implode liberal reality in ways that do not yield the "satisfaction" of understanding, let alone resolution. But, did either of the white speakers in these two incidents derive *jouissance,* some "surplus of enjoyment," from uttering the words that abruptly revealed an incoherence in the liberal positions from which they spoke? Who can say? Rather than speculate about those speakers' individual sensations, I think it is more instructive to consider some of the national press response to the forced resignation of David Howard, the D.C. official. Without trying to guess anything about Howard's private experience of the sequence of events, we can nonetheless use aspects of the press response to elucidate some of the psychological and sociopolitical dynamics at play for several commentators who took commonsense positions on the eruption that stained, rendered murky, the liberal space inside Howard's office.

Howard reportedly said, "I will have to be niggardly with this fund because it's not going to be a lot of money" during a budgeting dispute with a lower-ranking African American aide. The latter heard him as having said "nigger" and angrily left the meeting. After the aide complained to Mayor Anthony Williams and to others, the mayor met with Howard and accepted his resignation. Several days later, Howard was rehired.

Many journalists and public figures disagreed with the mayor's initial termination of Howard's employment. ("Seems to me the mayor has been niggardly in his judgment on this issue," then NAACP chair Julian Bond wryly told the Associated Press.) By contrast, some others concurred with Howard himself, who admitted that he had "used poor judgment in using that word" and who told the *Washington Post* that he hoped his own mistake would serve as "a signal flag to all of us."[11] After some searching, however, I was unable to find a mainstream editorial page that agreed with Howard's own assessment of the incident. On the contrary, major editorial pages gave much more blame to the black mayor for the egregious mistake of accepting Howard's resignation. Moreover, for certain editorial and op-ed writers, Howard's forced resignation for having said "niggardly" occasioned outcry.

Interestingly, editorialists and columnists expressed outrage not only on behalf of Howard but also on behalf of the word "niggardly," dwelling on its "long-honored" history of usage by canonical British writers ranging from William Shakespeare to Samuel Richardson to Charles Dickens.[12] Implicitly claiming the word as part of America's proud colonial inheritance from Europe, Colbert King of the *Washington Post* recommended that the complaining black aide be given a "New World" dictionary.[13] The editors of the *Boston Globe* found it "sad to think that a brave word could die from disuse because of ignorance compounded by hair-trigger sensitivities."[14] In a syndicated column from the same paper, columnist Jeff Jacoby saw the need to defend both Howard and the "venerable English word" against what Jacoby called "other people's ignorance of English." For Jacoby, Howard had been "thrown to the wolves." Reporting that one of Howard's "black friends" had described him to the *Washington Post* as "the most gentle, purest guy you'd ever want to meet," Jacoby emphasized, "the victims of mindless racial resentment so often are." In his column's final paragraph, Jacoby admonished his readers that "people everywhere are laughing about this incident. But at the heart of it is the trashing of a decent man, and there's nothing funny about his pain."[15]

The racist and colonialist fantasy into which Jacoby inserts the District of Columbia incident is not difficult to recognize. The "purest" white "gentle" man and the "venerable English" language had both been mindlessly attacked by dark-skinned "wolves" aligned with "ignorance" and, as Jacoby adds, "idiocy." An editorial in the *Atlanta Constitution* summoned the same imagery of a bestial attack when it said that those responsible for Howard's resignation were engaged in "a peculiar and predatory form of race-baiting."[16] (Also fitting with the imagery of a potentially deadly predator would be the *Boston Globe*'s editorial reference to the "hair-trigger sensitivities" of offended black people.[17]) Jacoby himself obviously identified with the "victim." Immediately prior to bringing forward Howard's black friend as a character witness on the fired official's behalf, Jacoby recounted a time when he was himself "denounce[d] as a racist" because he revealed that "the Jacoby family cat" was named Jemima ("—because the cat is named Jemima," he repeats in exaggeratedly innocent disbelief).

The *Jouissance* of White Male Victimhood

Jacoby's vision of the D.C. event—the essentials of which were shared (albeit in less vivid language) by several other newspaper columns and editorials—demeans the African American listener offended by "niggardly" as both subhuman and murderously dangerous.[18] The offended listener is aligned with "ignorance" and "idiocy" for not recognizing the difference between the words niggardly and nigger. (The SAT strikes again: David Howard told a *New York Times* reporter that he learned the word as a junior in high school when preparing for the exam.) Yet interwoven with racist aggressivity, a powerful masochistic impulse also animates Jacoby's vision of the event. His column moves with increasing fervor toward the "pain" that is its last word and in which Jacoby himself, identifying with the wounded Howard, seems to luxuriate. Jacoby theatrically claims in his last paragraph that at the "heart" of the D.C. event is the "trashing" of a decent man. Moreover, in Jacoby's masochistic vision, the public humiliation of this "trashing" is amplified by a large circle of laughing spectators.

In *Taking It like a Man: White Masculinity, Masochism, and Contemporary American Culture*, David Savran traces the postwar "ascendancy of a new and powerful figure in U.S. culture: the white male as victim."[19] Savran's analysis includes versions of white masculinity prevalent among such varied groups as white hipsters of the 1950s and far-right militias of the 1990s. Prominent throughout this terrain, Savran demonstrates, are "masochistic fantasies" of white masculinity as painfully victimized and wounded. These white male fantasies have arisen, he argues, largely in response to relatively modest economic and political advances achieved by white women and minorities since World War II and to the decline since the 1970s in the real wages of white working-class and lower-middle-class men. For Savran, white men imagining themselves as suffering victims ultimately serves as part of a strategy by which they seek to retain their "cultural hegemony" and their "enormous economic, political, and social power."[20]

Savran's description of widespread white-male-as-victim fantasies provides an apt explanatory context for mainstream press reactions to David Howard's losing his job for having said "niggardly." To defend the "venerable" English language against the "ignorance" of racial others is also to defend traditional Anglo-American cultural hegemony. To emphasize the tragedy of Howard's resignation and, moreover, to position the D.C. mayor as the stupidly culpable agent is implicitly to undercut African Americans who supervise white professionals. Yet what about the perverse *pleasure* usually associated with masochism? Such pleasure plays a surprisingly small role in Savran's account.[21] Are these white male masochistic fantasies connected to *jouissance,* to "pleasure in the real"? What is the relationship between white male masochism and *jouissance*'s explosive "intensity," which may be experienced as a "loss of ego controls and boundaries" that "may be felt as horror or delight"?[22] Most pertinent here, do the scenarios of white male pain provoked by the D.C. event derive their energy from the overwhelming excitement that, as I have argued, can arise in the disjunction between liberal reality and an underlying racist real?

When recalling his own experience as a "decent man" victimized by "mindless" charges of racism, Jacoby mentioned that the name of his cat, for which he was attacked as a racist, came up in a column that he wrote criticizing the motor voter law. Trying to show the potential for abuse in a system that allows people to register to vote when renewing their driver's licenses, Jacoby's column claimed that, using the new law, he had succeeded in registering his cat Jemima as a voter in three states. Angry readers, Jacoby related in the tone of an innocent still wounded by a burst of inexplicable hostility, "called and wrote to denounce me as a racist—because the cat is named Jemima." Although Jacoby did not say so, however, the motor voter law aimed to make voter registration more easily accessible to working-class and especially working-class minority citizens. So Jacoby's attempt to use ridicule to undermine the law was also an attack on an attempt to increase minority access to the franchise. The "real" structure of Jacoby's mockingly registering his cat Jemima to vote included the racial dynamics of debate about the motor voter law. It also included the history, ever since Reconstruction, of both ridicule and demeaning animal comparisons used as weapons against African American voting rights. In addition, of course, "Jemima" evokes "Aunt Jemima" and a long history of stereotyping black women. Now, whatever conscious awareness Jacoby may have had about the racial real of the context in which he first disclosed his cat's name (and in this case I do suspect a relatively high degree of conscious awareness), that real could not in any case be acknowledged in a column bemoaning the fate of a "pure" white man, whether David Howard or Jacoby himself, trashed by mindless racial resentment.

Jacoby's column is thus necessarily fractured between its representations of white male innocence and its active participation in a continuing history of white racist disenfranchisement of African Americans. Covertly making the column into non-sense, the friction between its argumentative assertions and its unacknowledged "real" generates an eruptive charge of dissolution or *jouissance*. I suggest that this dangerously explosive sensation is displaced or channeled into the masochistic fantasy of white male "pain" in which Jacoby, by the end of his column, comes luxuriantly to rest. Masochistic fantasies of pain and humiliation (heightened here by Jacoby imagining a circle of laughing spectators) can be scary and painful. But, as scenes that are freestanding and coherent, and that offer the added virtue of psychic familiarity, they are easier to manage than the more traumatic dissolutions associated with *jouissance*.

Huck Finn and the Antiracist Teacher's Enjoyment

An ever-growing body of secondary literature focuses on the vexed intersection of the American literature classroom and the many appearances of the word "nigger" in *Adventures of Huckleberry Finn*. Mark Twain's novel "is generally acknowledged as the literary work most frequently taught in U.S. colleges and high schools," but struggles continue over how best to deal with the racial epithet that appears on almost every page.[23] In contrast to the aversion evinced by some students, parents, and secondary-school teachers, the currently dominant approach to the problem among literary scholars is to treat the word as an especially loaded focal point for a more general question about Twain's text: "Does *Huckleberry Finn* Combat or Reinforce Racist Attitudes?" (This is a section title from the recent Bedford Books edition, *Adventures of Huckleberry Finn: A Case Study in Critical Controversy*.) However, posed within a mainstream academic context, the symmetrically balanced question is something of a set-up, insofar as the great majority of *Huck Finn*'s academic critics will answer that, taken as a whole, the book combats rather than reinforces racist attitudes. Those who argue that Twain's novel serves primarily to reinforce racism are far fewer, and they tend not to derive their primary professional identities from the critical academy.[24]

Many scholars go so far as to view Twain's novel as an unambiguous, uniquely powerful indictment of a racist culture. Critics including David L. Smith, Justin Kaplan, and Shelley Fisher Fishkin see Twain's use of the word "nigger" as always occurring, in effect, within ironic quotation marks.[25] For these scholars, Twain uses the word so often not merely for historical verisimilitude but because he wishes to undercut or hollow out the late-nineteenth-century white construct of the stereotypical "nigger." The task of the *Huck Finn* teacher then becomes to help students recognize the implicit quotation marks around the offensive word, and the subversive work that they perform. As Jonathan Arac has pointed out, however, no one can ensure that students and others will "get" the supposed irony in Twain's use of the word. Nor, in fact, is there any certainty that its local appearances in the text will, or even *should,* be taken synecdochically to refer to some larger "message" from Twain regarding race and racism. This latter interpretive move remains a fairly recent one in the book's history of reception.[26]

Arac traces the fascinating process by which *Adventures of Huckleberry Finn* achieved "hypercanonicity" in the overlapping contexts of the Cold War and the Civil Rights movement. In the 1950s and 1960s, Twain's novel became an "idol" in the academy and in liberal American culture more generally. The book was taken as *the* literary expression of America's democratic spirit. From the 1950s on, Arac shows, *Huck Finn* has been vigorously defended by scholars and mainstream newspaper editorialists alike against charges that it functions to support racism or racist values, in the classroom or anywhere else. Among other effects of *Huck Finn's* hypercanonization, Arac believes, "the idolatry of the book has served, and—remarkably—continues to serve, as an excuse for well-meaning white people to use the term *nigger* with the good conscience that comes from believing that their usage is sanctioned by their idol (whether Twain, or his book, or Huck) and is made safe by the technique of irony." Thus, "even though *Huckleberry Finn* is claimed as a talisman of racially progressive thought and action, one of its major effects is actually to license and authorize the continued honored circulation of a term that is both explosive and degrading." Arac documents, for example, a remarkable pattern of writers praising the impressive humanity that Twain gives to "Nigger Jim"—even though that offensive sobriquet for Jim does not appear anywhere within the novel itself.[27]

As a teacher, I hope that my approach to the novel has stopped short of "idolatry." But when it comes to the word "nigger" I have tended to resort to the Twain-uses-it-in-ironic-quotation-marks approach. I have drawn my students' attention, for instance, to the well-known moment in chapter 32 when, in response to Huck's fib about a steamboat and an explosion, Aunt Sally Phelps asks him if anybody was hurt and he answers, "No'm. Killed a nigger." Here, it is relatively easy to argue that Huck's literally dehumanizing use of the word is part of his clever attempt to play into Aunt Sally's evident assumptions about an expected visitor (who Huck is pretending to be). Especially because of its slightly overdone neatness—Huck's response can be felt as a quick punch line in a patter that continues with Aunt Sally's saying, "well, it's lucky; because sometimes people do get hurt"—it makes sense to see the moment as showing Huck's canny reading of Aunt Sally's likely prejudices, and thus to read his use of the epithet under the sign of irony.

I have not given up raising questions about how "nigger" may function ironically at specific moments in Twain's novel or, perhaps, in the book as a whole. During the past several years of teaching *Huck Finn,* however, I have tried to devote a full class session to having what might be thought of as a "metadiscussion" about the word "nigger." Because my classes often focus on close textual analysis of specific passages, when we study *Huck Finn,* I regularly find myself reading the word aloud, or asking a student to read it aloud. In addition, during discussion, the word will sometimes be used in paraphrases of or informal references to Twain's text, usually by students, but occasionally by myself. In such cases, even when we don't twitch our fingers in the air, our unsaid presumption is that the word is being spoken with *extra* implicit quotation marks around it to show that it is being cited from the text or from "back then," rather than emanating from ourselves. During our discussions, I ask my students to consider possibilities for how the word operates in Twain's book, as well as in pertinent sociolinguistic contexts both from the 1840s (when the book is set) and from the 1880s (when it was written); I provide secondary materials pertinent to those questions. In addition, however, I try to get them to reflect about what actually is happening when "we" in the classroom sound and re-sound "nigger" at the turn of the twenty-first century.

In June 2003, Justice Sandra Day O'Connor wrote for a 5–4 majority in the Supreme Court reaffirming that public universities have "a compelling interest in obtaining the educational benefits that flow from a diverse student body."[28] Ever since the recent wave of organized legal attacks on affirmative action began in the mid-1990s, however, both the meaning and the importance of a "diverse" student body have been much debated on campuses throughout the country, a debate that has continued unabated even after the Supreme Court's decision. At UT-Austin, a study of fall 2002 course enrollments showed that 65 percent of the university's smaller classes (classes with between five and twenty-five students) had no African American students in them, while 90 percent of such classes had either one or no African American enrolled. Eighteen percent of the courses had no Hispanic students enrolled, and 43 percent had only one or no Hispanic member. The university's largest classes were only a bit more racially and ethnically diverse.[29]

In this context, my initiating classroom discussion about "our"—my and my students'—saying "nigger" when analyzing *Huck Finn* has an ulterior pedagogic aim. I hope to provide a concrete classroom demonstration for my students of the importance of diversity in college education. Specifically, I hope to lead white members of my very predominantly white English classes to note and reflect upon the classroom's prevailing hue, and upon how the overwhelming whiteness of the room might limit the reach of our discussion both of Twain's novel and of its contemporary relevance. I hope to foster, that is, an experience-based insight about how a lack of diversity could limit their own learning and growth. As for the one or two African American students who might be enrolled during a given term, beyond hoping that they would not be offended I have usually found myself unable to think coherently about what educational value, if any, they might derive from this discussion. In fact, my "lesson" paradoxically relies upon deemphasizing the presence of black students in the classroom—although I nonetheless remain acutely aware of these students. In conceiving the discussion's goals, I was certainly guilty of reducing the problem of racism to the question of what white people think or feel.[30]

I realize that to take my own classroom reactions as the next "text" through which I continue to explore the issues discussed in this chapter's earlier sections will be to engage both in self-revelation and, unavoidably, in a degree of self-aggrandizement, the full dimensions of which I likely don't even see. But this is not the place, in any case, for maintaining a posture of dignity and detachment. I have so far been presenting my own attempts at antiracist pedagogy in a rational, intellectualized vein. Yet when I am leading my classes in analytic discussions of the word "nigger," my physical and emotional temperature is hot, not cold. I feel my face turning red and often intensely wish that I could transport myself elsewhere. I squirm at my white students' foolish or "inappropriate" remarks, including: "the word is only used for a joke these days"; "black people use it among themselves all the time"; or "my grandparents still use that word but they don't know any better." My underarms get damp as I try to counter that the word continues to possess demeaning implications. Why am I, the liberal and responsible teacher who is doing a liberal and responsible thing, in such a state?

It is easy to identify sources for at least some of my awkwardness and embarrassment. In the first place, who am I to speak about this topic? Second, since many of the white students assume that racism lies safely in the past and plays no role in their own lives or minds, how do I challenge their remarks that appear almost transparently racist—or at least blind to their own race privilege—without seeming to claim a holier-than-thou status (a status that I am just sophisticated enough to know I do not deserve)? Third, and most uncomfortable of all, if there are African American students in the room, who may or may not be contributing to the class discussion, what are they thinking and feeling? Have I made a horrible mistake in forcing them to sit through this? Do they feel ambushed, as if now they "should" say something on a topic that they may have no desire to discuss in this context? Have I made these students angry with me or ensured that they will be more than usually self-conscious about coming to my class for the next several weeks? I am sharply cognizant of the possibility that this is a classic example of those situations that purport to confront racism, but where minority subjects "end up . . . bearing the burden of the lessons imparted to the more powerful while learning nothing themselves that is new or helpful."[31]

To me, these sessions always feel stressful and frustrating, sometimes almost unbearably so. But I also experience them as uniquely intense. They twist my viscera and sensitize the surface of my skin. I leave with churning feelings, mostly of guilt, confusion, and shame, as well as a sort of depressive helplessness. It is a dictum of Freudian thought, however, that where there is guilt there is also unconscious desire. What does it mean that I feel as if I have been caught red-handed in some shameful act every time I embark on a pedagogical attempt to discuss the word "nigger"? What secret desire or, to recur to Wharton's term, "fire" might underlie the guilt? It goes beyond, I think, excitement at breaking a taboo, at the repeating out loud of a forbidden word (which, of course, I know quite well before class that I will do). What strikes me, as I look back over the pattern I have just described, is that for all the pedagogical experience and planning that goes into these sessions, by the time the discussion is over and I walk out of my classroom I am overwhelmed by one question: what was I just doing in there? Not, it is clear, having the teacher's famil-iar and gratifying experience of achieving knowledge regarding some aspect of reality with my students. As Copjec puts it, *jouissance* arises "pre-cisely there where we do *not* know."[32] Part of my charged discomfort when discussing the word "nigger" with my students, I suspect, comes from the eruptive sensation of a collision between my own symbolic position as lib-eral professor and, on the other hand, the racial real of my university, my classroom, and my own psyche.

Regarding the Lacanian concept of the "real," Foster has observed that what operates as the internal blockage or limit for a given reality is not "general or universal . . . the same everywhere for all people." Every struc-tured reality will have its own "real," which depends on the "particular qualities in the forms of symbolic representation at work for a given sub-ject."[33] For the symbolic system that governs my avowedly antiracist class-room at a prestigious and predominantly white state university, the inas-similable real begins with the crazy persistence of racial exclusion. This persistence, which is visible as soon as one becomes conscious of the over-whelming whiteness in the room but remains invisible as long as white-ness continues to be unmarked, can be called "crazy" because, as liberal commentators have noted, it simply does not *make sense* some thirty-five years after the Civil Rights movement is supposed to have changed

America. Indeed, as discussed in chapter 1, the Fifth Circuit Court's ruling in *Hopwood* categorically denied that affirmative action was still necessary to compensate for the University of Texas's admitted history of racial discrimination. Given the university's long-running efforts to make up for past racism (through affirmative action, minority scholarships, and other recruitment and retention efforts) and given that it is now peopled almost entirely by those who had nothing to do with past practices of segregation, most of whom regard those practices with revulsion and anger, the court demanded, how could it make sense to depict the University of Texas as an institution that participates in or perpetuates racism? Yet despite the reality of the university's genuine efforts against its white-supremacist heritage, one has only to look around to see that a real of racist hierarchy and exclusion persists. Soundings of the word "nigger" within my liberal, almost entirely white classroom cannot help but engage this real, from which, moreover, everyone in the dominant group continues to profit. Within what Foster calls the particular "forms of symbolic representation at work for a given subject," I would further specify the real as the unwillingness—or the inability—of most white people in the room, including myself, fully to recognize and to imagine surrendering that unfair profit.

Moreover, if, as M. Garlinda Burton argues, the word "nigger" inevitably conjures up, summons into presence, the violent *history* of white supremacy grounded in the degradation of black people, then speaking the word in my class puts that history into impossible simultaneity with the liberal (arts) tenets ostensibly underlying our discussion. We operate under the assumption that all voices deserve an audience, and that fairness, rationality, and mutual respect should govern our class discussions. Yet, as noted in chapter 1, the history of white supremacy has helped in multiple ways to shape my own and other universities. The University of Texas was founded in 1883, during the post–Reconstruction heyday of white racism. Eighteen eighty-three was also the year that Twain finished writing *Huckleberry Finn,* with its more than two hundred uses (ironic or not) of the racially denigrating word. Several statues commemorating the "lost cause" of the Confederacy, which date from around the turn of the twentieth century, remain on campus. A popular student dormitory is named after a known leader of the Ku Klux Klan.[34] It might seem as if it should be relatively easy to separate the University of Texas at Austin's objectionable and obviously outdated statues and dorm names from its mission, which defines itself in relation to Enlightenment values of reason, truth, neutral expertise, civilization, service, and progress. And it might seem the merest common sense to claim that the open racism of many of the university's founders does not intrude into the practices of my own classroom. After all, the goal of my teaching is to empower students and to improve society through offering guidance in the tools and protocols of critical thought.

Yet recent scholarship has begun to demonstrate the disturbing extent to which the emergence and shaping of these same Enlightenment ideals, in both Europe and America, was entangled with racist and colonialist epistemologies. For foundational Enlightenment thinkers such as David Hume, Immanuel Kant, and Thomas Jefferson, "'reason' and 'civilization' became almost synonymous with 'white' people," while unreason and savagery were equated with non-whites.[35] David Theo Goldberg considers "*the* irony" of Enlightenment modernity to be that, given its universalist claims about human reason, "race is irrelevant, but all is race." In the work of key Enlightenment writers, "racial specificity and racist exclusivity" enfold the very "content and applicability of reason."[36] Thomas DiPiero suggests that, in its colonialist encounters with what it conceived as racial otherness, the Enlightenment constituted whiteness as not "a mode of being but one of knowing." More than a simple form of identity, that is, whiteness was equated with Enlightenment epistemology, which was "intimately bound up not only with the discourses of law . . . but those of logic and reason as well."[37] When teaching *Huck Finn,* I attempt to use critical investigation, logic, and reason to undercut white supremacist assumptions (in part by showing, along with Mark Twain, that such assumptions are arbitrary and irrational). Can the Enlightenment "modes of knowing" that I rely on at such moments ever fully be detached from their recent history of—indeed what might be considered their original entanglement with—"racial specificity and racist exclusivity"? Such questions again point in the direction of an unacceptable real fissuring through liberal American claims to "racial progress," especially when that progress is imaged, as it sometimes is, as increasing enlightenment. (A student in one of my classes once said, for example, "both of my grandfathers are completely unenlightened about race.")

The hot, face-flushing charge that I seem to experience when, in front of a roomful of students, I suddenly sense myself to be embodying a conflict between one "reality" that organizes white liberal identity and another, far more recalcitrant "real" of white supremacy might be metaphorically compared to the sensation of putting one's finger onto some wires assumed to be "dead" and experiencing a jolt of electricity. It would be hard to connect my visceral churning at such moments to "ecstasy" as that term is commonly understood, but Lacanian theory explicitly contrasts *jouissance* with feelings of satisfaction or pleasure. Regarding media responses to the D.C. incident, I have suggested that one place such a charge or jolt might go is into sadomasochistic fantasies of punishment or humiliation. The almost rhythmic incantations of "nigger" during class-room discussions devoted to analyzing and critiquing the word likewise evoke something resembling a sadomasochistic scenario, at least for me as a teacher. To adapt Freud's famous phrase, "a child is being beaten," the syntax of which allows for mobile fantasized identifications with the positions of victim, abuser, and observer, "a word is being said," and said, and said. But, if sadomasochism does come into play here, what are its specific vectors? And who is the child being beaten? I probably take some pleasure in being able to view my white Christian students (than whom, as a Jewish New Yorker, I sometimes feel less white—or, rather, more marked) in the humiliating position of showing themselves to be more discursively naïve, more crudely provincial than I am.[38] They do not know enough to avoid such remarks as "black people use it among themselves all the time" or "the word is only used for a joke these days." As for any students of color in the class, and especially black students, my guilt tells me I must be enjoying something of the voyeur's sadism. Throughout the discussion I glance covertly in their direction. (How does it feel to be a problem? I wonder, not at the moment realizing that I am echoing the famous "unasked question" W. E. B. DuBois perceived in the faces of well-meaning white interlocutors: "Unasked by some through feelings of delicacy; by others through the difficulty of rightly framing it."[39]) Here I enjoy the voyeur's sense of safety because, ultimately, I feel that the word "nigger," no matter how many times it is said, can never really touch or hurt me: I am white.

Apparently at odds with the sensation of invulnerability just mentioned, however, there is also a masochistic sense of myself as a noble victim: as teacher I embody the narcissistic pathos of the committed white liberal, painfully entrapped within paradox and irony. I have sacrificed pedagogical safety and comfort by staging such a discussion, by subjecting myself to oppressive anxiety about my students' feelings, by risking the revelation of my own embarrassed lack of cognitive mastery over this subject. Moreover, there is a masochistic frisson in feeling myself "forced" (by my own sense of political and teacherly responsibility) both to repeat the "n-word" and then to listen to my students as they recite "nigger" in turn. They are licensed to do so, I keep realizing, by my own expectation that they contribute to the discussion. But the masochism here is, by definition, light. These discomforts leave no welts. The one day each term devoted to discussing the word becomes, at least for me, a session of stinging, but ultimately limited and controlled, encounters with the real. My own "suffering" no doubt also helps me feel just a shade less implicated in the persistence of white privilege.

My remarks in this chapter may seem to promote skepticism and pessimism, if not despair, about white antiracist pedagogy, at least as practiced within privileged, mostly white educational contexts. Put most pessimistically: if I am saying that white liberal pedagogy often does not go beyond rubbing heatedly against the racist realities that in fact continue to define and subtend the place of its own enunciation . . . then what's the point? For myself, anyway, I hope that gaining a better grasp on how I "get my enjoyment" will help me develop renewed and, yes, recharged possibilities for participation in real social change. Chapter 6 returns to guilt, cynicism, and hopelessness as immobilizing, inescapable—and potentially productive—modes of white leftist identity.

PART TWO

Gender, Liberalism, and Racial Geometry

S tarting with Kate Chopin's novel *The Awakening* (1899), a literary realist text once in need of recovery but now widely taught and anthologized, and then turning to Steven Soderbergh's Academy Award–winning film *Traffic* (2000), Part Two continues this book's exploration of white liberal identity. In the following two chapters, I investigate the triangulation within both texts of new, "liberated" versions of white gender identity with Africanist and Mexicanist signifiers. I do so with two interrelated aims. First, I wish to show that what Robyn Wiegman refers to as the United States' "contemporary reconfiguration of white power and privilege"—a reconfiguration anticipated in *The Awakening* by Edna Pontellier's accession to a liberal and relatively unmarked whiteness—should be understood as occurring in conjunction with the rise to prominence of "new" white gender identities, identities significantly progressed from sex-role orthodoxy.[1] Second, I hope to begin addressing what I perceive as a limiting presumption that still operates in many literary-studies and cultural-studies treatments of American whiteness: a presumption that the racial two-category system of black and white that became so rigid in the southern United States is the only pertinent system of racial meaning.

The juxtaposition of these quite different texts emphasizes the roles played by Mexican characters and Mexico-associated signifiers in the development of a "new" white femininity (the New Woman) in the late nineteenth century and of a "new" white masculinity (the sensitive, nurturing—yet nonetheless empowered—man) in the late twentieth century. For both works, what Toni Morrison calls "real or fabricated" Africanist elements function in tension and collaboration with real or fabricated "Mexicanist" elements to help define white liberal gender identities that are, in each text, relatively freer from old-fashioned sex roles.[2] Further, these new liberal identities deemphasize their own whiteness and thus become available to figure, whether within or outside their texts, as harbingers of a liberal and ostensibly color-blind American nation.

Compared to literary critics, historians of U.S. whiteness have responded more quickly to the need at least to complicate what Carl Gutiérrez-Jones identifies as "a tendency in U.S. race discourse to pose black/white dynamics as the defining characteristic."[3] Historians working in whiteness studies have striven to trace the *uneven* emergence and spread of a two-category racial system across the nation, dwelling on the many powerful variations and exceptions to that system throughout the nineteenth and twentieth centuries. For instance, Neil Foley's *The White Scourge: Mexicans, Blacks, and Poor Whites in Texas Cotton Culture* explores what it means that, in Central Texas's "triracial borderlands," "whiteness meant not only not black but also not Mexican," and that the latter two categories also shifted their meanings in relation to one another.[4] Historian Matthew Jacobson's *Whiteness of a Different Color: European Immigrants and the Alchemy of Race* traces a shifting geometry of racial significations through the nineteenth and well into the twentieth centuries. It is a geometry of relationships which at varying moments and locations included several different groups that were each considered, both popularly and scientifically, as distinct "races."

By contrast, even such astute literary and cultural critics as Robyn Wiegman, Eric Sundquist, Linda Williams, and Toni Morrison herself still tend to read "whiteness" as constructed only in opposition to "blackness" or, in Morrison's term, Africanism.[5] It is as if our recent decades of literary criticism devoted to analyzing portrayals of black-white race relations, especially in literature set in the South or involving African American migrants from the South, predetermined that, for most literary critics, the emergent field of "whiteness studies" would remain fixated on the two-category system. I do not deny that the black/white axis has been and still remains the single most powerful and pervasive influence on constructions of American whiteness throughout U.S. culture and literature. It is the axis upon which the current book's first two chapters turn. Rather, I am arguing against a default critical assumption that, if a black/white binarism appears within a given literary text, it entirely subsumes whatever other racialized dynamics may simultaneously be at play. Whiteness critics concentrate so intently on understanding and critiquing the complex set of strategies by which literary whiteness establishes itself in relation to literary blackness that they may miss opportunities for recognizing the distinct roles played in certain U.S. texts by other nonwhite categories in defining whiteness (as well as in defining blackness).[6] Critics sometimes substitute the binary "white/of color" for the binary "white/black." However, when the omnibus "of color" is effectively treated by whiteness critics as if it were a unitary category, as is often the case, this nod to multiplicity still risks oversimplifying the complicated, often asymmetrical economies of racialization that contribute to representations of American whiteness.[7]

Moreover, analyzing how more than just one binary set of racial meanings contributes to shaping literary portrayals of whiteness can also sharpen our awareness of divisions *within* literary whiteness. Indeed, if it does not make sense to regard "of color" as a unitary category in a work such as

The Awakening, neither does it make sense to regard "whiteness" as unitary within Chopin's text. Rather, *The Awakening* emphasizes ethnic differences between its white Protestant female protagonist Edna Pontellier and the Old World, Catholic, French-speaking white "Creoles" among whom she finds herself. I argue in chapter 3 that, through the play of descriptions and connotations among the novel's Africanist presence, its Mexicanist presence, its portrayal of Old World whiteness, and, finally, Edna's white Protestantism, Edna herself emerges as an American New Woman, a national figure seemingly beyond ethnicity and thus ready for adoption by white feminists of the 1970s and 1980s.

Understanding such dynamics in *The Awakening* provides both a framework and useful points of reference for the reading that then follows the "new" version of liberal masculinity developed by Michael Douglas's character in *Traffic*. Douglas's new masculinity emerges most vividly through its uneven triangulation with an African American drug dealer (who in a racially charged scene takes sexual advantage of Douglas's iconically white American daughter) and a layered but ultimately opaque Mexican police officer. As we will see, this triangulation also helps Douglas's character, Judge Robert Wakefield, distinguish his liberal American masculinity, still empowered but now relatively unmarked as white, from the eminently white centers of power he begins the film by representing.

CHAPTER THREE

Awakened White Femininity and a Shaping Mexicanist Presence

Since the appearance in 1992 of Toni Morrison's paradigm-changing *Playing in the Dark: Whiteness and the Literary Imagination,* critics have striven to respond to her mandate that we develop a new "critical geography." Offering both eloquent argumentation and brilliantly developed critical examples, Morrison urged that readers must learn to recognize the "informing, stabilizing, and disturbing" role played throughout the United States literary terrain by a "dark, abiding, signing Africanist presence." That presence has always, since before our nation's beginnings, helped to constitute "America" as such. If the United States is "the oldest democracy in which a black population accompanied (if one can use that word) and in many cases preceded the white settlers," then, perforce, "American literature could not help being shaped by that encounter." *Playing in the Dark* asks, how has the United States' pervasive Africanist presence helped to organize, to give texture and meaning, to "literary 'whiteness'"?[1] Trying to answer Morrison's question has produced remarkable results throughout U.S. literary studies, ranging, for instance, from Shelley Fisher Fishkin's *Was Huck Black?* to Kenneth Warren's *Black and White Strangers* to Eric Sundquist's *To Wake the Nations.*

Despite the vast border Mexico and the United States share, comparatively little scholarship has been devoted to a question that might be taken as analogous to Morrison's: How has the centuries-old encounter between the United States and what José Limón (following Américo Paredes) calls Greater Mexico helped shape literary whiteness in the body of material that U.S. critics often think of simply as "American literature"? (By Greater Mexico, Limón means people of Mexican descent from "either side of the border," "with all their commonalities and differences."[2]) If a black population accompanied and, as Morrison emphasizes, in many cases preceded white settlers to this country, so too a Mexican population inhabited significant areas of what became the United States long before those areas' mid-nineteenth-century incorporation. (Roughly 20 percent of the U.S. population now lives on land that was once part of Mexico.) Moreover, of course, Mexican-descended people have continued to inhabit these and other parts of the United States ever since, exercising incalculable influence on the cultural, financial, and political economies of the regions.

In the field of literary studies, much important work has been done by scholars associated with the Recovering the U.S. Hispanic Literary Heritage Project, as well as by other scholars, in locating and elucidating a richly diverse tradition of Mexican American and Chicano literature. Such recovery work, however, does not take literary whiteness as a primary concern. Thus, few scholars working primarily with literary materials have asked how paying fuller attention to the abiding, signing "Mexicanist" presence (adapting Morrison's terminology) in the United States might also help us reread certain "Anglo" texts, ones that are usually seen as unrelated to the nation's Hispanic literary heritage. Again, adapting Morrison's terms, how has "a real or fabricated" Mexicanist presence been used "to limn out and enforce the invention and implications of whiteness"?[3]

The lack of critical attention to the influence of "Mexicanism" on constructions of whiteness is especially striking, given the long and continuous significance in U.S. culture of Mexico, Mexicans, and Mexican Americans. For scholars of what Morrison calls "literary whiteness," models for understanding textual relationships between it and literary or textual Mexicanism seem an especially important need now, in light of census data from 2000, which reveal that Hispanics, primarily Mexicans and Mexican Americans, already outnumber African Americans in such key states as California and are on the verge of becoming the nation's largest minority.

Explicitly responding to Morrison's challenge finally to *see* American literature's shaping Africanist presence, the most powerful recent line of argument about Kate Chopin's *The Awakening* contends that the sexual, political, and creative dimensions of Edna Pontellier's "awakening" all depend upon an unacknowledged "racial midwifery." Citing, for instance, the domestic labor (childcare, cleaning, cooking, and errands) provided for Edna by "nameless, faceless black women," Elizabeth Ammons insists that "the very liberation about which the book fantasizes is purchased on the backs of black women."[4]

Michelle Birnbaum, who has developed this line of argument about *The Awakening* most fully and subtly, emphasizes in particular how Edna's access to a freer, richer sexuality is facilitated, even structured, by the many black women who surround her. Highlighting a series of implicit, oblique, and even hidden textual connections, Birnbaum shows that Edna does not only take the physical labor of African American women for granted. She "employs as well their tropological potential, their associations with the marginal and, ultimately, with the erotic." Birnbaum draws, for instance, on Hortense Spillers's suggestion that the mere presence of a mulatto in works of American literature serves to evoke illicit sex: the mulatto presence permits dominant white culture "to say without parting its lips that 'we have willed to sin.'" Using this logic, Birnbaum argues that the "quadroon" nursemaid who frequently appears near Edna carries a "literary inheritance" of libidinal connotation. Despite the fact that in Chopin's portrayal the nursemaid seems to lack both subjectivity and sexuality, for Birnbaum the aura of illicit sex that hovers about the mixed-race woman's very existence helps emphasize Edna's own awakening desires.[5]

This is true, to the extent that racist cultural assumptions linking African American women and ungoverned sexuality can never be far away when African American women appear in a text such as *The Awakening*, which deals explicitly with a white woman's emerging desires. It is important, however, to recognize the differences in how *The Awakening* treats its African American women characters and how it treats Mariequita, a local "Spanish" or Mexican girl on Grand Isle.[6] For instance, Chopin gives no mention or even hint of active sexual desire on the part of any African American women in the book. But Mariequita, by contrast, explicitly regards Edna as a sexual rival for Robert and, later, Victor, both of whom, as the text openly implies, she has had some previous sexual connection with. With her "round, sly, piquant face" and "coarse" bare feet with the "sand and slime between her brown toes" that especially draw Edna's gaze, Mariequita is the one female character in the novel who takes adulterous sex for granted as an ever-present possibility. She says as much to Robert when she asks if Edna is his "girlfriend," and she teases Victor later in the book that she "could run away any time she likes to New Orleans with Célina's husband."[7]

Why does it matter if African American women *connote* unsanctioned sex in *The Awakening* because of the book's literary and cultural context while Mariequita more directly *denotes* it? It matters, I suggest, because there is a shaping *Mexicanist* presence in Chopin's novel, one that is not simply collapsible into the larger category "women of color." *The Awakening*'s Mexicanist presence works complementarily with the Africanist presence that Birnbaum and Ammons, following Morrison in this case perhaps too literally, have helped elucidate. But the novel's Mexicanist presence also has its own different valences, its own specificities. The most striking of these centers on the book's constructions of white gender identity, both feminine and masculine.

Consider, for example, the freighted question of Robert Lebrun's masculinity. Part of what, at least initially, makes Robert a good catalyst for Edna's emerging desire is that he stands somewhat outside the paradigm for normative bourgeois masculinity represented by Edna's husband. But this also makes his masculine status uncertain. Léonce Pontellier is an eminently desirable man, both sexually and financially. Edna's marriage to him makes her the "envy of many women whose husbands were less generous than Mr. Pontellier" (48). The group of ladies who hover around the box of "toothsome" sweets that he sends to her choose "with dainty and discriminating fingers, and a little greedily," as they declare "that Mr. Pontellier was the best husband in the world" (9). By contrast to Léonce, who leaves home every weekday for eight hours of hard but lucrative work on "the street" (Carondelet Street, the center of New Orleans's financial district), Robert Lebrun's primary occupation seems to be assisting his mother to run her hotel. He never visits the local men's club, Klein's, where the vacationing Mr. Pontellier goes to smoke cigars, gamble, and talk about business. A grown man of twenty-six years, the "boyish" Robert is permitted to flirt with his mother's female guests only because, as Edna's friend Madame Ratignolle humiliatingly reminds him, nobody thinks of taking his attentions seriously. When he protests—"Am I a comedian, a clown, a jack-in-the-box? . . . Am I always to be regarded as a feature of an amusing programme?"—Madame Ratignolle squelches his complaint: "You speak with about as little reflection as we might expect from one of those children down there playing in the sand" (38).

Unlike Alcée Arobin, for instance, a bachelor whose attentions to a woman always arouse sexual suspicions, Robert's removal from the categories that Edna's society associates with grown-up masculinity makes him a "safe" male companion for Edna. He can spend endless hours with her without it even occurring to Mr. Pontellier to object. Yet while Robert's innocently juvenile status smooths the way for the early stages of his and Edna's relationship, this status must alter for him to develop into the central object of her mature and acknowledged sexual desire. How does Robert's figuration shift to that of an adult, sexualized masculinity? This shift, which also enables a crucial jump in Edna's awakening (specifically, her conscious recognition of her desire), occurs via *The Awakening*'s Mexicanist elements.

I have mentioned already the novel's suggestion of a previous sexual affair between Robert and Mariequita. The suggestion is made most strongly just after Robert has left Grande Isle for the long trip to Mexico that keeps him absent until almost the end of the book. The artist Mlle Reisz tells Edna an anecdote about Robert thrashing his handsome younger brother Victor a year or two earlier over "a Spanish girl, whom Victor considered that he had some sort of claim upon." When Edna asks, "Was her name Mariequita?" Mlle Riesz answers yes, continuing, "Oh, she's a sly one, and a bad one, that Mariequita" (68). In addition to emphasizing Robert's physical strength and triumph in combat, the anecdote places Robert as intimately involved with a "bad" woman, one whom men fight over. Visioning Robert in a sexual relation with Mariequita helps Edna bring him into focus as the man whom her own "impassioned, newly awakened being" craves. Robert's connection with Mariequita allows him to appear to Edna as an active sexual agent. Toward the end of the book, when Edna is moving toward her attempt at seducing Robert, a similar triangle—this time involving "a transcendently seductive vision of a Mexican girl" whom Edna jealously fantasizes Robert having met during his trip—adds to Robert's status as a sexually experienced, sexually desirable man (97). Just as important, Edna's imagination of this "seductive . . . Mexican girl" helps fire up her own determination to act as an assertive sexual agent.

The Awakening's specific setting in and around New Orleans, and in particular the book's frequent allusions to nineteenth-century New Orleans's highly systemized indices of African American identity, helps explain why Chopin's novel places Mexicanist women more explicitly into the racist slot of darkly lustful than it does Africanist women. As Birnbaum suggests, one effect of placing the book's black servants and nannies onto a fixed grid of racial ratios and hierarchies (categories The Awakening deploys include "mulatto," "quadroon," and "griffe") is paradoxically to make them serve as "stable counters to Edna's flights." By contrast to Edna's rebellions against a conventional social order, New Orleans's complex but rigid traditions of racial hierarchy render "the mulatto" and "the quadroon" into, as Birnbaum has explained it, "reminders and reinforcements of cultural tiering."[8]

As is symbolized by Mariequita's first introduction on an unanchored boat, however, as well as by the fact that the "transcendent" Mexican seductress whom Edna later imagines is supposed to live in far-away Vera Cruz, the novel's Mexican women do not bear this same association with New Orleans's traditional order. The Mexican women are thus free to represent a wild space, one outside the regular rules and denominations of New Orleans society. At the same time, however, this wild space is literally contiguous with New Orleans. The "seductive," "sensuous" sea that figures so prominently in Edna's awakening is, after all, the Gulf of Mexico (14).

We see none of Robert's actual sojourn in Mexico, but his trip there plays a key role in his assumption of a socially readable, full masculinity. When he returns, Edna perceives in Robert's attentions "an added warmth and entreaty that had not been there before" (93). Mexico has long functioned in the southern and southwestern U.S. imaginary as a liminal zone for American males, a place from which American boys return as men to be reckoned with. This U.S. figuration of Mexico has been operative at least since Civil War–era discourse about the Mexican War. There, we find Confederate and Union officers' experience in the invasion of Mexico described as transformational in their development into formidable fighters and leaders. (Civil War enlistment posters invited potential recruits to fight side by side with the "heroes of the Mexican War.")[9] The trope of Mexico as a site for the passage of (white) boys into manhood has remained important, especially for Westerns and other genres that locate themselves near the border.[10]

In addition, as befits New Orleans' nineteenth-century status as the primary port for U.S. trade with Mexico, Robert's ostensible motive for his trip is finally to enter the male world of business and moneymaking. When his mother's guests express disbelief about his forthcoming trip, Robert protests in the same tone of frustratedly defensive pique in which he had responded to Madame Ratignolle's assumptions that his flirtations could never be serious: "'I said all along I was going to Mexico; I've been saying so for years!' cried Robert, in an excited and irritable tone" (40). Once it is clear that Robert really is going, Mr. Pontellier himself confirms Robert's achievement of recognizable masculinity, finding it "altogether natural" for a "young fellow . . . to seek fortune, and adventure in a strange, queer country." As he narrates to Edna, when he encountered Robert making final preparations for his trip on Carondelet Street, the two of them "had gone 'in' and had a drink and a cigar together" (45). The extra quotation marks that Chopin places around the word "in" within Léonce Pontellier's speech call attention not so much to Pontellier's use, in conversation with his wife, of a polite euphemism for drinking establishment. Instead, the emphasis on "in" here signifies the adult masculine space into which Robert finally gains inclusion by heading off on a Mexican quest.

Even as this Mexican trip helps change Robert's status into that of a man among men, the conventional masculinity into which the trip allows him to enter will also, ironically, motivate the novel's and Edna's own final refusal of patriarchal structures and assumptions. Edna's suicidal swim out into the ocean constitutes a rejection of—even an escape from—all the other scenarios she sees as open to her. Most notably, and often surprising to students, she refuses any possibility for a familiar love story ending, one that would allow her and Robert, having finally declared their feelings for one another, to be together happily ever after.

Edna does not fear that Mr. Pontellier would never agree to a divorce—
she concurs with Robert that "we have heard of such things" (102). Nor
does she fear public opinion, as is made clear by her actions since the relatively early moment when she simply stops attending her own Tuesday
reception hours. Rather, she gives up on the possibility of a future with
Robert because she senses that his passage into socially recognizable manhood implicates him in a system that can only ever imagine her as an
object of exchange, whether as a wife or as a mistress. Robert's voyage to
Mexico, where he will supposedly seek "fortune, and adventure in a
strange, queer country," allows Mr. Pontellier to invite him "'in,'" as he
puts it, to share a cigar, but once Robert has been thus recognized as a full
member of the grown-up men's club, he also joins Mr. Pontellier as a
potential owner and exchanger of women.

When, having returned from Mexico, Robert proposes to Edna that
perhaps her husband will set her free so she can become his wife, Edna
responds, "I am no longer one of Mr. Pontellier's possessions to dispose of
or not. I give myself where I choose. If he were to say, 'Here, Robert, take
her and be happy; she is yours,' I should laugh at you both." Robert is as
disturbed as Mr. Pontellier himself would be at Edna's explicit withdrawal
not merely from one particular marriage but from the culture-shaping system of female exchange that marriage subtends: "His face grew a little
white. 'What do you mean?'"(102). The whitening of Robert's face here
indicates not only his shock but also his by now complete identification
with the entitlements of adult white masculinity. (After his trip to Mexico
he makes it a point that he now buys his own cigars, "a whole box" at a
time; before the trip, the still-boyish Robert had smoked symbolically less
phallic cigarettes because "he could not afford cigars" [100, 5].)

Similarly revealing a certain structural equivalence between Robert and
what had previously seemed to Edna the contrasting significations of
patriarchal entitlement is Alcée Arobin's conversation with Robert about
the alluring beauty of Mexican women. In his early discussion with
Madame Ratignolle, Robert enviously cites Arobin as a man whose
advances toward women are, unlike his own, taken to have a genuine
force to them. After Robert's return from Mexico, however, Arobin himself expresses a friendly jealousy over Robert's apparently having gotten
"so deep in their regard" that one of Vera Cruz's "stunning girls" had given
him a silk pouch (96). (The hint of sexual imagery here—a silk pouch
supposed to represent, like a trophy, Robert's having gotten "so deep in"
with Mexican women—further reinforces the idea of his Mexican trip as
a rite of masculine passage.) Edna's witnessing this moment of classic male
bonding between Robert and Arobin, her seeing the two men connect,
however casually, over the girls of Vera Cruz, prepares for her recognition,

just before committing suicide, that even the strength of her feelings for Robert will not lift her above the options of wife or degraded mistress: "'Today it is Arobin; tomorrow it will be someone else. It makes no difference to me.'" "She even realized that the day would come when [Robert], too, and the thought of him would melt out of her existence, leaving her alone" (108).

Mexico and Mexicans, even when they are only invoked in conversation or in a character's imagination, play a key role in defining both Robert's white masculinity and Edna's "awakened" femininity, the latter both in its empowering mode of sexual agency and desire and in its final mode of despairing insight. I want now to consider a brief yet complex moment in the text where the invocation of Mexico serves somewhat differently to further *The Awakening*'s articulation of gendered whiteness. I am interested here in how the text's Mexicanist presence helps position Edna to serve, as she would for many readers in the 1970s and 1980s, as an icon for a specifically national, as well as specifically liberal, white feminism, albeit one that unselfconsciously assumes its own cosmopolitan universality. Although scholars who have written on whiteness in *The Awakening* do not emphasize this complicating factor, the book itself often reminds readers of the ethnic, cultural, and linguistic differences between Edna's Kentucky Protestant identity and the New Orleans "Creole" society in which she finds herself, a white Catholic aristocracy descended from Louisiana's first French and Spanish settlers. How does the novel's emphasis on these white ethnic differences intersect with the Mexicanist presence in the book to create space for a New Woman, a universalized figure seemingly beyond ethnicity? Defined in part against the emphatically white Creole identities of New Orleans, Edna emerges ready for adoption by a later generation of white American feminists who sometimes ignored their own relation to white privilege.

When Robert surprises his mother and her summer guests by announcing that he will be leaving that very afternoon for Mexico, it provokes among them a "general and animated conversation . . . concerning Mexico and Mexicans" (43). As with most of the participants in this conversation, Madame Ratignolle's contribution seems almost comically irrelevant to the purposes of Robert's trip. Her comment is noteworthy, however, as the most explicitly racist reference in the book:

> Madame Ratignolle hoped that Robert would exercise extreme caution in dealing with the Mexicans, who, she considered, were a treacherous people, unscrupulous and revengeful. She trusted she did them no injustice in thus condemning them as a race. She had known personally but one Mexican, who made and sold excellent

tamales, and whom she would have trusted implicitly, so soft-spoken
was he. One day he was arrested for stabbing his wife. She never knew
whether he had been hanged or not. (41)

Most crucial here, I believe, is the slightly mocking indirect discourse with
which the narrative voice distances itself from Madame Ratignolle's
remarks. The narrative voice compresses Ratignolle's lurid anecdote into
flat reportorial language and continually reminds readers that the conclu-
sions drawn from it are hers and not its own by such phrases as "she considered," "she trusted," and "Madame Ratignolle hoped." The distancing
note in this paraphrase serves two functions. For one, it allows the narrative voice to signal its own allegiance to the generous liberalism supposed
to characterize the high realism championed in the U.S. at the time by
William Dean Howells. The narrative voice, that is, wants it to be clear
that only Madame Ratignolle, not itself, "trusts" that she does Mexicans
"no injustice in thus condemning them as a race" despite her having personally known "but one Mexican."

In addition, however, Madame Ratignolle's grasping after crude stereo-
types and her obvious failures of empirical reasoning emphasize the limits
that inhere in her particular version of white femininity. Like Howells's
idealized "cardboard" grasshopper, which he famously adduced as an
example of the romantic artifice that literary realism must move beyond,[11]
Ratignolle's "mother-woman" or domestic angel is set up from the start as
foil to Edna's progressively awakening real female self. (Chopin emphasizes
Madame Ratignolle's almost allegorical status as antitype to Howellsian
realism by saying that her appearance suggests "the bygone heroine of
romance and the fair lady of our dreams" [9].) But Ratignolle's silly and
biased remark about "Mexicans" also provides an opportunity to cast her
domestic angelicism as, so to speak, too *white*. Ratignolle's artificially protected whiteness embodies an innocence that actually translates into
embarrassing provincialism, or even offensive ignorance. Implicitly created is a space in which Edna's version of awakened white femininity can lay
claim to a femaleness not overtly marked as white, a femaleness that lends
itself to being taken as both natural and universal.

Throughout the book, Madame Ratignolle's whiteness is underlined
not only by her description as "pure white," "the fair lady of our dreams"
with "spun-gold hair" and blue eyes, and not only because she personifies
the Creole woman's "lofty chastity," but also because she is visibly "more
careful of her complexion" than Edna (9, 10, 15). By contrast to Edna,
Madame Ratignolle always wears veils and gloves so as not to tan, and she
never forgets to carry a protective parasol when outside. I suggest that
Madame Ratignolle's "lofty" display of ignorance about Mexico and

Mexicans, along with her insistence that she has only ever come into contact with one representative of the Mexican "race," connote the same thing as does her overscrupulous protection of her complexion—that is, an overcareful, even forced, and thus *marked* white femininity. The Creole woman functions in Chopin's text to embody an unnatural Old World whiteness, proper only to a "bygone heroine."

When the Creole woman is put into relation with Edna, as well as with the text's "real or fabricated" Africanist *and* Mexicanist presences, the Creole woman allows Edna's American Protestant whiteness to appear as simplified, contemporary, nonethnic, and normative. This normative whiteness has been accepted not only by those readers who have tended towards treating Edna as representative of "woman" under patriarchy. It has also been accepted, in a sense, by more recent "whiteness studies" analysts of *The Awakening*. Construing Edna's whiteness as part of a binary system whose other member is "of color" is the flip side of treating the latter as synonymous with African American.

CHAPTER FOUR

Trafficking in Liberal Masculinities

One hundred years after Kate Chopin's publication of *The Awakening*, director Steven Soderbergh and screenwriter Stephen Gaghan released *Traffic*, an epic movie about the interlocking economies of drugs and money that traverse the United States and Mexico. Michael Douglas stars as Judge Robert Wakefield, the film's central protagonist. The explicit concerns of Soderbergh's movie differ markedly from those of Chopin's novel, as do the gender and, hence, the relative freedom and social empowerment of each work's leading character. But, taken together, *The Awakening* and *Traffic* make a productive critical juxtaposition for the purpose of exploring connections between the achievement of "liberated" gender identities on the one hand and, on the other hand, the reproduction of unmarked liberal whiteness.

In a movement that parallels Edna Pontellier's changing relationship to conventional femininity, Judge *Wake*field "awakens" from unthinking allegiance to a traditional model of manliness into a new, more liberal masculinity. The "new" masculinity into which he awakens strives to free itself from hardened conventions about a man's familial and social roles. It thus becomes more available for contemporary white liberalism's universalizing processes of identification. As we will see, Wakefield's development of a new masculinity takes shape through the interplay of "real or fabricated" (recurring once again to Toni Morrison's terms) white, Mexicanist, and Africanist elements.

Released in the final year of Bill Clinton's presidency, *Traffic*'s depiction of Wakefield maps a trajectory of supposed liberal progress, from a Reagan-era style of law-and-order manhood to the nurturing, empathic style of masculinity projected by Clinton. Wakefield's new, Clinton-era style of liberal masculinity—in the film's final line of dialogue, he insists that his role as father is above all "to listen"—will allow him to reconstitute his own wounded family within a community comprised of people in "recovery" from addiction and its associated damages. *Traffic* ultimately proffers the "new" Judge Wakefield as a harbinger for a newly liberal American polity.

In his influential study, *Moral Politics: What Conservatives Know That Liberals Don't*, cognitive scientist George Lakoff has linked the "worldviews" held by conservatives and liberals on the contemporary U.S. political scene with two divergent models of child raising and family governance. Both conservatives and liberals, Lakoff asserts, share a "conceptual metaphor" of "Nation-as-Family," with the government in a parental role and citizens as children. But while conservatives support a "strict father" model of the family, and thus of the national polity, liberals believe in a "nurturant parent" paradigm for familial life. The latter framework, which "seems to have begun as a woman's model [but] has now become widespread in America among both sexes," serves as a cognitive "prototype" for the liberal vision of how government should function.[1] Whether in the "strict father" or the "nurturant parent" version, these family-based conceptual structures are "deeply embedded" in conservative and liberal viewpoints on a wide range of political and social issues. Moreover, it is because the nation-as-family metaphor usually functions at a level below conscious awareness that liberals and conservatives tend to misjudge each other's motives and values. Not recognizing the divergent cognitive paradigms that underlie either their own or their opponents' views, nor the basic family models on which the paradigms rest, both liberals and conservatives remain mystified by how the other can disagree on matters that seem merely common sense, such as the best ways to reduce crime.[2] Lakoff's cognitive modeling is unable to account for critical facets of Judge Wakefield's move from a conservative to a liberal constellation of identity—preeminently the role played in his transformation by racial and sexual fantasies. Yet Lakoff's emphasis on the nation-as-family metaphor and on two contrasting options for conceiving state and parental power, as nurturing or as strictly disciplinary, resonates with *Traffic*'s narrative elements and thus provides a useful starting point for our analysis. In Lakoff's terms, I begin by exploring Wakefield's shift from a strict father "worldview," which initially determines his approach both to his own family and to the nation's drug problem, to a nurturant parent model.

Appointed by his personal friend, the president of the United States, to be director of the Office of National Drug Policy ("drug czar"), Judge Wakefield works out of the White House itself. He begins the film, both in his "tough job" (Wakefield's own phrase) and in his family, as a hard-edged embodiment of the Law with a capital L. Almost his first line in the film, uttered while presiding over a trial, is "when you make the decision to have marijuana on your farm, whether it's one joint or an acre of plants, your property can be seized and your property can be sold." Wakefield is the leader and public face of the United States' "war on drugs" (with a special fondness, as his wife points out, for using military metaphors to describe his work). In the course of the film, events push Wakefield's identification with the law to its most extreme edge: a combination of the Charles Bronson–style "vigilante," kicking in doors and throwing people against walls to get them to talk, and the implacable John Wayne–style "searcher," dedicated to rescuing and redeeming the iconic white daughter from corruption by nonwhite men. Finally, however, Wakefield comes to recognize that the old-fashioned style of white masculinity in which he is expected to and does prosecute the drug war—as an authoritarian, hard-driving workaholic who usually has a glass of scotch in his hand—is in crisis. He ultimately comes to see this style of white masculinity as a hollow failure.

What is the relationship, I wish to ask, between Wakefield's movement toward a liberal mode of masculine identity and the triangular "traffic" that Soderbergh's film develops among its constructions of Mexicanist, Africanist, and white people and the spaces in which these characters are portrayed? The movie explicitly thematizes the intersections among racialized people and spaces that, in Chopin's 1899 novel, require interpretative teasing out. The film self-consciously illustrates a complex crisscrossing of drugs and money among such racially and economically diverse locations as Mexico City, a desert outside Tijuana, the Tijuana–San Diego border crossing, Washington D.C., wealthy suburban neighborhoods in California and Ohio, and an African American ghetto in Cincinnati. In certain ways, *Traffic* demonstrates a higher degree of self-awareness regarding its own deployment of racial signifiers than does *The Awakening*. For instance, the film's U.S. settings studiously include a minority prosecutor and judge. In addition, the two most visible street-level Drug Enforcement Administration (DEA) agents in the film, Montel Gordon (Don Cheadle) and Ray Castro (Luis Guzman), are African American and Latino, respectively. And Benicio del Toro won an Academy Award as supporting actor for his portrayal of Javier Rodríguez Rodríguez, the courageous if opaque Mexican police officer with a commitment to justice. The movie's explicit intention seems to be a multicultural portrait of interconnection and interdependence, one that breaks away from the simplicity of "us" (typically meaning white) vs. "them" (typically meaning nonwhite) that has been part and parcel of the drug war metaphor. Through most of *Traffic*, both good and bad guys come in at least three "colors" and at least two nationalities.

Yet despite *Traffic's* multiple characters and story lines, Michael Douglas's Judge Wakefield is at the film's center. Douglas is the biggest star in the film, and his is the only character, for instance, who crosses into each of *Traffic*'s primary locations.[3] In addition, although other characters also undergo development and growth, Robert Wakefield's character arc is most fully defined and, by comparison with other key figures such as Del Toro's Javier and Catherine Zeta-Jones's Helena, his arc is most accessibly readable. Judge Wakefield's sixteen-year-old daughter Caroline, moreover, serves as the film's most emotionally invested emblem for what Wakefield calls "our country's most precious resource, our children," a resource that has been "targeted" by the illicit drug trade.[4] With all its multicultural characters and international settings, *Traffic* remains a work whose most focused concern is the fate of the white American family and the father whose task it is to take care of them in a dangerous and corrupt world.

Awakening to a Crisis in White Fatherhood

In the primary (but by no means only) irony that *Traffic* sets up, sixteen-year-old Caroline Wakefield's descent into addiction, theft, and prostitution is paralleled by her father's first months in his new job as national drug czar. He takes the job because, in his view, "the war on drugs is a war that we *have* to win, and a war that we *can* win." Wakefield's view of how to win the drug war and thereby protect America's (white) children combines a tough-on-crime amassing of police and military resources to stop drugs from crossing the Mexican border with the encouragement of a zero-tolerance policy among American families, starting with his own. Making drug treatment more available does occur to Judge Wakefield, early in the movie, but only as an afterthought. When his daughter is arrested for drugs and spends a night in jail, he finds it ridiculous to consider whether she might need "any kind of therapy." He prefers instead to "clip her wings" by grounding her.

It becomes almost immediately clear both to viewers and to Wakefield himself, however, that his mode of strict paternalistic governance is failing. This failure is most forcefully articulated through Wakefield's increasing frustration that he cannot maintain either the United States' external border with Mexico or, more personally horrifying for him, the internal border separating the African American inner city from wealthy white suburbs, such as where his own family resides. Regarding the border with Mexico, Wakefield discovers that it is, in the words of one drug runner, "disappearing." Three times as many drugs are getting through now as six months ago, the movie claims. When Judge Wakefield visits the border, he sees, as described by the screenplay's stage directions, "anarchy." Here, the United States is losing (or, as a character insists, has "already lost") the drug war. The Mexican drug cartels have more money and more sophisticated equipment than does the DEA. Wakefield's predecessor in the post of drug czar, a retired army general, has no advice to offer him other than on how to prepare an exit strategy from the job. Law enforcement in Mexico is corrupt and Wakefield has trouble finding a counterpart, somebody to "interface with on their side." Mexico itself is mysterious and hard to read, visually depicted throughout the movie as grainy and ochre-tinged.

Mexico's lengthy and historically vexed border with the United States renders "Mexicanism" particularly available to evoke the crisis of an America unable to control foreigners and foreign substances crossing into it from outside. The seemingly insoluble difficulties presented by the United States' external border with Mexico threaten Wakefield's patriarchal sense of himself as guardian of boundaries and of the law. But the strict father's most personally gut-wrenching, life-changing failure occurs when he proves unable to maintain even the internal borders supposed to guarantee his own family's purity and privilege. Caroline Wakefield serves as *Traffic*'s symbol of the horrors that can ensue when middle-class white suburban youth, alienated from those who should offer them love, understanding, communication, and support ("nurturant" parenting, in Lakoff's terms) are sucked into drugs and drug culture. As played by Erika Christensen, Caroline is a visual icon of young white femininity, with blonde hair, large light-colored eyes, and luminous ivory skin. Caroline's craving for Mexican drugs leads her to steal from her parents, run away, and then become a prostitute for an African American drug dealer. One might say that she is the movie's traffic circle, around (and into) whose body flow not only drugs but the film's racialized, sexualized themes and fantasies. She is, furthermore, at the center of her father's movement from a conservative to a more liberal identity.

Cognitive science has no use for the unconscious in what Lakoff dismissively calls "the Freudian sense," an unconscious that struggles to repress unacceptable thoughts, desires, and fantasies. Instead, Lakoff makes it a point that the cognitive paradigms he elucidates can be considered "unconscious" only colloquially, meaning simply that we are not always as attentive as we could be to their role in structuring our thoughts.[5] Lakoff's disdain for psychoanalytic insights (a disdain widely shared by other cognitive scientists) means, however, that his "cognitive modeling" cannot explain the role that racialized, sexualized fantasy and paranoia play in a film such as *Traffic*. The eruption in the movie of a paranoid fantasy central to the history of American racism proves key in Judge Wakefield's eventual movement from a conservative, strict father to a more liberal and nurturing yet still masculine parent.

The scene in which drug dealer Sketch (Vonte Sweet) first has sex with

Caroline operates not only as the movie's most intense, but also as its most racially-charged, emblem of the degradation that drugs inflict on white America through its prized signifier of innocence, white children. (Tellingly, the scene has been treated by reviewers as the nadir of Caroline's downward trajectory—instead of, for example, the scenes in which her preppy white "boyfriend" Seth [Topher Grace] purposefully drugs her into virtual unconsciousness and then has sex with her.) In what follows, I dwell on *Traffic*'s portrayal of the sex scene or arguably, as we will see, rape scene between Caroline and Sketch because it is the moment in which the filmmaker's desire to be politically and multiculturally correct seems to break down. My close attention to the interracial sex/rape scene may risk participating in what I believe is the film's almost fetishistic need for that scene and also in the same narrowing of critical focus to white/black inter-actions that I have criticized within whiteness studies. Yet in order to understand *Traffic*'s specific geometry of racialized significations, and the manner in which that geometry ultimately produces a "new" white masculinity for Robert Wakefield, it is crucial to analyze why this liberal film includes a blatantly racist portrayal at almost precisely its midpoint. The scene between Caroline and Sketch adheres closely, in both form and content, to a primal fantasy within American racism, whose heyday was the white-supremacist, post–Reconstruction South: the fantasy of a white maiden violated by a black "brute," with the corollary of a heroic white man "rescuing" her at the last moment and enacting violent "justice" on the supposed perpetrator.

The restaging of this virulent racist fantasy serves two related functions in the movie. First, it offers an almost crystallized final opportunity to test Robert Wakefield's old-fashioned style of strong, uncompromising white masculinity. The director of national drug policy may not be able to control the confusing Mexican border, but he should be able to exert mastery over his domestic crisis—"domestic" in the sense of being both family-based and nationally familiar. A still-influential tradition of racist propaganda, including prominent pop-culture representations, urges that Judge Wakefield *must* rescue his daughter and punish her dark-skinned violator and, moreover, that he *should* be able to do so. But after Wakefield's increasingly desperate, cowboy-like attempts to act as heroic white rescuer fail, it becomes evident that an additional purpose, directly central to the film's liberal project, is served by *Traffic*'s projection of Sketch and Caroline's encounter through the lens of classic racist paranoia. *Traffic*'s liberal project requires this seemingly anomalous restaging of a classic racist scenario because it ultimately allows Michael Douglas's character to enact his own decisive "awakening" from a simplistic and often violent tradition of white identification with the Law. Wakefield's finally deliberate turn away from the heroic white role of violent rescuer and restorer has a meaning not unlike that of a white liberal's determination to *Never Say Nigger Again* (see chapter 2). White liberals need the word "nigger" in order *not* to say it, and to differentiate themselves from *other* whites who do say it. So too, when Wakefield rejects the heroic and violent white masculinity that is traditionally triggered by the racist fantasy of violated white womanhood, he solidifies his claim to a "new" kind of enlightened , flexible, and ostensibly non-racist masculine identity.

The movie—and Robert Wakefield—unconsciously require a restaging of the racist fantasy of black brute violating white daughter. The way the scene is shot makes clear that the movie also derives a certain cinematic pleasure or excitement from that restaging. The sequence in question begins with an exterior establishing shot of Caroline, who has run away from her rehab center and now wanders as the only white figure through the crowded streets of an almost entirely African American ghetto. She has crossed without protection into a threatening, internally foreign part of America. Wandering, Caroline is trying to find the building where her preppy boyfriend Seth previously took her to buy drugs. Suddenly, the scene cuts to a disorienting shot, blurry and uneven, of a partially blocked view of a dirty ceiling and an unshielded lightbulb. The right side of the visual field is blocked by a large dark form moving up and down. As we hear grunts we suddenly realize that we now occupy Caroline's point of view as the large black shape is (in the words of the screenplay) "pounding away" above her (us), on her (us), in her (us).

The startling temporal elision between this jerky handheld shot and the previous long-view exterior shot of Caroline on the street has edited out whatever talking or negotiating preceded the sex, thereby erasing Caroline's agency and giving the scene, as she lies there stoned and passive, a rape-like feel. Dimly lit from behind, Sketch (Vonte Sweet) initially appears without features but simply as a pitch-black and thrusting mass. His face only gradually emerges as an insistent knock at the door makes him curse and get up from Caroline. We watch the naked Sketch walk to the apartment door, receive some money through a slot, come back toward the bed to retrieve drugs from a duffle bag, and return to the door to pass the drugs through the same slot.

The brief sequence of shots depicting this doorway transaction focuses almost entirely on Sketch's naked body. His is the only body in the film that receives this sort of camera attention. As Sketch walks away from the bed toward the door, light glints off his brown skin, emphasizing the muscles of his back, buttocks, and upper legs, as well as the sheen of sweat derived from his exertions atop Caroline. The camera then roughly aligns with Sketch's own point of view as he returns to Caroline the second time,

Figure 1 (From *Traffic*)

where she is, adapting Richard Dyer's terms in an essay about Lillian Gish, "lit for whiteness."[6] Backlight trained on Erika Christensen's hair emphasizes her blonde curls, creating a distinct halo effect. Key lighting picks out her white throat, arms, and shoulders against an otherwise dark background. One sees the blue in her eyes very clearly.

Still lying down, Caroline gestures languidly toward the bag in which she now knows Sketch keeps his drugs. He takes out a syringe. It will be the first time she has received heroin in traditional junkie manner, by needle. A remarkable series of frames is filled by Caroline's lit face, with Sketch's black hands visible in the lower center holding the syringe upright. Testing it, his hands make liquid ejaculate from the syringe, so that white splotches shoot straight up from it, blotching or marring the visual image of Caroline's face (figure 1).

Finally, he moves down her body to pick up her right ankle, probing and turning it until, from above, he injects her in the upper foot, again penetrating her white skin. As Caroline's eyes lose focus and she swoons back, Sketch takes a moment to relish her face on the pillow and then lowers himself onto and into her body. The scene closes as it began, with him as a featureless black mass "pounding away" on top of her. Sketch's very name indicates his depersonalized and stereotyped function.

Caroline's passive white femininity, as it is penetrated, contaminated,

Figure 2 (From *Traffic*)

and obscured by Sketch's criminal black body, immediately places this scene within what Linda Williams has identified as "the most influential melodramatic story of all American culture: the story of black and white racial victims and villains."[7] In her incisive study *Playing the Race Card: Melodramas of Black and White from Uncle Tom to O. J. Simpson,* Williams has argued that this culturally pervasive melodramatic story about race exists in two complementary versions, "Tom" and "anti-Tom," both of which ultimately support white-supremacist logic. Each of these two forms of racial melodrama is epitomized in recurrent scenarios.

"Tom" melodramas repeatedly show a black male body beaten by sadistic white men.[8] By contrast, what Williams calls "anti-Tom" melodramas derive their force from images of stereotyped black "brutes" threatening or violating helpless white femininity. D. W. Griffith's *The Birth of a Nation* (1915), with its notorious scenes of former slaves trying to "claim" white women during the Reconstruction era, is an ur-instance in American culture of the "anti-Tom" melodrama. The *Traffic* scene that I have been discussing directly recalls the most viciously racist scenes in *Birth of a Nation.* Indeed, the shot with which *Traffic*'s "sex" scene closes, when Sketch's dark head pushes into the frame above Caroline's swooning white femininity as he again starts moving on top of her, visually echoes the moment in *Birth of a Nation* in which Silas Lynch (George Siegmann) is poised to force

Figure 3 (From *The Birth of a Nation*)

himself on the swooning Elsie Stoneham (Lillian Gish) (figures 2 and 3).

The classic supplement to this scene involves a white hero, often a vigilante, thundering to the rescue. Gwendolyn Brooks's poem about the vigilante lynching of Emmett Till captures "the beat inevitable" of this central white American fantasy, while also ironizing it: "The milk-white maid . . . Of the Ballad. Pursued by the Dark Villain. Rescued by the Fine Prince."[9] In Griffith's *Birth of a Nation,* the rescuing "fine prince" is Ben Cameron (Henry Walthall) dressed as a white-robed Klansman galloping on horseback down the road toward the interior room in which the dark villain Silas Lynch has confined the helpless milk-white maid, Elsie Stoneham.

So too, the resolute Robert Wakefield doggedly drives through the ghetto in his car, searching for Caroline, at one melodramatic moment barely missing her as she cuts across a street on her way back to Sketch's dark apartment. Wakefield's crisscrossing of the ghetto in search of

Caroline also evokes John Wayne's Ethan Edwards in director John Ford's *The Searchers* (1956), who rides hard back and forth along the western border desperately determined to reclaim his young niece from Scar, the evil Indian captor who wishes to make her his "squaw." Wakefield returns home only for sleep and brief mechanical interchanges with his wife Barbara (Amy Irving). The historical and psychocultural weight on Caroline's father of her specific sexual-racial "peril" pushes him here toward the embattled, antidomestic edge of his identification with law, mastery, and justice. During the search sequence, Michael Douglas comes closest to occupying the extreme "cowboy," white masculinity of a John Wayne or Clint Eastwood, especially at such moments as when he kicks in a flophouse door or storms into a classroom and roughly yanks Caroline's cocky prep-school boyfriend out of the room, growling to the frozen teacher that Seth has to go on a "field trip."

This explicitly more menacing version of Robert Wakefield's strict father identity has been elicited by his last encounter with Caroline before she runs away, a scene which makes evident that the embattled father's violent aggression can be directed not only toward those who threaten his family, but also toward his family itself. In that scene, Wakefield has burst his way uninvited into his daughter's bedroom. Caroline, oblivious, is seated on the toilet "cooking" her drugs in the private bathroom that opens from her bedroom. Wakefield turns the bathroom doorknob with increasing intensity, finally shouting in anger, "open your goddam door!" When she does open the door, having taken her hit, Caroline's face has the same vague smile and her head lolls just as it does later on Sketch's bed. Her father pushes her against the bedroom wall and takes her face in one of his hands. Turning it toward him so as to look at her eyes, he squeezes her cheeks, which forces her mouth to protrude and open. "Fuck you," she says to him, still smiling dreamily. "Well, FUCK YOU!" he screams back at her, three times as loudly. He puts his finger in her face: "You are not going *anywhere,* young lady." "You're like the Gestapo," she retorts. Wakefield's dictatorial posture, for all of its threatening and implicitly sexualized rage (almost shoving his finger into her open mouth), achieves nothing. The scene closes with Wakefield slumped against the wall, looking weary and defeated. Very shortly after this scene, Caroline is in the streets and then in Sketch's bed.

Technically, Wakefield's character does not witness Sketch's sexual "pounding" of Caroline, but that image is primal for the white-male subject position with which he becomes aligned during the search sequence. For him, the film's racially melodramatic portrayal of Sketch with Caroline—which the audience has viewed before Wakefield begins his search—hovers as an unspoken fantasy propelling his increasingly frantic

efforts to find his daughter. Unlike American prototypes of heroic and
relentless white defenders, however, Judge Wakefield's final confrontation
with the transgressing racial other proves fruitless and humiliating.
Wakefield finally arrives at Sketch's apartment (to which he has forced
Seth to bring him) and hammers angrily on the door. Sketch opens the
door to Wakefield with a big gun, which he holds to the head of the suddenly trembling federal judge. Threatening to kill Wakefield and put his
body in a dumpster, Sketch warns him never to come back. When
Wakefield offers to pay him a thousand dollars for information, Sketch
tells him scornfully that if he wanted Wakefield's money he would simply
take it. For all Wakefield (or, for that matter, the viewer) knows, Caroline
is behind the door of Sketch's apartment at that very moment, either desperate to be rescued or eager for her father to be chased away, or perhaps
too drugged-out to know what is happening. Unlike John Wayne, Clint
Eastwood, or the Klansman in Griffith's film, Wakefield's rescue of
Caroline will succeed only when he abandons what Seth calls the "vigilante thing."

Judge Wakefield stumbles out of Sketch's building, blinking, into the
glaring daylight of a dirty street. Walking several yards ahead of him, Seth
(who rarely shuts up) says patronizingly, "Look . . . man, I'm telling you.
Don't do this vigilante thing." At the remark, Michael Douglas stops
dead in his tracks, startling Seth who has now reached the parked car.
Douglas stares at Seth as he takes something out of his pocket, his face
growing darker, more frustrated and more grim. The viewer feels his frustration, his alienation, and his desperate rage. Because the camera stays
above his waist and hand, we can't see what Judge Wakefield is holding.
He slowly lifts his arm and pauses, clearly pointing something at Seth,
but we can't quite make out what. It might be a gun. Here it comes, we
for a moment think: Michael Douglas will now turn to the "vigilante
thing" in earnest, ready to blow away all those who have hurt his daughter. Called vividly to mind is Douglas's character in *Falling Down* (1993,
directed by Joel Shumacher), where the actor played a frustrated divorced
white male, known in the film by his license plate D-FENS (he worked
for a defense contractor before being laid off), who snaps and starts
shooting minority residents of Los Angeles in an attempt to recover his
sense of patriarchal mastery. But in *Traffic,* when Robert Wakefield finally "shoots" we discover that he was holding only a remote control key to
his car's front door. The car beeps and Robert quietly gets into it, returning to the domestic sphere of his wife and home. He is reunited with his
daughter shortly thereafter.

This key moment of transition—in which what might have been a gun-
drawing gesture of macho vigilantism turns into a movement back toward

the domestic sphere—constitutes Judge Robert Wakefield's most distinctly marked step away from the old version of white masculinity up to which he has heretofore tried to live. Using his remote control to open his car door and drive home at scene's end—and, more broadly, becoming a liberal, "nurturant parent"—represents a change of policy and posture for him. In another movie, Wakefield might have returned to Sketch's apartment with a gun even bigger than the drug dealer's or with a "posse" of police and federal agents. Here, it is as if *Traffic's* liberal conscience suddenly shakes itself awake and steers its protagonist away from the alluring white revenge fantasy. Wakefield pointedly extracts himself from the *Birth of a Nation* scenario: black brute violates white daughter; white hero destroys black brute, restoring racial order. Instead, he drives back to his home and enters into a newly tolerant, enlightened version of manhood. In so doing, Wakefield also establishes a protective zone of distance between himself and the racialized, sexualized fantasies of violent domination that help drive the U. S. government's strict father mode of prosecuting the war on drugs.

Yet it is crucial that Wakefield's switch of "worldview" to that of the liberal nurturer by no means eliminates the law's need for violence in the world that *Traffic* portrays; it merely shifts the enactment of that violence onto the shoulders of an African American DEA agent in the United States and a Mexican policeman working the border. Meanwhile, the political organization and bureaucratic administration of this violence are left, when Wakefield resigns as drug czar, in the hands of the notably white staff of the White House. This set of displacements is integral to Wakefield's assumption of a liberal, relatively unmarked whiteness analogous to that attained by Edna Pontellier in *The Awakening.*

A Dirty Job

It is no simple accomplishment for *Traffic* to portray Robert Wakefield's giving up the fight against Mexican drug cartels and black street-level dealers as a renewal of white fatherhood, and ultimately of the American nation itself, rather than as their joint defeat. After all, the cartels still send drugs across the border at will, supplying dealers who then seek to push the drugs into every intimate fold of American life. The dangers to America's children continue, and will perhaps even escalate. In ironic counterpoint to Wakefield's resignation from his public post as hard-edged guardian of America's children, California-based Carlos Ayala (Steven Bauer) dubs his new, supposedly foolproof technique for smuggling cocaine "the project for the children": it involves shaping an odorless version of the drug into what look like innocent plastic toys.

Indeed, Ayala's naïve wife, who until recently had no idea that her husband was anything but a law-abiding businessman, herself descends into the underworld to arrange a hit against the star witness in her husband's trial; the witness is killed despite the cadre of cops supposed to protect him, and charges against Carlos are dropped. Even as Ayala, a "handsome, charismatic second-generation American in expensive conservative clothes" (as Stephen Gaghan's screenplay puts it), enjoys his son's lavishly overdone birthday party, staged in what the screenplay calls a "starter castle," he uses his cell phone to arrange for his best friend and lawyer to be killed.[10] Intended to exhibit home, family, friends, and wealth, the child's birthday party—which constitutes the film's third-to-last scene—instead exudes pretension, ruthless greed, and ready violence. Given such ever-spreading webs of corruption, crime, and danger, how can Judge Wakefield abandon his hard-edged persona as drug czar—how can he walk away from his public mandate to protect "our nation's most precious resource, our children"—without appearing culpable or derelict?

Traffic is too committed to a gritty aesthetic of hard-boiled realism (and to the "realistic" view of crime and criminals that characterized Bill Clinton's version of liberalism) to imply that the war on drugs can ever be concluded, let alone won. The movie makes clear that somebody still has to keep putting away the bad guys. As Wakefield himself puts it when he first takes his job, drug busts are crucial as "symbols," ways of "sending a message" to drug gangs that the law remains "serious about putting the top people away."

Differentiating what he calls the "hard-boiled" crime story from the classic "English country house" genre of detective fiction, Raymond Chandler writes that the former do not encourage the belief that "murder will out and justice will be done—unless some very determined individual makes it his business to see that justice is done." Such individuals were "apt to be hard men, and what they did, whether they were called police officers, private detectives or newspaper men, was hard, dangerous work. It was work they could always get. There was plenty of it lying around. There still is."[11] Judge Wakefield passes through and then moves beyond the role of a "very determined individual who makes it his business to see that justice is done," a role located at the hardest edge of strict father American masculinity. But Wakefield's transcendence of that role does not mean that the "hard, dangerous work" of representing the interests of justice and law in a corrupt world is no longer necessary. There is still "plenty" of such work "lying around." It may no longer be Wakefield's personal "business" to embody hard justice, but a *noir* world such as that which *Traffic* has spent almost three hours establishing, in which corruption, hypocrisy, and violence always hover, continues to require "hard men" to take up the classically male task of confronting the corruption and violence with uncompromising resolve, courage, and physical force. Given the vicious, power-hungry criminals *Traffic* has already so vividly portrayed, criminals that threaten America both internally and externally, the film's representational economy demands the continued presence of a dedicated and credible counterweight, "some very determined individual" who, as Wakefield initially says of himself, has signed on "to do a tough job," indeed to organize his identity around it.

Judge Robert Wakefield can "awaken" into a new and less constricting masculinity, one defined by openness, empathy, and emotional connection, only because of the presence of two minority characters in the film who serve to absorb the hard, dangerous work of personally ensuring that justice is done. As Wakefield's personal transformation gradually develops, parallel plot lines in *Traffic* follow two other representatives of the law, Don Cheadle's black DEA agent Montel Gordon in the United States and, in Mexico, Benicio del Toro's police officer Javier Rodríguez Rodríguez. After witnessing his longtime partner and friend Ray Castro (Luis Guzman) get torn apart by an Ayala hit man's car bomb, a fiercely determined Gordon starts over again at the end of the film with the difficult task of bringing the California-based Ayalas to justice.

Meanwhile, Rodríguez shifts into an active and high-level fight against Tijuana's drug cartels (he had previously worked for one of them). At extreme risk, Rodríguez personally initiates busts of several "top people" in the Juarez cartel, including his own former mentor. Rodríguez and Gordon become "very determined individual[s]," the "hard men," who, by movie's end, have assumed responsibility for the "hard, dangerous work" of ensuring that justice is at least sometimes done. Having effectively portrayed the primary threats to white American children as originating from bad, violent Mexican, Mexican American, and African American people and places, *Traffic* now concludes that these threats should be met on the "front lines" (in a phrase Wakefield himself formerly used) by African American and Mexican agents of the law.

But in taking on the personal identification with law and strict justice from which Wakefield extricates himself, Rodríguez and Gordon also assume the emotional and other isolations that come with that "tough job." Steely resolve and sealed-off interiority come with the territory of planting oneself in between insidious, aggressive evil and vulnerable innocence. Neither Rodríguez nor Gordon is portrayed as having a family. Indeed, the victory *Traffic* gives to liberal identity against strict father conservatism in their competition to define the "worldview" of the movie's protagonist renders the normative nuclear family as the exclusive preserve of white liberalism. By movie's end, both Rodríguez and Gordon seem quintessentially alone; each has accepted the classically American roles not only of hard-boiled *noir* hero, but also of cowboy loner. Even their respective best friends have been killed by drug traffickers.

Consider as a pair the film's last and third-to-last scenes. The two scenes sandwich Robert Wakefield and his family's final appearance at a recovery meeting (which I conclude by discussing below). In the ante-penultimate scene, the now partnerless Gordon walks alone, without a warrant, into the Ayala house during the little boy's almost parodically luxurious birthday party. In the midst of tussling with two burly bodyguards, Montel achieves his goal of planting a surveillance bug under the dining table. He allows himself a small smile of success as the guards toss him out. Our last sight of Gordon is of his back, as he walks alone down a road.

In *Traffic's* final scene, Javier sits among a crowd of Tijuana families enjoying the new well-lit baseball field as dusk descends over the game. The field, a valuable and unifying amenity for the community, was secretly funded by the DEA as Rodríguez's payment for his dangerous machinations against the Juarez drug cartel. At this point, Rodríguez's partner Manolo Sanchez (Jacob Vargas) has been executed by drug dealers, and Rodríguez has lied to Sanchez's wife about it, trying to paint Sanchez as having died a hero's death. Rodríguez's own parents are dead from a flood because they lived in substandard housing. Rodríguez himself has turned over for arrest and torture the corrupt general who first promoted him to a position of power.

Director Steven Soderbergh makes visually clear in this final scene that, despite his being surrounded by an animated crowd, Rodríguez is essentially alone, separated as if by an invisible wall. When Rodríguez's face comes into focus, those of the happy families become blurred. When all around him clap for a good play on the field, he waits several moments before joining in, and even then he claps more slowly than the others, in a different rhythm. Rodríguez's status here recalls that of John Wayne in *The Searchers'* bittersweet last scene. As Ethan Edwards, Wayne stands with his body framed by the doorway of the happy family that his heroism has made whole again; because of what he has seen and done, and because of what he still must do, he cannot enter the house and join them. Edwards turns and walks away; the door closes and the screen goes black.[12] Updating *The Searchers, Traffic* reassigns Edwards's isolating task—the task of preserving the homely values of family and community by going after the ruthless and immoral non-white "savages"—from white Robert Wakefield to Mexican Javier Rodríguez and black Montel Gordon.

In a version of the same crossings and interchanges that constitute *Traffic's* titular theme, Gordon's lonely walk down the road and Rodríguez's status as among but not part of the crowd of Tijuana families help make possible Wakefield's immersion in the warm space of the U.S. recovery meeting, which is placed exactly between these two other images. The presence of these two hard, dedicated men in the film's closing sequences, one inside the United States and one working the Mexican border, ensures that Wakefield's shedding the military metaphor of "drug war" from his own outlook, and seeking to reconstruct himself as part of an egalitarian, emotionally sharing recovery community, will not leave a glaring hole in society's protection against irredeemably bad people.

Recovery Nation

Robert Wakefield hangs up his badge, so to speak, as hard-line enforcer of law and order so he can become part of a community of individuals recovering from addiction. He has come to realize the value of human connection, emotional vulnerability, and intimacy. He now grasps that these are rendered impossible when one strives to embody justice and the law. Moreover, he has encountered the law's own inescapable relationship with obscene violence; he understands that this obscene violence may take as its desired object not only lawbreakers but also those whom the law is supposed to protect. As he says when quitting his job, "If there is a War on Drugs, then our own families have become the enemy. How can you wage war on your own family?"

It is important to emphasize the distance that Robert Wakefield has traveled. Edna Pontellier's awakening into New Womanhood in *The Awakening* entailed her differentiation from the heavily marked whiteness of the New Orleans's ruling Creole establishment, a whiteness that was part and parcel of that establishment's rigidly defined sex and gender roles. It was not only Pontellier's movement away from the expected female role of (as Chopin puts it) "mother-woman," but also, I have argued, her disaffiliation from aggressive modes of whiteness that made her available for her reception in the 1970s, 1980s, and early 1990s as a general symbol of rebellious American woman. So too, when Wakefield literally walks away from his role as hard-line drug czar he detaches himself from a White House represented by English actor Albert Finney as White House chief of staff and D. W. Moffett as Jeff Sheridan, Wakefield's smarmy and officious assistant. Wakefield also dissociates himself from the arrogantly privileged (and ironically named) neighborhood of "Indian Hills," the affluent Cincinnati suburb in which his family lives and which seems most fully personified by the conceited and preppy Seth.[13] (All of the Indian Hills teenagers and adults we meet in the film are white.) In separating himself from these two contexts, Wakefield renders himself seemingly more marginal to the trappings of power and privilege in

America. His whiteness thereby becomes less ostentatious, less obvious. He is more available for identification with the normal, the average, the universal, as well as more available for alignment, I suggest, with what *Traffic* envisions (or hopes for) as the nation's liberal future.

Caroline's recovery meeting constitutes the Wakefield family's final appearance in the film. The meeting is replete with language and phrases derived from such "twelve-step" programs as Alcoholics Anonymous or Narcotics Anonymous. Despite the anonymity adhered to within real life twelve-step programs, though, the film implies that the presence of Caroline's parents at the meeting is crucial to her recovery. Caroline's first attempt at battling her addiction failed at least in part because her parents simply dropped her off at a treatment center but did not themselves join her recovery community. Now, however, the Wakefields sit gratefully in the audience during Caroline's turn "sharing" at the podium. When asked if they want to share as well, Judge Wakefield introduces himself and his wife by their first names and, after pausing a moment, says that they are here to offer "support" and "to listen."

It is noteworthy that the first, failed recovery sequence in *Traffic*, when Caroline runs away from the treatment center and directly to Sketch's drugs and bed, depicts only white participants. The final, more successful recovery sequence depicts a group still primarily white but now strategically sprinkled with people of color, including Latinos and African Americans. A middle-aged Hispanic woman nods with sympathetic approval as Wakefield says that he is there to support and to listen. One catches a glimpse of the top of an African American man's head, with a squared-off haircut that appears very similar to that of Sketch. However, if Sketch's body-as-penis represented a visceral threat, the body and face of this black man are blocked from the screen, all threat erased, by a white group member sitting in front of him. The discussion leader at the recovery meeting is a white man named Jim. One can say here of *Traffic* what Rosalinda Fregoso has argued is true of John Sayles's film *Lone Star* (1996), that the re-envisioning of a "multicultural order" is "subsumed and contained within the point of view of whiteness and masculinity which is privileged in the narrative."[14]

Traffic's American portion closes with the recovery meeting in order to model a new liberal polity, one that serves to complement Michael Douglas's "new" white masculinity and that intimates the film's hope for a saner and more tolerant post–drug war America. Safe within a therapeutic space, the recovery community both turns away from and substitutes itself for a militarized nation devoted to the Sisyphean task of policing its borders yet rent by ugly internal divisions and hierarchies of race, class, and power. The meeting, where everyone is given at least the option to "share," proffers a

seemingly liberal alternative to the failed national polity. Replacing the alien-
ating hypocrisies of the United States' official ruling circles, the multicultural recovery community acts as a kind of liberal utopia, one which provides
sincerity, emotional connection, shared purpose, and a sense of egalitarian-
ism.[15]

When a choked-up Robert Wakefield, unable to continue delivering his
written speech, walks out of his final press conference as drug czar and gets
into a cab, with the White House still in the background, the only words
he utters are directed to the driver: "National Airport." Of course this bit
of dialogue fits into the plot's diegetic surface, but it also carries the suggestion that when Wakefield leaves the putative seat of the nation for the
space of the recovery meeting (where we next see him), he is heading for a
truer and more real "National" space, a truer and more real America. The
camera stays on his face for a lengthy close-up during the cab ride, emphasizing Robert's newly opening interiority. The scene ends only when Judge
Wakefield reaches up to loosen his constricting tie. He is, as Chopin says
of Edna Pontellier, "casting aside that fictitious self which we assume like
a garment with which to appear before the world" (Chopin, *The
Awakening*, 108). This marks a new beginning for him, as a father, a citi-
zen, and a man. Yet Wakefield's new beginning as a nurturing liberal has
been rendered possible in *Traffic* not by eliminating the strict father, but
by racializing him and his functions. The strict father's functions both of
embodying and administering the law have been divided and distributed
among a tough and lonely African American cop, a mysterious Mexican
police officer with vigilante characteristics, and the overmarked whiteness
of the White House. In thus refiguring the strict father, this liberal movie
succeeds in rewriting his national role from solo star to supporting cast.
Center stage is cleared for the liberal, relatively unmarked whiteness of the
new Robert Wakefield.

PART THREE

American Innocence
and Liberal Guilt

Federal Agent Jack Bauer: "I don't think you can justify killing millions of innocent civilians."
Terrorist Marie Warner: "Nobody is innocent in this country!"
Fox TV's popular drama "24" (February 25, 2003)

American innocence, a theme with a long national and prenational history in the United States, showed up with renewed prominence after the terrorist attacks of September 11, 2001. For many sources, liberal and conservative alike, the attacks marked the "loss" of American innocence, an innocence that, it was thus implied, had existed up to the moment of the first plane's impact. But American innocence in this context seemed to mean different things to different commentators. For some, what was lost on September 11, 2001, was a supposedly national sense of invulnerability, which had now been proved illusory. Here, American innocence appeared to connote something like physical virginity for the national body, a status or at least a feeling (now lost) of never having been violated by foreign others.

For other commentators, the lost American innocence in question was a widespread absence of knowledge about places and peoples outside of the United States. We had not realized that other people could be so different from us, and so angry at us. For some, American innocence signified more metaphysically as a failure to grasp the nature and malevolent persistence of "evil" as such. The loss of this innocence meant our belated recognition of omnipresent and ubiquitous danger in the world, exacerbated by modern technologies such as cell phones and passenger jets. Our national safety would henceforth require ever-expanding suspicion and vigilance, both inside and outside the United States. Indeed, from now on we would have to be prepared to exert deadly force even before our nation was itself attacked.

In response to the widespread discourse of lost American innocence that followed the September 11th attacks, more than one historically minded writer pointed out that Americans had been widely reported to have lost their innocence after other national traumas as well, from the

Civil War to Pearl Harbor to the assassination of President Kennedy and the Vietnam War. They asked what it meant that American innocence seemed perpetually available for "losing" yet again. Much more controversially, however, certain leftist intellectuals insisted that the September 11th attacks served to emphasize America's *lack* of innocence, the nation's current and historical *guilt* for pernicious actions around the world. These leftist intellectuals uniformly condemned the terrorist attacks: despite right-wing attempts to imply otherwise, they did not take the extreme point of view represented in my epigraph by the television character Marie Warner, who plots to destroy Los Angeles because of what she sees as her own nation's irredeemable international guilt ("Nobody is innocent in this country!" she screams). Many leftists nonetheless insisted that Americans could be construed as "innocent" only in their naiveté, whether willful or otherwise, about their own nation's past and current role in the world. Still, claims about American innocence and virtue continued to function as ideological touchstones in the nation's mobilization for its so-called "war on terror," including the invasion of Iraq.

Albeit with larger and more widely visible stakes than usual, post–September 11th back-and-forth exchanges about American innocence and guilt exemplify a dynamic with which leftist intellectuals and academics have become frustratingly familiar. That is, working in diverse registers, we analytically "strike through the mask" (to borrow words from Herman Melville's Ahab) of American innocence, exposing the ambiguities, ambivalences, and actual history that lie beneath it. In so doing, we help produce varying degrees of liberal guilt for those paying attention—and perhaps most of all for ourselves—only to see a presumption of American innocence emerge unscathed as central to most Americans' (or at least to most white Americans') sense of their national identity. The two chapters that conclude *Liberal Identity, Literary Pedagogy, and Classic American Realism* read novels by Henry James and Edith Wharton in the context of present-day political and cultural discourses of American innocence and American guilt. A critically presentist approach to this fiction, I believe, can help us at least begin to frame possibilities by which the Left might move beyond its repetitive but seemingly futile attempts to dismantle the ideology of American innocence.

CHAPTER FIVE

"A Good Fellow Wronged":

CHRISTOPHER NEWMAN AND THE
FEELING OF AMERICAN EXCEPTIONALISM

Scholars agree that "American exceptionalism" has been a remarkably persistent dimension of U.S. culture and identity, even though the term tends to be used somewhat differently within different disciplines. For scholars of American literature, American exceptionalism usually refers to a set of presumptions and desires concerning the unique status, unique character, and, above all, unique mission of America.[1] Originating even before the birth of the United States, American exceptionalism in the latter sense initially took shape as the Puritans' vision of founding "a city upon a hill," a community elevated by God with the mission of modeling Christian charity and virtue to the rest of the world. This exceptionalism subsequently evolved beyond its early religious manifestations to appear in various secular and quasi-secular versions. During and after the Revolutionary period, for instance, there was a widespread, almost millennial conviction among many influential Americans that the United States was destined to model democratic self-governance for the rest of the world, which would soon follow in our footsteps. In the nineteenth century, Catherine Beecher contended that "the Disposer of events" designed that America should "go forth as the cynosure of nations." Hence, "to American women . . . is committed the exalted privilege of extending over the world those blessed influences, which are to renovate degraded man."[2]

Ironically, scholars first adopted the actual term "American exceptionalism" from the Communist Party, which introduced it during the 1930s in an attempt to theorize why the Party's attempts to build a large-scale socialist movement in the United States kept failing, unlike in most European countries. For frustrated Party theorists, American exceptionalism referred to a prevalent ideological belief among Americans that their nation was different from other industrialized societies because it lacked social classes. Today, considerations of American exceptionalism in such fields as political science, economics, and sociology continue to investigate the truth-value of specific exceptionalist notions—for example, that religion plays a decisively different role for Americans than for Europeans and Canadians—as well as the social and political implications of Americans' beliefs about their nation's exceptional nature, regardless of whether those beliefs are accurate or not.[3] Although social-scientific interrogations of American exceptionalism often overlap with questions literary scholars ask, the latter tend to concentrate on exceptionalism's cultural expressions. Literary scholars have been especially interested in analyzing literary and cultural artifacts that manifest, whether blatantly or subtly, Americans' messianic sense that their nation has a unique role to play in the world.

In what follows, I juxtapose a work of classic American realism, Henry James's novel *The American* (1877), with a recent nonliterary articulation of American exceptionalism, as expressed in an address then-Senator Jesse Helms delivered to the United Nations Security Council in January 2000.[4] My aim in this brief chapter is not merely to draw parallels between the stances of American exceptionalism assumed by Helms and by James's protagonist Christopher Newman (although the parallels are striking—and to a degree amusing). Rather, by reading James's novel and Helms's speech together, I seek to sketch key elements of a constellation of American political identity that is today markedly prominent in international contexts. Adopting a phrase employed by James's text, I call this constellation of identity the "good fellow wronged." It is an identity grounded in an unyielding presumption of American innocence and of the United States' purity of motive, transparency of character, and absolute forbearance from morally unjustifiable actions. For the good fellow wronged, American exceptionalism operates less as a collection of discrete, potentially falsifiable beliefs about the United States and its actions than as feeling and form: a mode of functioning emotionally, psychically, and interpersonally. Exceptionalism here is a stance, a posture—a template—for positioning and presenting oneself, simultaneously for one's own gaze and for the gazes of "foreign" others.

The feeling that oneself as an American—or the United States as a nation—has been wronged, taken advantage of, or misunderstood by foreign others is by no means uncommon among those who would locate themselves on the liberal side of the U.S. political spectrum. As a consistently inhabited mode of being, however, the good fellow wronged is an identity that tends to be based farther to the Right than the various liberal and leftist identities explored in other sections of this book. Under the George W. Bush administration, the position of good fellow wronged (which, as we will see, is a stance that authorizes various forms of violent response) has become the predominant character that the United States images for itself in the "war on terror." Despite its not being a specifically liberal or leftist style of identity, I devote this chapter to investigating the good fellow wronged as a structuring disposition because that figure's defining insistence on the essential innocence of America and Americans serves as a provocative counterpoint to the topic of chapter 6, which returns to a focus on leftist modes of political subjectivity. Chapter 6 concludes our study of liberal identity by using critically presentist reading to explore the problem of liberal guilt. As will become plain, liberal guilt is generated and regenerated by its continual practice of demystifying American "innocence." Using the lens of Edith Wharton's *The Age of Innocence,* chapter 6 enunciates an alternative relation to American innocence, one perhaps more productive than the simplistic "good fellow wronged" innocence insisted on by American exceptionalism, which is both opposed and complemented by liberal guilt.

I choose to work with Helms's year 2000 speech to the United Nations instead of post–9/11 interactions between the U.N. and such high-ranking U.S. officials as President George W. Bush and Secretary of State Colin Powell, which focus on such topics as the "war on terror," and the invasion of Iraq, because these more recent interactions have been dominated by the rhetoric of immediate life-and-death crisis. Helms's speech foreshadows many of the same postures and presumptions that appear especially in Bush's United Nations–related discourse of 2001–2003, but Helms's earlier performance of exceptionalist feeling, while not exactly calm, is more everyday, less self-conscious than later performances by Bush. What I find most interesting is how Helms's speech and James's novel together help illuminate the American "good fellow wronged" as a quotidian, habitual mode of subjectivity.

A speech by Jesse Helms and a novel by Henry James may seem an especially odd couple to link through critically presentist reading. James, after all, was a richly gifted, cosmopolitan, multilingual American writer, who early on decided he did not wish to reside in the United States. Helms retired from the U.S. Senate at the beginning of 2003, but remains a political force, in part through his involvement with the Jesse Helms Center, located in his home state of North Carolina. Helms is a populist politician who, in vivid contrast to James, has always presented himself as exemplifying America's "common" people. He has been a prominent opponent of public support for the arts and humanities, both of which he approaches with hostility and fear. James possessed a subtle and complex literary imagination; Helms often seems to take pride in a certain crude reductionism. In chapter 1, the social, psychological, and temporal intricacies of Edith Wharton's *"Autre Temps . . ."* helped give figure to difficult aspects of *Hopwood v. Texas:* for instance, the paradoxical possibility that racial exclusion at the University of Texas might be more powerful for having lost whatever rationale or coherence it may once, at least on its own terms, have possessed. In the current chapter, James's portrayal of Christopher Newman in *The American* helps provide interpretative leverage on Helms's version of American exceptionalism. But the lens of critical presentism is also, so to speak, turned around, as we reread a canonical realist text with the new perspective created by setting it next to a recent political event. Indeed, in this case, the purposeful, almost ostentatious avoidance of subtlety in Helms's words means that his speech serves as a magnifying glass that aids in the deciphering of underlying fantasies, structuring formulations, and political implications inherent in James's literary imagining of the American as a good fellow wronged.

Quadrupeds and Foreigners

Near the beginning of his U.N. speech, Jesse Helms announces, "I am not a diplomat, and as such, I am not fully conversant with the elegant and rarefied language of the diplomatic trade. I am an elected official, with something of a reputation for saying what I mean and meaning what I say. So I trust you will forgive me if I come across as a bit more blunt than those you are accustomed to hearing in this chamber." Helms's self-presentation as an uncomplicated good fellow requires him, not merely to avoid, but to make a *visible point* of avoiding "elegant and rarefied language." His insistence here on the strict identity between his saying and his meaning (he means what he says and he says what he means) fits squarely within American pragmatist accounts of language. Similarly, the narrator of *The American* insists that, for Christopher Newman, "words were acts and acts were steps in life, and that in this matter of taking steps curveting and prancing were exclusively reserved for quadrupeds and foreigners."[5] Newman's canonically pragmatist view of language as itself a form of effective action (a view developed by William James, among others) is, for the American businessman, explicitly posed against "foreigners" and implicitly posed against effeminacy.

   Indeed, those who practice verbal "curveting and prancing" may become, in a familiar homophobic paradox, so "overcivilized" as to be excluded from the normatively human, figuring instead as artificially-trained "quadrupeds" performing in a show ring. The body of the Frenchman Urbain de Bellegarde, as the name "Urbain" might suggest, epitomizes this overcultivation, which constitutes the hollow opposite of Newman's active and substantive American masculinity: "Here was a man towards whom he was irresistibly in opposition; a man of forms and phrases and postures."[6] By contrast to the straightforward transparency of Newman's language, consider "the conscious, ironical smile of his host.

What the deuce M. de Bellegarde was smiling at he was at a loss to divine. M. de Bellegarde's smile may be supposed to have been, for himself, a compromise between a great many emotions" (139).

For both James's and Helms's versions of the American good fellow, the eschewal of language's diplomatic potential for ambiguity and for compromises of meaning sets up the good fellow's own direct, one-to-one correspondence with "America" as such. Matching his pragmatist claim to eliminate any gap between his saying and his meaning, between his signifiers and what he intends as their signifieds, Helms posits himself as perfectly representative of, even perfectly *coincident* with, "the American people." Integral to the figure of the good fellow wronged is an identity that, transcending its individual bearer, instantiates the literal essence of America as a nation and of American-ness as a quality.

Helms begins his speech with the unmistakable implication that he represents the American people more perfectly even than do the U.S. president or the president's appointees—more perfectly, in fact, than other U.N. diplomats represent their own countries: "Distinguished Ambassadors, Ladies and Gentlemen. . . . You are distinguished world leaders and it is my hope that there can begin, this day, a pattern of understanding and friendship between you who serve your respective countries in the United Nations and, those of us who serve not only in the United States Government but also the millions of Americans whom we represent and serve." There is a reason that Helms's syntax here is so strained. His not quite tautological phrasing strives to establish a difference between "serve" and "represent." A distinguished ambassador *serves* a government and a "country." By contrast, an "elected representative" such as Helms not only serves but also stands in for, without any gap or mediation, the real-life individuals who together comprise a unitary "people." When referring to America's people, Helms always uses the direct article: "Let me share with you what *the* American people tell me." James's Christopher Newman fills out "*the* national mould." His body perfectly reflects "*the* American type" (again, use of the direct article is important) with "almost ideal completeness" (18; my emphasis). When asked if he is American, Newman responds "don't you see it?" To wound an American good fellow such as Newman or Helms would be, in the very same act, to wound "America"—not only as a nation and a people, but also as an idea.

"Trustful, Generous, Liberal, Patient, Easy"

Henry James's *The American* depicts the attempts of self-made western American millionaire Christopher Newman to marry Claire de Cintré, beautiful widowed daughter of one of France's oldest, most aristocratic, and most politically and socially conservative families, the Bellegardes, albeit a family whose economic fortunes have ebbed. For many centuries, the Bellegardes had married only within a restricted circle of high-ranking European nobility. Despite the pernicious prejudices of the Bellegarde elders against him as a vulgar commoner, the wealthy American does manage to win Madame de Cintré's love and the family's apparent consent to their marriage. The Bellegardes even take the unusual step of hosting a party to announce the engagement among their distinguished friends, many of whom have never even seen an American before. (One elderly duchess does remember meeting Benjamin Franklin, however, when that famously representative American lived in Paris [146].) At the party, the large and international audience to Christopher Newman's seeming acceptance amplifies the American's "cheerful sense of success, of attainment, of victory" (191). When the marriage itself draws near, however, Claire's mother and brother finally find themselves unable to "swallow" such a close family connection with Newman and his tainted "commercial" "antecedents." They call off the match. Unable to defy her mother's "command" and marry Newman anyway, Claire withdraws to a convent, one which forbids her ever to exchange human words again (221, 245, 112, 217).

Newman is both infuriated and heartsick, partly on Claire's behalf but mostly on his own: "His sense of outrage was deep, rancorous, and ever-present." Throughout his dealings with the Bellegardes, Newman sees himself as having been "trustful, generous, liberal, patient, easy, pocketing frequent irritation and furnishing unlimited modesty" (245). Now, however, Newman is consumed by "the feeling that after all and above all he was a good fellow wronged," a phrase that is repeated three times in the text of *The American* (245, 303). James's 1907 preface confirms that the "essence" of Newman's experience in Paris is that he has been "wronged," "cruelly wronged," and "ill-used" (3, 2, 11).

It is crucial that the "wrong" Newman suffers in the novel is not merely the loss of his fiancée, Claire de Cintré. Worse, for Newman, is the wound of having been judged "not good enough" by Claire's family (284). "To lose Madame de Cintré after he had taken such jubilant and triumphant possession of her was as great an affront to his pride as it was an injury to his happiness" (220). Worst of all, Newman has been judged and rejected in public, on an international stage. Newman repeatedly insists that his humiliation has occurred "before the world—convened for the express purpose" (284). James's preface envisions the wrong done to Newman as occurring "on a high and lighted stage. . . . [H]e would be wronged with just that conspicuity, with his felicity at just that pitch and with the highest aggravation of the general effect of misery mocked at"

(3).[7] Newman's overwhelming sense of his rejection as occurring on a lighted stage begins even in the first "startled and pained" moment when he hears the bad news: "He was amazed, bewildered, and the presence of the old marquise and her son seemed to smite his eyes like the glare of a watchman's lantern" or, we might add, a spotlight (214). He later describes his experience to the Bellegardes' former servant, Mrs. Bread. "They [the Bellegardes] took me up into a high place and made me stand there for all the world to see me, and then they stole behind me and pushed me into this bottomless pit, where I lie howling and gnashing my teeth" (257).

Eric Haralson has recently argued that Sigmund Freud's famous essay about masochistic fantasy, "A Child Is Being Beaten," helps explain Newman's response to his rejection. Haralson shows that, intermingled with Newman's obvious anger and pain at the Bellegardes' successful interference with his marriage, the American also experiences a "strange satisfaction," even "pleasure" in his own loss and humiliation. Haralson quotes James's description of the "singular sensation" Newman feels, that "of his sense of injury almost brimming over into jocularity." Haralson observes, moreover, that Newman seems extravagantly invested in his "ordeal as one of extreme, and extremely public, humiliation." Especially in light of James's own emphasis on the "lighted stage," Newman's description of his humiliating rejection as having occurred "before the world—convened for the express purpose" seems the same sort of imagined masochistic "scenario that would do credit to the most inventive of Freud's fantasists."[8]

Although Haralson has arrived at a valuable insight in recognizing the ways in which Newman's experience with the Bellegardes resembles masochistic fantasy, I would emphasize that, unlike the classic masochist, Newman never imagines that he deserves punishment, or that he has done anything bad. For Newman himself, envisioning his rejection as a painfully public humiliation primarily serves to motivate and authorize his rancorous outrage. People he conceives of as foreign judges using foreign standards have delivered the negative judgment of him, and this is the "sensation" Newman finds "intolerable" (220). The mode of American political subjectivity we are exploring here—that of the good fellow wronged—emphasizes, even draws out, the sensation of woundedness consequent upon public humiliation inflicted by foreign judges. But the pain of having been so misjudged above all serves the good fellow as an occasion and justification for aiming at aggressive domination over those who have cast judgment upon him. The overweening agents and witnesses of his wronging must be forced to recognize and confirm his American moral, political, economic, and even, as we have already witnessed through the examples of both Newman and Helms, his linguistic exceptionalism.

Helms's speech to the U.N. Security Council shares Newman's vivid sense of having been demeaned before an international audience. Helms enumerates several offenses both of behavior and of attitude that the United Nations has committed against the United States and "the American people." He dwells on specific scenes in which the American people are made a spectacle, as they receive humiliating abuse directed at them by the other U.N. countries. Helms emphasizes, for example, that the American people "see the majority of the U.N. members routinely voting against America in the General Assembly. They have read the reports of the raucous cheering of the U.N. delegates in Rome, when U.S. efforts to amend the International Criminal Court treaty . . . were defeated. . . ." Six sequential clauses or complete sentences begin with Americans' sensory or cognitive taking in of humiliation: "They have heard," "they see," "they have read," "they read," "The American people hear." In these sentences, Helms positions the American people simultaneously as victim and spectator to the abuse almost ritualistically meted out to them by "U.N. members."

Most important again, however, is that, unlike in the masochist's classically preferred scene, in Helms's construction, the American people do not claim to have been "bad" or to deserve punishment. The American people, Helms tells the Security Council, "know instinctively that the U.N. lives and breathes on the hard-earned money of the American taxpayers." In 1999 alone, "the American people have furnished precisely TEN BILLION, ONE HUNDRED AND SEVENTY-NINE MILLION DOLLARS to support the work of the United Nations" (capital letters in original). (Christopher Newman also enjoys the "magnificent sound that large aggregations of dollars put on . . ." especially when that magnificent sound serves to underline his own exceptional generosity [128].) "No other nation on earth comes even close to matching that singular investment," Helms adds. "And yet," he continues, the American people "have heard comments here in New York constantly calling the United States a 'deadbeat.' They have heard U.N. officials declaring absurdly that countries like Fiji and Bangladesh are carrying America's burden in peacekeeping." Helms is determined to impress upon his audience of U.N. diplomats that "The American people hear all this; they resent it, and they have grown increasingly frustrated with what they feel is a lack of gratitude."

James's "international theme" includes as a key component the abuse by foreigners of our American good nature. This same motif plays a structuring role in Helms's imaginary, as well as in the stance subsequently projected by the Bush administration both within the United States and around the world. Moreover, as for the Bush administration and a significant portion of the American population since September 11, so too in both Helms's speech and James's novel there exists an almost voluptuous sense

of having been outrageously and publicly *wronged*. This outrage becomes
the occasion for a reverberating assertion of American wealth and power,
as well as a reassertion of America's status as unique and superior. Henry
James through Christopher Newman and Jesse Helms in his speech both
dwell in the sensation of having been publicly wronged, but at almost the
same time they also loudly and derisively repudiate what Helms calls "foreign judges." Foreigners cannot judge the American (people), Helms and
Newman insist, because the latter are always already superior to their
would-be judges. The American people, Helms asserts, do not want or
"need . . . the approval of an international body, some of whose members
are totalitarian dictatorships." He is astonished that "a U.N. 'Special
Rapporteur' decided his most pressing task was to investigate human
rights violations in the U.S.—and found our human rights record want-
ing." Experiencing his rejection by them as "preposterous," Newman
angrily informs the Bellegardes, "I mean to show the world that, however
bad I may be, you are not quite the people to say it" (220, 284).

Because of their shared conviction of America's essential innocence,
both Jesse Helms and James's Christopher Newman experience any criticism of America or American-ness by "insolent foreigner[s]" (James's
phrase for the Bellegardes in a letter to William Dean Howells) as an
undeserved, outrageous, even exceptional wrong.[9] In an international context, the good fellow's feeling of American exceptionalism paradoxically
requires outside confirmation of the nation's unique virtues, confirmation
even from "enemies" who must be given no grounds for criticizing or dis-
missing the American experiment. The Puritans' sense of their special mission and status in God's eyes occasioned feelings of intense pressure and
anxiety, not only from the fear of disappointing God but also from the fear
of licensing "the world" to regard God's chosen people as having failed.[10]
If the Puritans were "made a story and by-word through the world" as failures, not only would they themselves be "consumed" but the world itself
also would be given over to evil. Becoming a negative example, a story and
a byword, is intolerable. The separateness often implied by American
exceptionalist thinking should thus be recognized as only *pseudo*-isolation-
ist because it requires the approving gaze of others to maintain its sense of
its own identity.[11]

America's Clear Intention to Help

Christopher Newman and Jesse Helms both give expression to a sure conviction that, despite what might temporarily appear as morally suspect
behavior in others' eyes, America is essentially, unchangingly good.

Despite their possessing great power, and despite their sometimes having exerted it on morally ambiguous terrain, "the" American people, for Helms, or "the American," for Newman, have never crossed the line separating right from wrong. "I may be dangerous," Newman tells his friend Mrs. Tristram, "but I am not wicked. No, I am not wicked" (305). Thinking back on his "old efforts, old exploits . . . examples of 'smartness' and sharpness," Newman feels "decidedly proud" of some of them. Of others, "it would be going too far to say that he was ashamed of them. . . . Newman knew the crooked from the straight at a glance" and he "had never had a stomach for dirty work" (74). He is pleased to reflect "with sober placidity that at least there were no monuments to his meanness scattered about the world" (301). Helms argues that every occasion on which the United States has involved itself in the affairs of another country, and every method that it has used, including what he lists as "moral, financial, and covert forms of support" (in Newman's rhetoric, "examples of 'smartness' and sharpness") has been designed to produce an "expansion of freedom."

Indeed, the good fellow wronged constellation of identity we have been sketching professes an overriding devotion to freedom, not only for Americans themselves but also for foreign others. This devotion to freedom underlies an investment in fantasized scenarios of rescue both in *The American* and in Helms's U.N. speech. Within these imagined scenarios, the masculine heroic mission of the good fellow (America) is to save victimized foreigners from their bondage to totalitarian dictators. On the ticklish question of respecting other nations' integrity, Helms has no choice but at some level to recognize the possibility of provoking irony in a speech that insists on the absolute inviolability of American sovereignty, given the United States' lengthy past of intervening in the internal affairs of foreign countries (what Newman might refer to as its "old efforts, old exploits"). Thus Helms several times emphasizes what he calls "the American people['s] long history of coming to the aid of those struggling for freedom." He insists that helping others who are "struggling to break the chains of tyranny" is an "inherently legitimate" form of action. "During the 1980s," Helms adds, "we called this policy the 'Reagan Doctrine.'"

Some twenty years prior to America's embrace of an analogous structure of justification for its war to "free" Cuba from Spanish tyranny, Christopher Newman asserts that he wishes to take Claire de Cintré out of her family's orbit so as to make her "perfectly free." "Your family exert a pressure upon you, interfere with you, annoy you," Newman exclaims in an early discussion with Claire (115). Later, he insists, "they have bullied you, I say; they have tortured you" (241). "Let me come in and put an end

to it," he virtually demands of her when proposing marriage (113). To
Newman, the Bellegardes have locked Claire into an ideology of family
conformity that is, as Claire herself says, "like a religion" (242). Speaking
of the multiple interventions launched under the "Reagan Doctrine,"
Helms asserts, "in each case . . . it was America's clear intention to help
bring down Communist regimes that were oppressing their peoples—and
thereby replace dictators with democratic governments."

In the eyes of the American good fellow (whether Newman, Helms, or,
most recently, George W. Bush), for foreigners to judge such actions—as
when, as Helms puts it, "the U.S. effort to overthrow Nicaragua's
Communist dictatorship by supporting Nicaragua's freedom fighters and
mining Nicaragua's harbors was declared by the World Court as a viola-
tion of international law"—is itself almost literally profane. Such judg-
ments, Helms declares, threaten "the God-given freedoms of the American
people" to rescue and protect others who wish to exercise their own
"inalienable, God-given rights" to freedom. Newman is convinced that for
the Bellegardes to block his project of making Claire "perfectly free" (by
marrying her) is to contravene both nature and the God-given privileges
of white heterosexual American masculinity: "To see a woman made for
him and for motherhood to his children juggled away in this tragic trav-
esty—it was a thing to rub one's eyes over, a nightmare, an illusion, a
hoax" (246). "A man can't be used in this fashion," he proclaims. "You
have got no right. You have got no power" (217).

Although Helms's "American people" are not as overtly masculine as
Christopher Newman, the United States of Helms's Reagan-era rescue
scenario is implicitly male.[12] It deserves emphasizing, moreover, that the
vision of America as a good fellow wronged conceives the good fellow as
unambiguously white. Although the Bellegardes seek to assume the position of "ethnologist" in regard to Newman as American specimen, he
deftly parries by taking for granted that they could not possibly mean to
render *white* Americans as objects of ethnography: "An ethnologist?"
Newman responds, "Ah, you collect negroes' skulls, and that sort of
thing" (124).

In Helms's U.N. address, the status of "the American people" as white
emerges most clearly in the senator's insistence that intervening "when the
oppressed peoples of the world cry out for help" is "not a new concept for
the United States [because] the American people have a long history of
coming to the aid of those struggling for freedom." Implying that an
essential aspect of American identity has always been the rescue of "peoples" from "widespread oppression and massive human rights abuses,"
Helms erases America's own history of slavery, genocide, chauvinism, and
convict labor. In asserting America's long history of support for "*nations*

struggling to break the chains of tyranny and claim their inalienable, God-given rights" (my italics), Helms elides the historic contradiction that is at the heart of the Declaration of Independence's assertion that "life, liberty, and the pursuit of happiness" are "unalienable rights": a contradiction African Americans have pointed out ever since the Declaration's signing.[13] For the Helmsian, Newman-esque American exceptionalist, un-freedom is always out there, on terrain clearly distinct from the land of the free.

Ever hovering above the American good fellow's melodramatic fantasy of rescuing the un-free is the threat of anger and retribution if either the victim supposed to require rescue or the melodrama's *audience* does not decisively enough recognize the hero's impeccable intentions. Part of Newman's American good-fellowness throughout James's novel has been his seeming willingness to "pocket . . . frequent irritation," to accept small slights. When the Marquis and Marquise de Bellegarde publicly reject him, however, Newman finds himself possessed by a "sense of outrage [that] was deep, rancorous, and ever present" (245). He now feels more than justified in releasing his "deep" rage. No longer "easy," he still claims the moral high ground—after all, he remains "a good fellow wronged"—even while he unleashes a desire for violent mastery. "I want to bring them down—down, down, down!" he exclaims to Mrs. Bread, the repetition of the word "down" evoking the severity of the ringing mortification he wishes to inflict (257). Newman immediately develops a plan of "vengeance" by locating evidence of a scandalous crime committed by Madame de Bellegarde, the mere publicizing of which would forever disgrace the proud Bellegarde name. By letting the Bellegardes know what he has discovered, Newman succeeds in frightening them. Ultimately, they flee Paris for an isolated country home.

Before finally loosing his "thunder-bolt," however, Newman relents (269). He burns up the evidence against the Bellegardes simply "out of his good nature," as James puts it in his letter to Howells. Having repocketed his irritation, and thereby reclaimed his status as "generous, liberal . . . easy," Newman returns to America. James's preface describes Newman as having "let them go, in short, his haughty contemners, even while feeling them, with joy, in his power" (2). Although the novel's narrative voice not infrequently takes an ironic tone regarding Newman (when describing his opinions on art, for example), Henry James clearly admires what he describes as this act of "practical, but quite unappreciated, magnanimity" (which thus already is *not* "unappreciated"). Newman's gesture is, James writes in the preface, one of "the large and easy impulses *generally* charac-teristic of his type" (James's emphasis)—his "type" being that of a New World man. Newman's admirable move has been "to simply turn, at the supreme moment, away" from his vengeance, having "sacrifice[d] it in disgust" at the Bellegardes and the unworthy conflict in which he had almost become entangled.

Note, however, that if the "very force of his aversion" for the foreign family and their foreign values drives Newman to his isolationist "turn . . . away" from them, this is still an isolationism that must explicitly be *viewed* in order for the American's exceptional generosity, ease, self-sufficiency, and strength to be rendered iconic in the figure of the "good fellow wronged." As if through the fourth wall of a stage or on a movie screen, Newman's turning away becomes a spectacle in need of an audience, even though Newman must at the same time appear not to know (or care) that an audience watches: "One's last view of him would be that of a strong man indifferent to his strength and too wrapped in fine, too wrapped above all in *other* and intenser reflexions for the assertion of his 'rights'" (2–3).

After detailing the public injuries "the American people" have suffered at the hands of the U.N., Jesse Helms first imagines himself, like Newman, as a punishing agent, one who will inflict a degrading physical fall upon the U.N.'s "insolent" foreigners. Helms threatens that if the demands of the American people are not met, the U.N. can expect "retaliatory measures," which will ultimately force the international organization to "collapse under its own weight" ("down—down, down, down!" as Newman might put it). If Newman is repeatedly characterized as a good fellow wronged, a phrase that, by extension, I have suggested, also describes the constellation of identity that Helms both inhabits himself and claims for "the American people" as such, then the anachronistic pun suggested by Martin Scorsese's film *Goodfellas* can help emphasize the menacing possibilities of violence summoned up when American "good fellows" are wronged.[14]

Like Newman, Jesse Helms chooses to ease back from his threat. He will not try to make the U.N. collapse under its own weight, and, more important, he will allow the U.N. to receive over $500 million, money that he has been blocking and that the organization desperately needs. Helms relents, however, only after he believes he has forced the U.N. to accept "the American people" on their own terms. One year after his unprecedented Security Council speech, Helms announced in the Senate that, after months of "cajoling, and maybe even a little browbeating, some of our friends at the United Nations," the United States had succeeded in pushing through most of the specific changes that Helms had demanded. These included changes in the U.N.'s overall dues structure and in the organization of its peacekeeping missions.[15]

Romance and the Real

In his 1907 New York Edition preface to *The American,* Henry James famously admits that, although he had assumed when writing the book thirty years earlier that it was a realist novel, he now discovers that he had all along "been plotting arch-romance without knowing it" (4). For James, *The American* becomes romance instead of realism when the "cable is cut" that had connected events and characters in the book to "our general sense of 'the way things happen'" (11). Specifically, James now realizes that Newman's marriage would indeed have gone forward. Real-life Bellegardes, attracted by his money, "would positively have jumped . . . at my rich and easy American," "taking with alacrity everything he could give them, only asking for more and more, and then adjusting their pretensions and their pride to it with all the comfort in life" (12).

To James, the genre of "romance" connoted fantasies of remaining untouched, pure, separate: disconnected from the contaminations and enmeshments of real life. In romance, not only the individual but also experience itself is "liberated, so to speak." Human experience, whether that of characters or of readers, is "disengaged, disembroiled, disencumbered, exempt from the conditions that we usually know to attach to it and . . . drag upon it." Romance defines itself, above all, through breaking with "the inconvenience of a *related,* a measurable state, a state subject to all our vulgar communities" (10).[16] James's notion of the romance correlates with an important dimension of American exceptionalism that insists on and presumes American innocence: the United States' continuing status as a New World, free from the moral compromises and entangled corruptions of older civilizations, guilty of nothing in relation to others save "practical, but quite unappreciated, magnanimity."[17]

As we will see in chapter 6, liberal guilt arises from precisely the opposite feeling. As Julie Ellison asserts, liberal guilt stems from our "complicated awareness of the human costs of national and imperial economies": it blossoms from our awareness that there is no way to cut the "cable," so to speak, that ties our material, social, and political privileges at home to other peoples' experiences of suffering and deprivation.[18] In the vocabulary of literary genre, liberal guilt would be a "realist" formation.

CHAPTER SIX

Liberal Guilt and
The Age of Innocence

> Members of this Left find America unforgivable. . . . This leads them
> to step back from their country and, as they say, "theorize it." . . . It
> leads them to prefer knowledge to hope.
> —Richard Rorty, *Achieving Our Country: Leftist Thought in
> Twentieth-Century America.*

> American academic feminism operates out of fear, I believe, of
> repeating the definitional exclusions, violences, and imaginative laps-
> es of feminism since '68, of repeating American/white feminism's
> imperialist, racist, heterosexist, class-biased, culture-bound, and
> overoptimistic parochialism.
> —Lauren Berlant, "'68, or Something"

Knowledge, Theory, and Paralysis

Richard Rorty and Lauren Berlant share similar worries about today's academic Left. Both are concerned that certain forms of knowledge and theory currently influencing many on the academic Left also act as constraints on the Left's vital tasks of imagining and constructing a better
future. Both Rorty and Berlant want to combat the intellectual, emotional, and political blockages, the tendencies towards inertia and risk avoidance, that they see as byproducts of intellectuals' dwelling on past failures
or mistakes. Berlant finds a fear of making political mistakes on the academic Left, as well as suspicion of and even hostility toward the utopian
energies associated with the "revolutionary projects" of the 1960s, which
many leftist academics today dismiss as naïve and narcissistic.[1] Rorty
insists that a generation of academic leftists has become obsessed with the
United States' failure to live up to its democratic, egalitarian promise. He

worries that, in the minds of these intellectuals, "the two-hundred year history of the United States—indeed, the history of the European and American peoples since the Enlightenment—has been pervaded by hypocrisy and self-deception."[2]

Possessing no hope that their country can be authentically changed, Rorty claims, leftist intellectuals in the United States find a posture of "national self-mockery and self-disgust" more congenial than any attempt at democratic political action. But such emotions are luxuries, Rorty insists, "which agents—either individuals or nations—cannot afford."[3]

Despite meaningful differences in their perspectives and aims, Rorty and Berlant together help frame what became an increasingly problematic question for me as I researched and wrote earlier chapters of this book.[4] What did it mean that my work seemed to be participating in, maybe even contributing to, a feeling that I also recognize on the academic Left, not least as an intimate facet of my own political subjectivity: the feeling that we *know too much* to act effectively? Among other things, as Berlant indicates, we know that 1960s radicals were indeed overly naïve in their beliefs about social, economic, and political change. We know that some of their worst failures were due to the fact that they did not sufficiently theorize power, subjectivity, or representation. We also know that putative liberation movements have sometimes rested on the continuing oppression of others.

Our well-informed anxieties, based as they are on some of the most compelling historical and theoretical knowledge that we have acquired, can debilitate thought and action. Although such feelings no doubt affect people in different forms and to varying degrees, it is safe to say that many leftist academics at least sometimes feel paralyzed because: 1) they have difficulty imagining that whatever they do as scholars and teachers will ever bring about meaningful social change, and 2) they cannot help but recognize ways in which they themselves will inevitably continue to participate in—and to benefit from—regimes of social, economic, or epistemological injustice.

Wendy Brown's explication of Walter Benjamin's term "Left melancholy" describes a stance that previous chapters of this book might be read as supporting. "Left melancholy" characterizes "a Left that has become more attached to its impossibility than to its potential fruitfulness."[5] In her discussion of liberal guilt, Julie Ellison emphasizes that the "liberal superego demands direct action," but at the same time it assures us that our actions are useless or worse. This is why, "in the throes of liberal guilt, all action becomes gesture, expressive of a desire to effect change or offer help that is never sufficient to the scale of the problem. Actions are carried out in sorrow. One is sorry in advance for the social consequences of one's acts."[6] Although

I hope that my previous chapters are not reducible merely to such a stance, I have indeed elaborated upon, for example, the "impossibility" of a white antiracist teacher of *Huck Finn*. I have argued that the University of Texas, and by implication other universities, are constitutively unable to confront that the Enlightenment commitments defining their mission, as well as the ongoing quotidian practices sustaining their institutional existence, might both be inextricable from white supremacy. I have sought to demonstrate that, in culturally symptomatic cases, achieving more liberated, more progressive-seeming gender identities for white men and women participates in a complex dynamic of displacing representational and material burdens onto racial and national others. Nonetheless, I hope in this final chapter to develop at least some beginnings of a response to the essential question that emerges from both Rorty's book and Berlant's essay: Given all of our knowledge and theory, how do leftist intellectuals retain what Berlant calls a "radical openness" at least toward the act of continuing to think about "possibilities" for "broadscale social transformation."[7]

In what follows, I link liberal guilt and its potential for paralysis together with the fear of political error, failure, and humiliation whose constraining effects Berlant addresses; with Left melancholy as Brown understands it; and with the forms of knowledge and theory that Rorty sees as so enervating to political agency. Treating these phenomena as continuous with one another involves certain slippages of definition. Yet guilt, humiliation, and melancholy share many attributes, including self-denigration and difficulty moving or even looking toward a future different from the past. As for liberal guilt's relationship with knowledge and theory, Ellison's illuminating history of the phenomenon explains that it has long had a symbiotic relationship with both: "Guilt spawns theory. As the structuring of painfully interrelated information, theory induces guilt."[8] The more systematically we come to understand our own position in unjust, pain-causing structures, the more implicated, hamstrung, and guilty we feel. And the guiltier we feel, the more theorizing we do.

Ellison traces liberal guilt's emergence as a culturally prominent category to the eighteenth century. Theatrical and literary forms increasingly offered access to "a concept of nation, empire, economy, or some other system that was understood to produce suffering for some and privilege for others," particularly racialized others.[9] She argues that, both on and off the stage, educated white "men of sensibility" emotively displayed their "moral embarrassment," including literal tears of sympathy shed over "the pain caused by political arrangements from which artists and intellectuals knowingly benefited but at the same time could not control."[10] Today, as George Packer writes, liberal guilt "leaves people with the best will in the world feel[ing] thoroughly enmeshed in the current arrangements and powerless to do more than express a vague wish. . . ." As a result, we find ourselves allowing chronic social ills to go untreated, enduring "them with the self-contempt of a man who can't stop overeating even though his joints are swollen with gout and his face keeps breaking out."[11]

Many on both the Right and the Left see liberal guilt as functioning ideologically in *support* of exploitative relations. They take its meaning to be: "As long as I *feel* sufficiently guilty, I can retain both my material privileges and my personal virtue."[12] Although Ellison does not entirely reject this interpretation of liberal guilt as self-excusing, self-aggrandizing bad faith, she also insists on taking it seriously as a multivalent phenomenon.[13] If liberal guilt spurs, as it often does, the continuing production of more complex and nuanced forms of understanding, then, Ellison argues, the potentially salutary effects of that understanding should never simply be dismissed. Bruce Robbins concurs, insisting that there are many good reasons today to nurture even the "constraints, obscurities, hesitations, and self-questionings" imposed by liberal guilt and its related forms of awareness, which usefully temper our urges toward the "illusory satisfactions of immediate action in a domain of ostensible political transparency and ethical universality."[14] Berlant observes that academic feminism's urgent desire to avoid reiterating harmful academic and political practices has helped propel the field toward cultivating "importantly non-optimistic relations to global capitalist forms, to national identities, to liberal promises for universal suffrage."[15] And for critic Daniel Born, the "alteration of the liberal voice from confidence to despair, from prescription to guilt," which he finds occurring in such nineteenth-century English novelists as Dickens and Eliot, "signals an enlargement and maturation of liberal concern." The effect on the writers' middle-class audiences was to bring home "the necessity of enlarging [their] sense of social breakdown to encompass social and not merely individual terms of explanation."[16]

Yet most commentators equally recognize the perils of "paralysis and inertia" that lie just on the other side of our knowledge about overarching systems in which we are implicated.[17] The challenge, then, is how to remain infiltrated and instructed by what Ellison calls our "complicated awareness"—whether of the disturbing history of white middle-class "liberation" movements, or of our own implication in both local and global economies of exploitation—without being politically immobilized by that awareness.

Choosing against Liberal Guilt?

Rorty's own recommendation, drawn from his reading both of the American pragmatist tradition in philosophy and of canonical American literature, is that we should self-consciously choose *Hope in Place of*

Knowledge, the title of a 1999 collection of lectures. Leftist intellectuals must determine to replace any "shared knowledge of what is already real with social hope for what might become real."[18] We must opt to believe that meaningful social change lies within our grasp. To counter the influence of overly negative understandings of the United States, Rorty celebrates a long-standing liberal view of American exceptionalism, which holds that "America has always been a future-oriented country, a country which delights in the fact that it invented itself in the relatively recent past." To enable a progressive political vision and the possibility of acting on that vision, leftist intellectuals must embrace a quintessentially American "willingness to turn one's back both on the past and on the attempt of 'the classical philosophy of Europe' to ground the past in the eternal."[19] We should just say no to modes of knowledge or theory that might induce feelings of cynicism, despair, or political pessimism.

As I have tried to demonstrate in this book, however, a future-oriented determination to regard the past as a time distinct from our own now—a determination which would seem to allow us to make ever-increasing "progress" in separating ourselves from what we find unacceptable in the past—renders us obtuse to the past's persistently shaping effects on our institutions and ourselves. Such misrecognition ensures that the past will continue covertly to rub against the present, producing both continuing injustices and uncomfortable pleasures. Moreover, to trade our guilt- or despair-inducing knowledge "of what is already real" in return for "social hope for what might become real" (or for that matter even to bracket off negatively or ironically charged knowledge for our private moments, as Rorty elsewhere recommends[20]) is not a psychological exchange achievable within anything except the most impoverished versions of the psyche found in inspirational self-help books, with titles such as *Good-Bye to Guilt.*[21] Especially when "knowledge" of one's own (liberal) guilt manifests itself in the extreme forms of "hopelessness," "self-loathing," and even "bottomless self-disgust" that Rorty invokes, how could anything be as simple as his voluntarist language of "choices" would suggest? As George Shulman aptly observes, "for Rorty, people simply get over the past, or willfully 'choose' not to repeat it."[22] But one cannot simply make the "choice" to "deny" theoretically informed recognitions of one's own guilty implication in oppressive structures, and thereby, à la Walt Whitman, Ralph Waldo Emerson, and John Dewey (as Rorty reads them), "make room for pure joyous hope."[23]

Both Rorty's diagnosis of left-liberal self-loathing among academics and his prescription that those laboring under it should simply decide to "deny" the "knowledge" that can lead to feelings of guilty implication are simplistic. They are simplistic because liberal guilt is *structural guilt:* that is, recognition of one's connection to immoral or unjust structures outside of one's direct control, structures so pervasive and complex that one cannot simply wake up one day and decide to dissociate from them, to leave them behind in the dust. Even worse, many left-liberal academics, certainly including myself, are not unambiguously certain that we would *want* to give up all of the advantages that these guilt-inducing structures provide to us and many of those closest to us, even if we could.

Edith Wharton's *The Age of Innocence,* a historical novel about elite society in "Old New York," may seem oblique to the questions about liberal guilt and its potentially immobilizing effects that are raised by Berlant and Rorty, as well as, implicitly, by earlier chapters of this book. In the self-consciously "presentist" reading that follows, however, I seek to refract these simultaneously psychological and political questions through Wharton's rich literary text. Wharton's novel cannot point us toward an "answer" to the "problems" posed by liberal guilt and leftist melancholia. Taken as a prism, however, *The Age of Innocence* can help both to defamiliarize these all too familiar phenomena and to offer fresh figurations of their dynamics. I will suggest that Wharton's novel may thus help us at least begin to imagine new approaches to this troubled terrain.

Theorizing Innocence

Although it would not quite be accurate to claim that Newland Archer, *The Age of Innocence*'s protagonist, is consumed by guilt over his own material and social privileges, Archer's ambivalent sense of self is expressed through his "complicated awareness" of interlocking systems that produce benefit for some and suffering for others; just this awareness, Ellison argues, is a defining element of liberal guilt. Through most of Wharton's novel, Archer both recognizes old New York's social structures as arbitrary, unfair, and often cruel, and also lives in such a way as to identify himself and his interests with those structures. Exclaiming over after-dinner cigars that "women ought to be as free as we are," he privately recognizes that "such verbal generosities were in fact only a humbugging disguise of the inexorable conventions that tied things together and bound people down to the old pattern" (89). Archer is often painfully aware of the clash between his trenchantly critical social views and his own rather conventional life choices: "Archer tried to console himself with the thought that he was not such an ass as Larry Lefferts . . . but the difference was after all one of intelligence and not of standards" (90). The result of this awareness is that he often feels his own "real life" is elsewhere, deferred, waiting for him to live it.

As for innocence, Archer initially defines his own identity against it. He aligns "innocence" with his fiancée, and then wife, May Welland. The novel's first pages introduce May to us at the opera, a performance of *Faust,* where we see her filtered through Newland's gaze as "a young girl in white with eyes ecstatically fixed on the stage-lovers." She carries a bouquet of white lilies, which she softly touches with "white-gloved finger tips." "The darling!" thinks Newland, "She doesn't even guess what it is all about" (59). By "it" he means Faust's attempts to seduce Marguerite. Newland takes for granted that May is innocent not only of sexual experience but also of any knowledge or representations related to sex. Looking forward to their honeymoon, Newland envisions himself exercising his "manly privilege" to initiate May not only into sexuality but, simultaneously, into the pleasures of grown-up literary classics such as *Faust.* Newland sets his fantasy of manly initiation abroad, outside New York society "in some scene of old European witchery" (60–61).

Newland Archer is himself the character most frequently aligned with knowledge and theory in Wharton's narrative. Describing May's absolute "purity," he situates himself outside innocence, looking in. He feels himself in several senses more experienced and sophisticated even than the other "white-waistcoated" gentlemen around him at the opera: "He had probably read more, thought more, and even seen a good deal more of the world, than any other man of the number" (61). Indeed, as critics have recognized, Newland explicitly uses theories and tools of ethnographic analysis to aid in his understanding of his own social group, which he thinks of as akin to a "primitive" "tribe."[24] Wharton herself read widely in anthropology (Bronislaw Malinowski was a personal friend), and she implies that Archer has assimilated at least what would have been available by the 1870s, including Edward B. Tylor's *Primitive Man* (1865).

Newland's analytic sophistication reveals itself a few chapters later, for instance, as, alone in his study, he reaches an anthropologically informed deconstructive understanding of May's "innocence":

> [A]ll this frankness and innocence were only an artificial product. Untrained human nature was not frank and innocent; it was full of the twists and defenses of an instinctive guile. And he felt himself oppressed by this creation of factitious purity, so cunningly manufactured by a conspiracy of mothers and aunts and grandmothers and long-dead ancestresses, because it was supposed to be what he wanted, what he had a right to, in order that he might exercise his lordly pleasure in smashing it like an image made of snow. (91)

Newland's analysis effectively turns inside out Western culture's most influential narrative of innocence and its loss, the *Genesis* account of Eden and the Fall. Newland displaces innocence from its primal position as humankind's original state, subsequently corrupted by the serpent who introduces guile and deception into Eden, and therefore into human experience. Instead of innocence, Newland asserts, guile and its twists are themselves primary. "Innocence" is a species of guile, secondary and derivative. Innocence is an "artificial product," "cunningly manufactured" for the marriage market via conscious and unconscious training.[25]

Still inverting *Genesis,* where the joint human fall from innocence renders humankind forever postlapsarian, Newland soon begins to theorize that what might really be in some deep sense irreversible is the transformation that occurs, among women of his own upper class, from humanity's original guile into feminine "innocence" as a historically specific form of artifice. May's mother, who insists on never being told anything "unpleasant," is for Newland an image of "the innocence that seals the mind against imagination and the heart against experience" (271, 171). Mrs. Welland's cunningly manufactured, "artificial" innocence has become impenetrable, a fixed identity. Although after their marriage May ceases physically to be a virgin, Newland continues to marvel "at the way in which experience drop[s] away from her" (221). May's own artificially constructed feminine "innocence," he fears, may soon constitute an obliterating "negation" that yields only blankness, and that can never be reversed (224).

Drawing on "some of the new ideas in his scientific books," in particular "the much-cited instance of the Kentucky cave fish, which had ceased to develop eyes because they had no use for them, Newland wonders what if, when he had bidden May Welland to open hers, they could only look out blankly at blankness?" (121). Newland's "scientific" theory that May's innocence may be an irreversible modification, analogous to the blindness of the Kentucky cave fish, is at the heart of why, as he sits in his study, "he felt himself oppressed" (91). He foresees that May's "invincible innocence," the "indestructible youthfulness" that keeps her forever "pure," will constrain his own freedom and individuality (171, 207). "He perceived with a flash of chilling insight that in future many problems would be thus negatively solved for him. . . . The worst of it was that May's pressure was already bearing on the very angles whose sharpness he most wanted to keep" (218).

Throughout, Newland's moments of "scientific" theorization about the people and social structures around him coincide with those moments in which he feels most trapped, most disabled. The best example occurs near the end of the book, at Ellen Olenska's farewell dinner. Archer analyzes the dinner party ethnographically as "the tribal rally around a kinswoman about to be eliminated from the tribe" (319). Although to a naïve witness the party would appear entirely "harmless-looking," Archer interprets it as a ritualistic expulsion or sacrifice, "the old New York way of taking life 'without the effusion of blood'" (319). Because the scene's social violence is never explicit, Archer must read and theorize aggressively. He construes even the faintest of implications, of unspoken analogical meanings, of pauses in conversation, as elements in the culmination of a vast "conspiracy" (Archer's word), patiently prepared for over months, to eliminate Ellen from the social group. I do not mean to suggest that Archer's analysis of the dinner party's meaning is paranoid or wrong (although it is worth noting that Wharton does not provide outside confirmation of his analysis). What I wish to point out is that the more completely Archer reads and theorizes the social technology involved in this sacrificial moment, in which he himself has a part to play, the more his emotional affect becomes one of numb paralysis: "[A] deathly sense of the superiority of implication and analogy over direct action, and of silence over rash words, closed in on him like the doors of the family vault" (320). The more he cathects onto the totalizing social power at work, the more robbed of agency he feels: "As these thoughts succeeded each other in his mind Archer felt like a prisoner in the centre of an armed camp" (319).

Newland Archer's understanding of Old New York's structures and modalities of power is comparable to the sorts of knowledge and theory that Richard Rorty finds so disabling for progressive political action, especially insofar as Newland takes the social power he analyzes to be both ubiquitous (employing "countless silently observing eyes and patiently listening ears") and inexorable in its workings (319). It is as if Newland has proleptically developed the perspective not merely of an ethnographer but of a Foucauldian cultural critic. For Rorty, however, this would mean that Newland has become a "rationalizer of hopelessness." "Foucauldian theoretical sophistication," Rorty insists, "is even more useless to leftist politics than was Engels' dialectical materialism."[26] Newland's sense of his own complicity in the "sacrifice" of Ellen—the sacrificial dinner is held in his own house, after all—adds, moreover, to his habitual sensation of weightlessness: Newland seems to himself "to be assisting at the scene in a state of odd imponderability, as if he floated somewhere between chandelier and ceiling, wonder[ing] at nothing so much as his own share in the proceedings" (319).

Yet although Newland Archer himself and, at least in part, Wharton identify him with theory, knowledge, and indirect guilt, I want to suggest several interrelated levels on which Newland, rather than May, simultaneously functions as the primary referent for the title's "innocence." I ultimately argue that Wharton's intertwining of guilt and innocence around the figure of Newland Archer offers a lens through which we might begin to envision how the theory-structured, potentially paralyzing, "knowledge" of the guilty liberal might potentially coexist with (rather than be replaced by, as Rorty would have it) a more open-ended orientation toward "the possibilities and politics of futurity itself."[27]

Innocence and the American Man

To begin with, Newland is wrong about May. She is not innocent, at least not quite in the way that he thinks she is. He has his first surprise when May indicates to him, just before their marriage, that she has known for two years about an affair he once had with a married woman ("poor silly Mrs. Thorley Rushworth"): "You mustn't think that a girl knows as little as her parents imagine. One hears and one notices—" (131, 174). If May recognizes one of the realities supposedly kept from young women, that many men in Old New York have premarital and extramarital affairs, then Newland's vision of her as she watched the *Faust* seduction scene—"She doesn't even guess what it's all about"—was incorrect, indeed itself overly innocent. Newland is again shocked, near the end of the book, to realize that for quite some time May has believed that he and Ellen are lovers, which is never technically the case. Still more unsettling, she conveys to him that she actively manipulated Ellen into leaving the country, playing on the latter's conscience by telling her at a strategic moment that she, May, was pregnant, although at the time she herself did not know whether it was true or not. Newland is astonished one last time in the book's final chapter, after May's death, when he learns that the wife whom he still thinks of as embodying "blindness" about both the real world and his own interiority in fact knew all about his struggle to break out of the marriage and then his decision to remain within it.

Newland's serial rediscoveries that May always knew more, saw more, and even acted more than he imagined suggest that it is his own belief in her feminine innocence that is invincible, rather than any actual quality of "invincible innocence" (171) that she possesses. From the beginning, Newland's sense of his own sophistication has relied on his gendered perception of May as utterly innocent: "[P]ride in his own masculine initiation was mingled with a tender reverence for her abysmal purity" (60). "Masculine initiation" derives its status by juxtaposing itself with the unfathomable naïveté of the young American girl. But if Newland seems recurrently unable to hold on to his repeated discoveries of May's lack of innocence, one might say equally of him what he says of May: certain experiences drop away or slide off of him, leaving no apparent trace. Further, almost as much as he insists on his own "masculine initiation"

relative to May, Newland himself emphasizes his inexperience, even ignorance, by comparison with the Countess Olenska. Ellen Olenska is an
American who has spent much of her childhood and all of her adult life
in Europe, the latter while married to the wealthy and decadent Polish
Count Olenski. Her sexual experience seems as unfathomable to
Newland as May's "abysmal purity" does. The countess, he is certain, has
"tasted mysterious joys" and had "exquisite pleasures" that he cannot
imagine, let alone name. In speaking with her about her past life, he feels
"as awkward and embarrassed as a boy" (136, 248, 142).

The countess's supposed sexual initiation is just one charged example
of her "depths of experience beyond his reach": "It frightened him to think
what must have gone into the making of her eyes" (283, 104). If, in
Newland Archer's scientific analogy, May Welland's enforced (and self-
enforcing) innocence has meant the loss of her ability to see at all, so that
even if he forced her eyes open, they would be able only to "look blankly
out at blankness," then by contrast Ellen Olenska has "had to look at the
Gorgon" (283). Rather than blinding her, the Gorgon has dried up her
tears, leaving no mediating screen between her and "the powers of evil"
with which she has lived for so long and so familiarly (117). More generally, whenever Newland's frame of reference shifts to the register of national identity, he unquestioningly aligns America and Americans with innocence and purity. Discussing the Olenski household with M. Rivière,
Newland's gaze wanders to a wall calendar with the U.S. president's picture on it: "That such a conversation should be going on anywhere within the millions of square miles subject to his rule seemed as strange as anything that the imagination could invent" (257).[28]

Fantasies of Innocence

In short, Newland has an almost lifelong investment in the category of
"innocence," whether he aligns it with May as the virginal embodiment of
Old New York; with himself as an American boy-man confronted by a
European woman; or with the territory and identity of the United States
itself. We turn now to the scene in which the most overbearing version of
Newland's investment in "innocence" emerges. During a carriage ride he
and Ellen share from the New Jersey ferry terminal to Fifth Avenue, he
articulates a "vision" for achieving absolute New World innocence, for
returning to a prelapsarian state in a world apart. He willfully chooses to
regard his "vision" as realizable. As Rorty might put it, Newland opts to
replace "shared knowledge of what's real with hope for what might become
real."[29] Because he refuses to accept this fantasy's status *as* fantasy, his

dream of escaping into a world outside of guilt will leave Newland feeling more entrapped, more implicated, in social realities than ever before. As we will see, his subsequently tortured relation to the fantasy of an escape from social implication—he will move from a desperate belief in the fantasy to a never quite successful determination to jettison it from his psyche—will constrain his sense of agency for nearly three decades.

Newland has been sent by May and May's mother to drive Ellen to her ill grandmother's house. He and Ellen have admitted their love to each other but have not sexually consummated their relationship. In the carriage, he insists to her that he does not want "an ordinary hole-and-corner love-affair," in which they would enjoy "stolen" moments of intimacy (281–82). Stealing intimate moments in hidden corners would make them criminals, albeit of the most ordinary kind, guilty of the same hypocrisy as those society men Newland knows who prate about morality and propriety while carrying on secret affairs with women of lower social classes. Newland desires an intimate relationship with Ellen, a woman not his wife, but a relation that would entirely avoid contradicting social law, no matter how frequently other men may bend or break that same law. He desires, that is, an "innocent" sexual relation. Ellen immediately points out the painful irony of their discussing such a vision in May's own carriage: "You choose your place well to put it to me!" That they are having the discussion inside the brougham of Newland's wife indicates the structuring realities of their situation. We must look, Ellen insists, "not at visions but at realities" (284). If they begin a sexual relationship, no matter where it happens, and no matter what Newland wants to call it, she will be his "mistress," with all the connotations of betrayal and immorality that attach to the word. At bottom, they would remain "only Newland Archer, the husband of Ellen Olenska's cousin, and Ellen Olenska, the cousin of Newland Archer's wife, trying to be happy behind the backs of the people who trust them" (285).

In response, Newland extrapolates from his initial vision of an innocent sexual relation to an entire "world" of innocence, a "new-land" in which his actions would not impact or implicate others. He insists that they can get "away" from the social world that he has spent the novel theorizing and critiquing, exempt at last from its guilty hypocrisies. Newland's notion for how he and Ellen can be together without guilt requires their escaping, somehow, from the "world" in which they live: "I want—I want somehow to get away with you into a world where words like that—categories like that—won't exist. Where we shall be simply two human beings who love each other" (284). Newland's vision here is that he and Ellen can relocate to what Richard Poirier has called "a world elsewhere." This vision, so pervasive in the American literary tradition, is itself an extension of American exceptionalism; it pictures a new world that is perpetually available as fresh, unmarked space, away from "old world" codes and constraints.[30] Newland's desire to leave society and its complications recalls, for example, Huck Finn's impulse to "light out for the territory" so that he can escape the constraints of "sivilization."

Ellen's response to Newland at first seems a jaded Europeanized deflation of his vision. There is no such place, she tells him: "Oh, my dear—where is that country? Have you ever been there? . . . I know so many who've tried to find it; and, believe me, they all got out by mistake at wayside stations: at places like Boulogne, or Pisa, or Monte Carlo—and it wasn't at all different from the old world they'd left, but only rather smaller and dingier and more promiscuous" (285). Those who go searching for some "new-land" outside of the social order discover that it does not exist: they find only another corner of their own world. If Ellen deflates Newland's vision of an innocent new world, however, she does so only to reinstate innocence, not as a place, but as a mode of behavior. If they cannot escape a social order that would render any sexual relationship between them as hurtful to others, then they must refrain from any relationship at all. That their love should cause no pain to others, and in this sense remain innocent, is, for Ellen, its most essential characteristic, even if that results in her rigidly paradoxical logic of renunciation: "We're near each other only if we stay far from each other" (285).

For Ellen, the imperative to eschew guilty behavior is also the heart of what differentiates America from the Europe she has left: "That's why I came home. I want to forget everything else, to become a complete American again, like the Mingotts and Wellands, and you and your delightful mother, and all the other good people here" (106). She loves Newland because it was he who first made her see that under America's seeming "dullness there are things so fine and sensitive and delicate that even those I most cared for in my other life" (such as art, beauty, and other, unnamed "exquisite pleasures") "look cheap in comparison" (247). For Ellen, "America" is a form of ethical behavior or it is nothing: "If it's not worth while to have given up, to have missed things, so that others may be saved from disillusionment and misery," then she might as well return to her decadent European husband (248). Her love for Newland will be dead. Hence, "I can't love you unless I give you up" (192).

In addition to American exceptionalism, both Newland's vision of exiting the social world, so that he can act beyond its hypocrisies, and Ellen's tortured renunciation of any active relationship with Newland, are also versions of what Berlant calls "liberal fantasies."[31] Liberal fantasies might best be understood as illusory attempts to evade the infamous "dirty hands" problem. Following Sartre, American liberal theorists such as Michael

Walzer insist that the problem of "dirty hands" is endemic to political and social action. For Walzer, to act effectively and morally in the real world, especially if one seeks to produce significant change, often means that at the same time one will find oneself forced to help perpetuate something that is morally ambiguous or morally wrong (even if only through remaining silent when one should speak up). A given political action or campaign, Walzer insists, "may be exactly the right thing to do . . . and yet leave the man who does it guilty of a moral wrong. The innocent man is no longer innocent." If this "man" insists on retaining his purity, however, he will tie his own hands and fail to do the right thing. The obvious and realistic response, Walzer contends, is that, to avoid impotence, we must recognize that sometimes our hands will get dirty.[32]

Literary realists, in their portrayal of a complex world where actions always have multiple ramifications and effects, are often read as advancing views analogous to those of political theorists such as Walzer. As Henry James himself says in his preface to *What Maisie Knew*, "no theme is so human as those that reflect . . . that bright hard medal, of so strange an alloy, one face of which is somebody's right and ease and the other somebody's pain and wrong." Whether in a political or literary register, the "realist" position asserts that we have no choice but to "live with all intensity and perplexity and felicity in [our] terribly mixed little world," where one person or group's "right and ease" is always connected to "pain and wrong" for someone (or someplace) else.[33]

Yet many leftist intellectuals continue to find it difficult to accept or operate within this realist logic. If not struggling in the throes of liberal guilt or leftist melancholia, then they are "caught" in such liberal fantasies as, for example, the fantasy "that ethical feminist knowledge will be safe for, will not do harm to, anyone who encounters it." Dreaming of modes of knowledge and praxis that exist beyond any possibility of causing harm leads some academic feminists, according to Berlant, to evade facing the "failure, loss, pain, and chagrin" that should be confronted alongside of any utopian imagining.[34] A similar fantasy of innocence also lies behind what Rorty claims he finds in left-wing "movements" that limit their own effectiveness by refusing to compromise on their ideological purity.[35] Ironically, these fantasies of political innocence constitute merely the obverse side of the same liberal guilt whose occasioning they are so determined to avoid. Like liberal guilt, they also end in immobility.

The sensible "realist" response to liberal guilt and fantasies of innocence alike is that one must learn to accept dirty hands, and just *let go* of the fantasy that one might do good—or do anything—without any possibility of causing harm. But it is a response that does not work for all, or not fully, including Newland Archer, protagonist of a realist novel. For Newland, the

determination to resign himself to reality, to let go of his fantasy of radical innocence, produces a dreary melancholia. By the time of the book's
last chapter, Newland has resigned himself to a life of limited aspiration:
"His days were full, and they were filled decently. He supposed it was all
a man ought to ask." A member of Old New York's wealthy elite, Newland
has reached a stage in his life where he takes a role in all of the "new phil-
anthropic, municipal, and artistic" movements responsible, in turn-of-
the-century New York, for "starting the first school for crippled children,
reorganising the Museum of Art . . . inaugurating the new Library," and
other good causes. He has been intermittently active in Theodore
Roosevelt's Progressive movement, although he was relieved to lose his seat
in the state legislature after serving for just one year (327–28). Newland is
heavily burdened by the knowledge that he failed in his primary attempt
at utopian reimagining, in which he envisioned constructing with Ellen
Olenska a whole new world without repressive social conventions or
oppressive power structures. He now views such visions as "unattainable
and improbable." Even to "repine" the failure would be excessive, "like
despairing because one had not drawn the first prize in a lottery" (329).
Having locked his utopian fantasy away in a vault that even he can no
longer open, Newland now feels himself to be "a mere grey speck of a
man" (335).

Wharton's much-discussed final chapter of *The Age of Innocence,* I suggest, begins to make visible another possibility beyond being "caught"
either by the liberal dream of "clean hands" or by the liberal disillusionment and melancholia that only appear to be opposed to that dream.
During the final chapter, Newland Archer suddenly comes to see his fantasy of establishing an innocent sexual/social relation with Ellen Olenska,
a utopian relation that would do no harm to others, explicitly *as* a fantasy, but, paradoxically, a fantasy that it is crucial he should never fully relin-
quish. When read next to contemporary American writings on liberal
guilt, Wharton's conclusion evokes possibilities for renegotiating, or at
least loosening the bonds of, our own paralyzing relationships with political guilt, fear, and melancholy—and renegotiating as well as our continuing (although often buried) investment in the vision of discovering an
innocent space or praxis.

Traversing the Fantasy of Innocence

The novel's last chapter jumps forward twenty-six years from the end of
the previous chapter, into the early twentieth century. It ends with the
now-widowed Newland Archer having just arisen from a Parisian street

bench, where he had sat looking up at the terrace of Ellen Olenska's fifth-floor flat. He has not seen Ellen since the ritualistic dinner party that simultaneously banished her from Old New York's social world and reaffirmed his own participating membership in it. With May dead, however, and his own son urging him to mount the stairs to Ellen's apartment, Newland and Ellen's coming together would no longer occur in the register of betrayal or guilt. It would not cause pain to others. Indeed, there no longer seems any social or institutional reason that they cannot finally enjoy a relationship that is simultaneously sexual and innocent. The central aspect of Newland's earlier vision of a new world—that is, his vision, while in May's carriage, of a nonguilty relationship with Ellen—now seems realistically within reach.

Nonetheless, Newland does not respond to his son Dallas's prompting. After Dallas himself has gone upstairs, Newland continues to sit on the street bench. "'It's more real to me here than if I went up,' he suddenly heard himself say." Finally, in the book's last line, "Newland Archer got up slowly and walked back alone to his hotel" (340–41). There is something inarguably perverse in Newland's final action, something that runs counter to common sense. His refusal to see Ellen Olenska provokes an "incredulous gesture" on the part of his son (340). As Renata Salecl emphasizes, "from a pragmatic point of view, this renunciation is stupid."[36] The ending bothers undergraduates, just as does Mrs. Lidcote's decision in "*Autre Temps . . .*" to return to exile (see chapter 1). They view these decisions as representing pointless sacrifices.

Rather than the sacrifice of his chance finally to enjoy a "happy ending" with Ellen, however, we can read Newland's arising from his seat in front of Ellen's window as signifying something else. Finishing her book in 1920, at the start of cinema's golden age, Wharton's language in the book's final few paragraphs evokes a man finally allowing a mesmerizing film to end, so that he can get up and leave. When Newland and his son Dallas first enter the Parisian square in which Ellen's building is located, Newland is struck by the light that the dome of the Hôtel des Invalides casts over the square: "By some queer process of association, that golden light became for him the pervading illumination in which she lived" (338). Newland stands for a moment and then sits down on the bench in front of Ellen's window, sending Dallas upstairs without him. As he sits, his mind's eye becomes like a mobile camera, tracking Dallas's ascent in the lift to the fifth floor, his ringing of the doorbell, his being "admitted to the hall, and then ushered into the drawing room." Next, reversing his angle of vision to a spot already inside the drawing room, Newland "picture[s] Dallas entering that room with his quick assured step and delightful smile." Then, quickly reversing his viewing angle once again, Newland "trie[s] to see"

Ellen's room from Dallas's point of view, finally tracking in on "a dark lady, pale and dark, who would look up quickly, half rise, and hold out a long thin hand with three rings on it. . . . He thought she would be sitting in a sofa-corner near the fire, with azaleas banked behind her on a table" (340; ellipses in original).

Newland finally turns away when a "light shone through the windows" and a servant "came out on the balcony, drew up the awnings, and closed the shutters." The lights have come up in the theater, as we might say, and the curtain has been drawn. "At that, as if it had been the signal he waited for, Newland Archer got up slowly and walked back alone to his hotel" (341). Newland finally grasps that to go upstairs would be to take his longstanding fantasy too literally, like a person trying to climb up and into a movie screen.

The book ends here. A blank space follows the final sentence. In sidestepping the conventional narrative closure that many readers expect, in which lovers finally join together—and which even Newland's son Dallas seems to have envisioned in bringing his father to Paris and then to Ellen's apartment—Wharton preserves an openness. Lacking the expected closure, the blank space at book's end becomes available, I believe, for readers' own projections. Certainly, one might find oneself disappointed by Newland's decision not even to try to connect with Ellen. One could quite plausibly fill in the blank with a future for Newland that is defined by disengagement and withdrawal from life. Taking willful advantage of the blank space, however, I would like to project, to imagine, that despite the conclusion's elegiac tone Newland's response to the "waited for" signal, to the closing of the shutters—at which he rises from the bench and starts to walk—represents a possible advance.

In my projection, Newland comes away with an importantly altered relation to his fantasy of a free relationship with Ellen. For much of his adult life, Newland has been captivated, captured, by the vision of a life that he and Ellen could and *would*, in a simpler, cleaner world, have shared. When he chooses not to enter her building and instead allows the screen to go blank, Newland for the first time recognizes his fantasy *as* fantasy. Lacanian theory uses the phrase "traversing the fantasy" to describe a process that results in the realization that the "fantasies that have been directing one's desire and contributing to one's suffering are both relative and doomed to remain unfulfilled."[37]

Traversing a fantasy, however, is not the same thing as repudiating it. Traversing a fantasy does not mean that one must now simply abandon it in favor of, say, the social "realities" Ellen had mentioned to Newland during their carriage ride.

In his latter decades, Newland's grimly realist attempts to force himself to let go of his fantasy even as, at some deeper level, he continued to organize his being around it left him feeling hollow, a "mere gray speck of a man." After years spent blindly pursuing/despairing of an impossible fantasy, like a moth banging up against a window, Newland Archer now chooses to walk away, this time holding on to the fantasy, rather than being held by it: "It's more real to me . . . than if I went up." In traversing his fantasy, Newland comes to realize that he can retain his thirty-year-old dream of connecting with Ellen in a world free of social complexity without also retaining the desperate belief that it will, that it *must,* come true. Fantasy, once recognized as such, just might come to play a productive role in his life. Archer can hold onto it as an emblem, even a metaphor, for other possibilities, just as a movie can energize and inspire us even when we recognize as fantasy the events that it depicts.

Paradoxically, it is only after Newland Archer recognizes and accepts his fantasy of achieving an innocent future with Ellen Olenska *as* fantasy that he has the opportunity to stop regarding his present moment as irredeemably diminished. It is only then that he has at least the chance to choose a new direction, even as he retains his fantasy as a signifier of utopian possibilities ("it's more real to me . . ."). Admittedly, the new relation to his fantasy that I am projecting for Newland is not directly signaled by any of his conscious thoughts or intentions at the book's end. Yet regardless of what he himself "actually" does after returning to his hotel, I would argue that the structure of the novel's concluding paragraphs still makes available to us, as readers, an opportunity to traverse his fantasy of innocence. What, then, might a critically presentist reading that "traverses" Newland Archer's fantasy of innocence illuminate regarding the question of liberal guilt?

The minor key tone of Wharton's ending, in which Archer walks off quietly and alone, might indeed lead one to think of what Daniel Born describes as an all-too-frequent trajectory of liberal guilt, "from a desire for involvement and activism to a fastidious withdrawal, a disengagement."[38] That trajectory repeats itself, spinning its wheels back and forth between the liberal dream of achieving a nonharmful, noncomplicit praxis, and leftist melancholia. A reading that "traverses" Newland's fantasy, however, presents us with at least an allegorical possibility for retaining, albeit in a new and altered form, a sense of openness toward the *image* of an innocent social relation, a relation in which, contrary to the dictates of both political and literary realism, trying to live and do "right" does not always involve complicity in "pain and wrong" somewhere else.

Taken as uncritical truth, "American innocence" has had, and continues to have, deadly effects both on the North American continent and around the world. The hegemonic ideology that Patricia Nelson Limerick has called the "Empire of Innocence" not only energizes a national self-view of the United States as a "good fellow wronged" by malevolent foreigners, as discussed in chapter 5.[39] It also continues to underwrite popular myths about the "settling" of the American West, white resistance to affirmative action programs, and literary and cultural celebrations of the canonical figure that R. W. B. Lewis dubbed "the American Adam."[40] However often it is demystified by activists, scholars, and teachers, or even "lost" as a result of national traumas, the feeling of American innocence remains an irreducible constituent of at least white American identity. Wharton's apposite phrase is "invincible innocence." In fact, insofar as liberal guilt takes a posture of confession and contrition, such guilt might itself be read as a bid to regain at least some form of spiritual innocence.

The Age of Innocence hints at a possibility for leftist intellectuals to move beyond the back-and-forth game of puncturing fantasies of American innocence, only to see such fantasies reemerge further downstream as still central to Americans' sense of their national identity. "American innocence," taken explicitly as a fantasy, would no longer signify a lack of knowledge, responsibility, or guilt regarding either the past or the present. Recognized as fantasy, and retained as such, "American innocence" would be by definition unrealizable. "Traversed," *the fantasy of American innocence* might yet remain "real" as a powerful tropological placeholder, a metaphor for leftists' need to maintain an orientation, a desire, towards futurity that is not entirely bound either by the preexisting social system or by the guilty intellectual's encompassing knowledge and sophisticated theory.

I conclude by arguing that, because of a crucial twist Wharton adds to her use of the genre of historical fiction, *The Age of Innocence*'s last chapter also foregrounds another form of "real" innocence. This latter is a built-in epistemological guilelessness regarding the future that we all share, including—or especially—the most sophisticated and knowing among us. The temporally based, structurally innocent dimensions of consciousness that Wharton's concluding chapter stresses both complements and energizes the necessary ability—whether Newland Archer's ability or the immobilized academic leftist's ability—to continue being motivated and sustained by something like what Lauren Berlant calls "concrete utopian imagining."[41]

Temporal Innocence

Returning briefly to the earlier scene in May's carriage, we see that in fact two seemingly unrelated sorts of fantasy or vision arise. There is what we have already discussed, Newland's "vision" that he and Ellen could escape to a new "world," outside the social, beyond categories of guilt and betrayal—which, as I have argued, does not yet know itself as fantasy. (At this point, Newland is, he insists, "just trusting to it to come true" (284). In addition, however, there is "the brotherhood of visionaries" that Archer muses upon as he waits for Ellen's train to arrive (280). "Their visions" dwell on the future and its possibilities, such as "a tunnel under the Hudson through which the trains of the Pennsylvania railway would run straight into New York," or "the building of ships that would cross the Atlantic in five days, the invention of a flying machine, lighting by electricity, telephonic communication without wires, and other Arabian Nights marvels" (280). As his reference to the Arabian Nights suggests, Newland—knowingly, in this case—locates this set of futuristic visions within the category of fantasy.

At a similar moment earlier in the novel, Newland Archer, Ellen Olenska, and the banker Julius Beaufort discuss early rumors about Alexander Graham Bell's invention:

> the fantastic possibility that they might one day actually converse with each other from street to street, or even—incredible dream!— from one town to another. This struck from all three allusions to Edgar Poe and Jules Verne, and such platitudes as naturally rise to the lips of the most intelligent when they are talking against time, and dealing with a new invention in which it would seem ingenuous to believe too soon. (163–64)

In the face of such an "incredible dream" about the future, knowledge and sophistication strive to avoid ingenuousness. The reflexive task of "the most intelligent" individuals, "talking against time," is carefully to evade naïveté. Their intelligent sophistication is pitted against any early belief in this "fantastic possibility" for future connection and communication.

Of course, the reader has the historical advantage of knowing that Archer, Olenska, and Beaufort's intelligent skepticism will turn out to have been misplaced. By the novel's end, "telephonic communication" has become quotidian reality, as Newland's son Dallas calls him from Chicago to arrange a last-minute trip to Europe on one of the new five-day steamers, a call which Newland receives in a room lit by "pleasantly-shaded electric lamps" (329). Indeed, each "fantastic possibility" for the future mentioned in earlier chapters is vindicated in the coda-like concluding chapter. Even Larry Lefferts's obscene and hyperbolic joke, uttered to Archer and the other men over cigars, that, one day, "we shall see our children . . . marrying Beaufort's bastards" becomes reality (322). Newland's "eldest son, the pride of his life," becomes engaged to Beaufort's illegitimate daughter Fanny, the wedding to occur in Grace Church, "and nobody wondered or reproved" (332).

In confirming the fulfillment of every "fantastic possibility" regarding both the technological and the social future, however "incredible" it originally seemed to the novel's "most intelligent" characters, Wharton gives a particular twist to the sort of dramatic irony generally available to the historical novelist. In any historical novel, the author and her readers will necessarily know more about the social and technological future than do the book's characters. At key moments in the *The Age of Innocence,* however, Wharton escalates this irony by calling our attention to how the book's most *sophisticated* characters—characters who think that their skepticism sets the example against any ingenuous, gullible, or naive relation to the future—are wrong.

Throughout, Wharton textures her novel so as to emphasize her readers' superior perspective and knowledge specifically in relationship to what passes for knowingness or sophistication in 1870s New York. In the first chapter, free-indirect discourse focalized in Newland Archer explains why he has arrived late at the opera: "New York was a metropolis, and [he] was perfectly aware that in metropolises it was 'not the thing' to arrive early at the opera" (58). The upper-class spectators at the opera constitute "what the daily press had already learned to describe as 'an exceptionally brilliant audience'" (57). Later in the same scene, the narrator refers to a character trying "to look as if he had meant to insinuate what knowing people called a *double entendre*" (68). In each of these examples, Wharton allows a whiff of quaintness to hover about the era's "knowing people." Imagine a time when *double entendre* was a daring new possibility, just beginning to circulate among the most advanced people. Think of the day when New Yorkers first began to conceive of their city as a "metropolis." Look backward from today (the 1920s), when mass media is already awash in formulaic, voyeuristic slickness, to an earlier era (the 1870s) in which such slickness actually seemed new and noteworthy. In addition, Wharton also allows her 1920s readers to recognize the silly arbitrariness of naturalized conventions of the 1870s, such as the "unalterable and unquestioned law . . . [which] required that the German text of French operas sung by Swedish artists should be translated into Italian for the clearer understanding of English-speaking audiences." This ludicrous "law" "seemed as natural to Newland Archer as all the other conventions on which his life was moulded" (58–59).

Alan Price's recent book on Wharton's activities during the First World War, which details her impressive, and personally very difficult, work on behalf of Belgian and French refugees, is titled *The End of the Age of Innocence.* A typical assumption about Wharton's work on *The Age of Innocence* in 1919 and 1920 is that she could perceive a valuable "innocence" in the rigid, old-fashioned world she had often severely criticized only after the "epoch" delimiting that world was irrefutably ended. This assumption takes its cue from sentences in Wharton's autobiographical memoir, *A Backward Glance* (1933), in which she asserts, "The world I had grown up in and been formed by had been destroyed in 1914." She describes her postwar writing of *The Age of Innocence* as an "escape" from the "grim" present, which allowed her imaginatively to return to her "childish memories of a long-vanished America."[42] Wharton's use of the word "escape" suggests her awareness that any "innocence" supposed to characterize "Old New York" ("Old New York" was an early title for the novel) is fiction, existing in a space self-consciously recreated in the mode of nostalgia.

There is an important sense in which an "age of innocence" (whether construed as an individual's childhood or a given historical epoch) can only ever be identified from a position after it or otherwise outside of it. For anyone who claims to speak from a position internal to the age of innocence—to speak "innocently," that is, of innocence—innocence will necessarily vanish in the very moment of its naming, like the "modern" in Paul de Man's well-known essay, "Literary History and Literary Modernity." De Man writes, "The spontaneity of being modern conflicts with the claim to think and write about modernity." So too, we might say that the spontaneity of being innocent conflicts with the claim to think and write about innocence.[43] If one "knows" that one is innocent, then one also has knowledge of something with which to contrast that innocence. One already knows too much. Innocence necessarily excludes its enunciator.

Thus, *The Age of Innocence,* from its title onward, positions its readers as a site of historical knowledge and sophistication relative to the novel's characters. But that reading position is only too familiar for the leftist academics whom we began this chapter by discussing, who feel blocked because they "know too much," whose theoretical sophistication has constrained their sense of political hope. To the degree that Wharton's text fixes innocence "back then," it would seem to militate against a presentist interpretation of the book as at least gesturing toward the chance for such a reader to reclaim innocence as a productive fantasy, as the emblem of an open future. Rarely recognized but absolutely crucial about *The Age of Innocence*'s concluding chapter, however, is that it does not take the narrative up to Wharton's actual time of writing: 1919–1920.

Living in the twentieth century's first decade, Dallas Archer serves as the representative of a new age, who judges his father's generation as "prehistoric" and notes how it "dates" him that he never left May for Ellen (336). Dallas takes utterly for granted those technological inventions and radical social changes (he is marrying "Beaufort's bastard," after all) that the most intelligent of Newland's generation declined even to believe were possible.

Able to recognize precisely how the most knowing of Newland's age were traduced by their temporal disadvantage, Dallas appears in the coda as something of a reader surrogate. Yet, although separated by less than twenty years from the moment of writing, the novel's last chapter is just as much "historical fiction" as is the body of the novel set in the 1870s. Above all, Dallas has no inkling that what Wharton later called the "catastrophe of 1914" draws near.[44] He is even more "innocent" in relation to the future than were his father, Ellen Olenska, and Julius Beaufort when they scoffed at the thought of "telephonic communication."

Wharton's working title for a projected sequel to *The Age of Innocence* was "The Age of Wisdom," in which she intended to follow the fortunes of Dallas Archer, Fanny Beaufort, and others of their generation. She never wrote the sequel. But given the world war that impended upon its group of protagonists, as a title "the age of wisdom" can only be read as deep irony. An alternate title might be something like "Age of Innocence: The Next Generation" or "Innocence Reloaded" (to borrow from popular science fiction of our own day). Here another meaning of "the *age* of innocence" emerges. Innocence may seem to belong to the young or to the prior generation, but it is itself of hoary age, insofar as it is forever reconstituted in relation to the future. This recurrent pattern emphasizes a kind of structural innocence that we all share in relation to the future, even or maybe especially the knowing and sophisticated. Today's sophistication may always be revealed as tomorrow's ignorance; today's knowingness may always turn out to be a form of ingenuousness. This temporally based epistemological innocence is one that in fact we can not escape, which means that despite all of our knowledge and theory, we do not know what is to come, or of what we can be sure.

From one point of view, Wharton's novel shows innocence as a state that is impossible. The "innocence" of an unmarried woman such as May is no more than a cultural artifact, "cunningly manufactured" via a historically specific process, because it is what men are supposed to want. More broadly, it is only a fantasy to believe that we could become somehow "innocent" of our participation or implication in burdensome, objectionable realities. At the same time, Wharton's novel also shows innocence to be always and unavoidably available. The point that I have been moving toward in this last section may seem to boil down to the truism that no one can really know what the future holds, no matter how knowing, sophisticated, or cynical he or she may be. Indeed, I do think leftist melancholia can lead us to forget the truth of this particular truism. Beyond the platitude, however, *The Age of Innocence*'s deployment of historical frames within frames serves to underline our real, structural "innocence" of determinate knowledge about the future.[45] The openness of futurity is a temporal reality that even liberal guilt's "complicated awareness" can never quite preclude. The novel's emphasis on a temporally based epistemological innocence, combined with the possibility of interpreting Newland as choosing to retain innocence knowingly *as* a fantasy, can, in a refractive presentist reading, help orient our imaginations toward a renewed relationship with the category of American innocence.

Now, More Than Ever

In 1950, composing his preface to *The Liberal Imagination,* Lionel Trilling felt assured enough about liberalism's ascendancy in U.S. culture to assert "the plain fact that nowadays there are no conservative or reactionary ideas in general circulation." He found only a few "isolated and . . . ecclesiastical exceptions" to this truism. Trilling viewed the lack of conservative or reactionary ideas in general circulation as a serious problem for liberals and liberalism. Unchallenged by intellectual opponents, liberals would never be forced to "examine their position for its weaknesses and complacencies."[1]

Suffice it to say that we no longer face the supposed problem of a lack of conservative antagonists, whether intellectual, ecclesiastical, or otherwise. Thanks to richly endowed right-wing think tanks, the new public prominence of Christian fundamentalism, and ever-more centralized corporate media, the "general circulation" of culture and ideas is now awash in conservative discourse. "Liberal" has become a pejorative epithet in national political campaigns.

I wrote most of this book during the first George W. Bush administration and concluded it during the run-up to the 2004 election. As 2004's oft-repeated phrase had it, I did indeed regard the upcoming election as the most important one in my lifetime. At the University of Texas, a large number of my students come from families and backgrounds that predispose them to be suspicious of the L-word and every person and idea associated with it. At the time, not a single Democrat held statewide office in Texas.

I kept wondering as I worked on this book whether now was the right moment to profess reading and teaching practices that uncover contradictions and tensions internal to liberal identity. Put most crudely, wouldn't some of the arguments articulated in this book, which in many cases I germinated in my undergraduate classes, provide aid and comfort to those already inclined to regard liberals as hypocrites who mouth politically correct pieties about equality and justice while enjoying privileged lifestyles? Wasn't now a time, if ever there were one, for liberal intellectuals to circle our wagons and send our critical gaze outward, rather than direct it inward?

In 1950, Trilling ignored, or he took so deeply for granted as to render invisible, what I view as the one factor that did then and still continues to shape American liberal identity more than any other: its predominant whiteness. Despite some meaningful steps toward diversifying their faculties, most university humanities departments remain overwhelmingly white, as do the larger academic structures of which they form a part. Yet humanities departments also remain one of the few institutional homes for unabashedly liberal thinking and research. Such spaces, in which the liberal imagination is still self-consciously cultivated and explored, must be valued and vigorously protected.

The humanistic academy has become an indispensable site both for the liberal imagination and for leftist imaginaries—even more so, I would argue, than in Trilling's day. At the same time, the humanistic academy is still deeply and disproportionately white. The tense combination of these two "plain facts" leads me to reiterate for our present moment Trilling's half-century-old words: "The job of criticism would seem to be, then, to recall liberalism to its first essential imagination of variousness and possibility, which implies the awareness of complexity and difficulty."[2] By comparison to today's most prominent forms of conservative American identity, liberalism is indeed a more difficult and complex political subjectivity to inhabit. It is textured by "nuance" (presidential candidate John Kerry's famous weakness in 2004). More profoundly, liberal identity is traversed by the series of structural dilemmas explored in the preceding chapters.[3]

But it is precisely those dimensions within liberal identity that are most difficult, vexed, or hard to speak or think about that must continually be pressured and examined: above all, the deep mutual dependence between liberal identity and hegemonic American whiteness. As several of my chapters suggest, hegemonic whiteness and American liberal identity have functioned, both historically and in the present, to construct and support one another. One might argue that in focusing so exclusively on *white* liberal identity—after all, there are multitudes of liberals in the United States who are not white, including many who are academics—the current book merely reinforces a culturally and socially dominant link between liberalism and whiteness. Indeed, whiteness studies as an approach often risks recentering and reuniversalizing whiteness, even as it critically analyzes the strategies by which whiteness acquires its status as empowered norm. I believe the risk is worth taking. The versions of liberal identity treated in this book are effectively hollowed out by a mostly unspoken, unselfconscious, and often repressed entwinement with white hegemony. That entwinement drains moral consistency from white liberals, leaches meaning from their political commitments and beliefs, and interferes with their ability to work actively for change. This book has been devoted to the proposition that, at least for white liberal critics, "the job of criticism" includes drawing on literature and its resources in order to "figure"—that is, both give legible figuration to and attempt to figure out—the gaps, contradictions, and incoherencies that our political, social, and personal investments produce, and to "figure" as well the economies by which white liberals maintain their often incoherent investments. Such acts of critical figuring are essential for a reimagination of liberalism to occur, particularly one that would alter—that would bring a new "variousness and possibility" to—American liberal identity's continuing alliance with racial, class, and global hierarchies.

NOTES

Introduction

1. Burke, *Permanence and Change,* 90.

2. See, for example, Patell, *Negative Liberties;* Newfield, *Emerson Effect;* and Bercovitch, *Rites of Assent.* Two excellent recent books, however, maintain a tight focus on the relationship between literature and political liberalism during the period of the 1930s: Szalay, *New Deal Modernism,* and McCann, *Gumshoe America.* Again, however, both of these studies take as a unifying theme the relationship between individuals and communal or social structures. While absolutely central to liberalism as a political *theory,* this theme is less immediately and insistently preeminent when considering the contemporary versions of left-liberal identity I concentrate on below. A slightly earlier group of books interested in liberalism and American literature—including new historicist criticism influenced by Foucault's notions of power—focuses on liberalism as a managerial practice that is also immanent in such literary genres as realism and naturalism. See Corkin, *Realism and the Birth of the Modern United States;* Howard, *Form and History in American Literary Naturalism;* Kaplan, *Social Construction of American Realism;* and Seltzer, *Henry James and the Art of Power.*

3. Turner delivered "the Significance of the Frontier in American History at the 1893 meeting of the American Historical Association, held in conjunction with the Chicago World's Fair. He concluded his speech by asserting, "the frontier has gone, and with its going has closed the first period of American history." The paper appears as chapter 1 of Frederick Jackson Turner, *The Frontier in American History.* See Garland, *Main-Travelled Roads;* Banta, *Taylored Lives;* and Morrison, *Playing in the Dark.*

4. On Howells and liberal identity, see Barrish, *American Literary Realism,* 30–47.

5. "We speak routinely and casually of the need to restore works to the 'historical situation' in which they were produced, or of sketching 'historical situations' for our own studies. The concept has turned slogan, and the inevitability with which it has accompanied efforts, especially programmatic efforts, to argue *against* certain kinds of formalism—New Criticism, Deconstruction—and *for* a certain kind of contextualism would be impossible to document exhaustively here; the practice has simply been too pervasive." Chandler, *England in 1819,* 37.

6. Knapp, *Literary Interest,* 107. See also Lane, "The Poverty of Context."

7. James, *Art of the Novel,* 5.

8. Rowe, *Other Henry James,* 192.

9. Ibid., 9.

10. Wiegman, "Whiteness Studies," 120.

11. Lipsitz, *Possessive Investment in Whiteness,* viii.

12. In choosing to take my own university as a focal point in Part One, I have

also been influenced by Henry Giroux's Gramscian insistence that a critical pedagogy "must always be contextually defined, allowing it to respond specifically to
the conditions, formations, and problems that arise in various sites in which education takes place. . . . Progressive educators need to engage their teaching as a theoretical resource that is both shaped by and responds to the very problems that
arise in the in-between space/places/contexts that connect classrooms with the
experiences of everyday life" (Giroux, "Pedagogy," 18–19).

13. Wiegman, "Whiteness Studies," 120.
14. Brown, "Resisting Left Melancholy," 26.
15. Ryan, "Liberal Political Theory," 4.
16. Williams, *Marxism and Literature,* 132.
17. Newfield, *Emerson Effect,* 10, 5.

Part One, Introduction

1. *Jennifer Gratz and Patrick Hamacher v. Lee Bollinger et al,* U.S. Supreme
Court, no. 02–516, Oral Arguments, April 1, 2003, p. 47. http://www.umich.edu/
~urel/admissions/legal/grutter/grutrans.html.
2. Glazer, "In Defense of Preference," 21–22.
3. De Man, *Blindness and Insight,* 187.
4. Wiegman, "Whiteness Studies," 128.
5. Stokes, *Color of Sex,* 13.
6. Dimock, "Non-Newtonian Time," 921.

Chapter 1

1. As in the title of his book, *Racism in the Post-Civil Rights Era: Now You See
It, Now You Don't.*
2. "*Autre Temps* . . ." was first published in two parts as "Other Times, Other
Manners" in *Century Magazine* 82 (July–August 1911). Wharton translated (or
retranslated) the title into French, italicized it, and replaced the second half of the
well-known French proverb (*autre temps, autre moeurs*) with ellipses for inclusion
in her 1916 collection, *Xingu and Other Stories* (New York: C. Scribner's Sons).
Future page references to "*Autre Temps*" will be from Wharton, *Roman Fever and
Other Stories.*
3. The key decision in the *Hopwood* case was actually issued by a panel of three
judges from the Fifth Circuit Court, who were assigned to consider the *Hopwood*
plaintiffs' appeal of an earlier District Court ruling in the case. The district court
judge, Sam Sparks, had found unconstitutional the specific affirmative action
mechanisms in place when Karen Hopwood et al. had applied to UT's Law
School, but he had awarded no damages to the plaintiffs. Moreover, following the
Supreme Court's 1978 opinion in *Bakke v. University of California,* Sparks's ruling
would still have allowed for a system that treated race as one (but never the sole
deciding) factor in admissions. The Fifth Circuit's three-judge panel went much
further, declaring in their "Decision Reversing and Remanding" that race could
not play any sort of role in admissions decisions by the Law School. (In doing so,

the panel controversially—and some argued illegally—set *Bakke* aside.) Although there was room for ambiguity about whether the panel's decree against giving race any consideration whatsoever applied to anything besides UT Law School admissions, Texas's attorney general at the time, Dan Morales, issued a binding interpretation that read the ruling as broadly as possible. All of Texas's public universities, Morales said, would have to cease any consideration of race not only in admissions but in financial aid and hiring. Four months after the three-judge panel's decision, the Supreme Court declined to become involved in the case. The district court ruling in *Hopwood, et al. v. State of Texas, et al,* 94 Ed 760 (S.D. Texas 1994), is accessible online at http://www.law.utexas.edu/hopwood/hoptxt. The Fifth Circuit panel decision, *Hopwood, et al. v. State of Texas, et al.,* 78 F.3d 932 (5th Cir. 1996), is accessible online at http://www.ca5.uscourts.gov/opinions/pub/94/94–50569-cv0.htm. (The latter decision will be referred to parenthetically in my text as "*Hopwood,* 5th Cir.") Texas Attorney General Dan Morales's Letter Opinion No. 79–001 (Feb. 5, 1997) is accessible online at http://www.law.utexas.edu/hopwood/morales.htm.

4. Catherine Gallagher uses a reading of Steven Spielberg's 1985 film *Back to the Future* to develop rich insights about the temporality of affirmative action and of proposals for racial reparation. Gallagher's argument about temporality and affirmative action is oblique to the ideas that I am developing here, but not incompatible with them. Gallagher, "Undoing."

5. Chandler, *England in 1819,* xiii

6. LaCapra, *Soundings in Critical Theory,* 39.

7. Benjamin, *Illuminations,* 260, 261.

8. Berman, "Politics," 323.

9. Flagg, *Was Blind but Now I See,* 53.

10. See Brodkin, *How Jews Became White Folks;* Jacobson, *Whiteness of a Different Color;* Roediger, *Wages of Whiteness;* and Ignatiev, *How the Irish Became White.*

11. Miller, *Afterlife of Plays,* 27.

12. Glavin, *After Dickens,* 1–4. Mary Poovey's review essay, "Creative Criticism and the Problem of Objectivity," contains a useful discussion of *After Dickens* as well as some other recent examples of what she calls "creative criticism."

13. "Introduction," in Elsom, *Is Shakespeare Still Our Contemporary?* 2

14. Contribution to "Session 1," in Elsom, *Is Shakespeare Still Our Contemporary?* 17

15. Ibid.

16. See Grillo and Wildman, "Obscuring the Importance of Race."

17. "*Hopwood,* 5th Cir." "Present effects of past discrimination" is a phrase cited not only in this but in prior and subsequent affirmative action cases as well.

18. *Barbara Grutter, Petitioner, v. Lee Bollinger, et al,* U.S. Supreme Court, No. 02–241, June 23, 2003, http://www.umich.edu/~vrel/admissions/legal/grutter/html.

19. Wharton, *Roman Fever and Other Stories,* 246; further page references will appear in the text.

20. Wharton, *Mother's Recompense,* 74.

21. For an analysis of the blush and its function in nineteenth-century fiction, see O'Farrell, *Telling Complexions.*

22. Morales, Letter Opinion No. 79–001 (see n. 3).

23. Motion of Thurgood Marshall Legal Society and Black Pre-Law Association to Intervene as Defendants, January 5, 1994, Binder I. Hopwood v. State of Texas Reserve Collection, Tarlton Law Library, Austin, Texas.

24. As the Thurgood Marshall Society and the Black Pre-Law Association summarized in a later brief, "The state declined to introduce the evidence or the testimony of the expert witness, presented no evidence concerning the validity of the Texas Index and raised no argument that race-conscious measures were required to mitigate the discriminatory effect of its use." Renewed Motion for the Limited Purpose of Allowing Evidence on the Predictive Validity of the Texas Index, July 1, 1994, Binder V. Hopwood v. State of Texas Reserve Collection, Tarlton Law Library, Austin, Texas.

25. Ibid.

26. Peller, "Toward a Critical Cultural Pluralism," 133. See also Cochran, *Color of Freedom;* and Montag, "Universalization of Whiteness."

27. Gould, *Mismeasure of Man,* 146–233.

28. Interveners representing minority students were allowed to present evidence about standardized tests and their racially disparate impact at early stages of the two Michigan cases. Their evidence was quickly dismissed by the presiding judges, however, and dismissed with a tone that at least one of the interveners' attorneys found "insulting." *Barbara Grutter v. Lee Bollinger, et al.* Civil Action No. 97–75928 (E.D. Mich), Rep. Joan L. Morgan, February 6, 2001: 127. http://www.umich.edu/~urel/admissions/legal/grutter/gru.trans/gru2.06.01b.html.

29. Matthew Cook, "Minority Applicants Less Likely to Be Accepted into Law School," *Daily Texan,* June 28, 2000, 1A.

30. Regarding individual "merit," Christopher Newfield contrasts ideas that were indeed floated in late-nineteenth-century discourse for more pluralistic modes of evaluation with the more rigid supposedly "meritocratic" systems of measurement that actually came to hold sway in research universities: "It is a bitter fact that the research university's great leap forward came in the decades, 1890–1910, during which Jim Crow segregation was being systematically installed in American life. Having cloaked stratification in the languages of nature and science, meritocracy insured that future attempts to value individual difference and diversify higher education would appear not to expand merit, but to compromise it" (Newfield, *Ivy and Industry,* 103).

31. Consider an exchange twice repeated, almost verbatim, in the Supreme Court on successive days during the oral arguments phase for each of the University of Michigan's two cases. Justice Antonin Scalia, one of the court's most conservative members, advanced to the university's lawyers that, if the State of Michigan chose and still chooses to develop an "elite" "super-duper law school," "one of the best law schools in the country"—which, he emphasized, is not a choice that the state or its university were ever compelled to make—then naturally it achieves this goal by "taking only the best students with the best grades and the best SATs or LSATs, *knowing* that the result of this will be to exclude to a large degree minorities" (my italics). Scalia then demands why, "considering [that the University of Michigan] created this situation by making that decision, it then turns around and says, oh, we have a compelling State interest in eliminating this racial imbalance that [we] ourselves have created." Scalia's racism is obvious: he assumes that the University of Michigan could no longer be a "super-duper law school" if it were to admit significant numbers of minority students. The univer-

sity's lawyers disagreed with him on this specific point by reminding him that minority students admitted under affirmative action are highly "qualified," just as are many other students whom the school is unable to admit. But what is most telling about the liberal university here is that Michigan's lawyers join Scalia in accepting "best," "elite," and "super-duper" (as well as "academic excellence") as neutral and transparent terms when applied to a law school, terms whose meanings they do not think of questioning. *Barbara Grutter v. Lee Bollinger, et al.,* U.S. Supreme Court, no. 02–241, Oral Arguments, April 1, 2003, p. 31, http://www.supremecourtus.gov/oral_arguments/argument_transcripts.html.

32. Richard C. Atkinson, "Standarized Tests and Access to American Universities," Robert H. Atwell Distinguished Lecture, delivered at the 83rd Annual Meeting of the American Council on Education, Washington, D.C., February 18, 2001, http://www.ucop.edu/ucophome/commserv/sat/speech.html.

33. Diana Jean Schemo, "Head of U. of California Seeks to End SAT Use in Admissions," *New York Times,* February 17, 2001, A1.

Chapter 2

1. If one were to make a point of always substituting "the n-word," as Burton suggests and as one of my white colleagues does even when he reads direct quotations to a class, the sudden break into artificially formal or "stilted" (Burton's term) speech would, as sudden emphasis on verbal form always tends to do, itself call attention to the word as material object. The pointed elision would "conjure up" the technically unspoken term as listeners were forced to pause, if just for an instant, to speak the translation of "n-word" in their heads.

2. See Butler, *Excitable Speech,* 7.

3. Williams, "Sensation"; David D. Kirkpatrick, "A Black Author Hurls That Word as a Challenge," *New York Times,* December 1, 2001, A16.

4. Wharton, 'Beatrice Palmato," Appendix C in Lewis, *Edith Wharton,* 547–48.

5. Copjec, *Read My Desire,* 122–23.

6. Ibid., 123, my italics.

7. Foster, *Sublime Enjoyment,* 161.

8. Claudia Grisales, "Hoelting Words Offend Some Staff," *Daily Texan,* February 5, 1999, 1A.

9. Foster, *Sublime Enjoyment,* 12.

10. Hortense Spillers makes a powerful argument that regarding race "as an aspect of the Real brings to light its most persistent perversity." "'All the Things You Could Be by Now," 150. See also Lane, "Introduction," to *Psychoanalysis of Race,* ed. Lane.

11. Linton Weeks, "Caught in a Verbal Vortex; One Word Leaves a Lot Still To Be Said about Former D.C. Official David Howard," *Washington Post,* January 29, 1999, C1.

12. Kathleen Parker, "Look in Dictionary before You Squawk," *USA Today,* February 3, 1999, A13.

13. Colbert King, "Much Ado about an N-Word," *Washington Post,* January 30, 1999, A19.

14. "The Last Word," Unsigned Editorial, *Boston Globe,* January 30, 1999, A18.

15. Jeff Jacoby, "It Wasn't the N-Word," *Boston Globe,* February 1, 1999, A15.

16. "Another N-Word Controversy," *Atlanta Constitution,* February 2, 1999.

17. "The Last Word," Unsigned Editorial, *Boston Globe,* January 30, 1999. The colonialist fantasy at work in this particular *Boston Globe* editorial is made still clearer when the author insists the mayor should have "stood up for . . . the English language, which is the envy of the world for its richness and nuance."

18. For example, see Al Neuharth, "Niggardly Not Racist but Thin-Skinned Are," *USA Today,* February 12, 1999, 15A; "Obsessing over the 'N Word,'" Unsigned Editorial, *Hartford Courant,* February 3, 1999, A14; Carl T. Rowan, "Country Getting Crazier over Racial Issues," *Houston Chronicle,* January 30, 1999, A36; and Dick Feagler, "Ignorance Was Trigger of 3-Syllable Time Bomb," *Cleveland Dealer,* February 1, 1999, 2A.

19. Savran, *Taking It like a Man,* 5. Curiously, Savran's history jumps from the English Renaissance and Restoration to post–World War II America, ignoring trajectories of male masochism in seventeenth-, eighteenth-, nineteenth-, and early-twentieth-century America. Yet the historical relationship between masochism and white American masculinity has been receiving significant critical attention over the past decade. For example, see Burgett, "Masochism and Male Sentimentalism"; Leverenz, *Manhood and the American Renaissance;* Newfield, *Emerson Effect;* Person, *Henry James and the Suspense of Masculinity;* and Silverman, *Male Subjectivity at the Margins.* For a comparative perspective that focuses on the German-speaking world at roughly the period of American literary realism, see Stewart, *Sublime Surrender.* Like Savran, Stewart argues that masochism "became the site by and through which masculinity was not only redefined but again made hegemonic" (9).

20. Savran, *Taking It like a Man,* 5, 37.

21. Sally Robinson develops an argument closely related to Savran's but, among other differences, she emphasizes "a pleasure in explorations of pain" on the part of "white men displaying their wounds as evidence of disempowerment." Such pleasure constitutes a facet of what she calls white masculinity's "identity politics of the dominant." Robinson, *Marked Men,* 11, 3.

22. Foster, *Sublime Enjoyment,* 161.

23. Leonard, *Making Mark Twain Work in the Classroom.* For teaching Twain's novel, in addition to Leonard's book I have found particularly helpful Richard C. Moreland's suggestions for juxtaposing Twain's novel with Toni Morrison's *Beloved* (Moreland, *Learning from Difference*), as well as the essays collected in Leonard, Tenney, and Davis, eds., *Satire or Evasion?*

24. See Smiley, "Say It Ain't So, Huck," and Wallace, "The Case against *Huck Finn.*" But Julius Lester, who has also written strongly against the book, is an academic. See his "Morality and *Adventures of Huckleberry Finn.*"

25. Kaplan, "Born to Trouble"; Smith, "Huck, Jim, and American Racial Discourse"; and Fishkin, *Was Huck Black?*

26. Arac, *Huckleberry Finn as Idol and Target,* 33.

27. Ibid., 16, 28, 24–28.

28. *Barbara Grutter v. Lee Bollinger, et al.,* 539 U.S. Supreme Court, no. 02–241, http://www.supremecourtus.gov/opinions/02slipopinion.html.

29. "The University of Texas at Austin proposes inclusion of race as a factor in admissions process," University of Texas at Austin Press Release, November 24, 2003.

30. For a small collection of descriptions by African Americans of what it felt like for them (or for their children) to study and/or teach *Huck Finn* in primarily white classrooms, see Mensh and Mensh, *Black, White, and Huckleberry Finn,* 107–13

31. Williams, *Rooster's Egg,* 28.

32. Copjec, *Read My Desire,* 123.

33. Foster, *Sublime Enjoyment,* 12.

34. For a discussion of seemingly "dated" monuments in locales ranging from Austin to Moscow, see Levinson, *Written in Stone.*

35. Eze, *Race and the Enlightenment,* 5.

36. Goldberg, *Racist Culture,* 4–6. Helena Woodard provides an illuminating analysis of eighteenth-century African-British writers' response to, and participation in, Enlightenment discourse in *African-British Writing in the Eighteenth Century.*

37. DiPiero, *White Men Aren't,* 55.

38. On the relationship between American Jews' *sometimes* not-quite-white status vis-à-vis white Protestants, on the one hand, and, on the other hand, their reliable "experience of whiteness and belonging vis-à-vis blackness," see Brodkin, *How Jews Became White Folks,* 2 and *passim.*

39. "All, nevertheless, flutter round it. They approach me in a half-hesitant sort of way, eye me curiously or compassionately, and then, instead of saying directly, How does it feel to be a problem? they say, I know an excellent colored man in my town; or, I fought at Mechanicsville; or, Do not these Southern outrages make your blood boil?" Du Bois, *Souls of Black Folk,* 9.

Part Two, Introduction

1. Wiegman, "Whiteness Studies," 120.

2. Morrison, *Playing in the Dark,* 6.

3. Gutiérrez-Jones, *Critical Race Narratives,* 27.

4. Foley, *White Scourge,* 11, 5.

5. Sundquist, *To Wake the Nations;* Wiegman, *American Anatomies* and "Whiteness Studies and the Paradox of Particularity"; Williams, *Playing the Race Card;* and Morrison, *Playing in the Dark.*

6. Whiteness critics who focus on the American West and/or on seventeenth-, eighteenth-, and even early-nineteenth-century American literature and culture do often pay careful attention to the role that constructions of "Indianness" play in literary whiteness. Some of these critics, moreover, also consider how Indianness and Africanism might work differently, yet complementarily, in shaping the meaning of whiteness. See, for instance, Nelson, *National Manhood,* and Brooks, *American Lazarus,* as well as Richard Slotkin's trilogy: *Regeneration through Violence, Fatal Environment,* and *Gunfighter Nation.* For an unusual example of nonbinary racial analysis focused on late-nineteenth-century American literature, see Coulombe, "Mark Twain's Native Americans."

7. See Perea, "Black/White Binary Paradigm of Race," 346.

Chapter 3

1. Morrison, *Playing in the Dark,* 3, 5, 8, 16, 9.

2. Limón, *American Encounters,* 3.

3. Morrison, *Playing in the Dark,* 6, 52. The phrase "Mexicanist presence" was suggested to me by Joseph Rodríguez. Some examples of U.S. works from the same period as *The Awakening* that contain a seemingly minor, incidental, or even negligible Mexicanist presence—but where that presence in fact plays an important role in helping to construct "whiteness"—include Jack London, *Martin Eden;* Frank Norris, *The Octopus;* William Dean Howells, *Rise of Silas Lapham;* and several short stories by Stephen Crane. José Limón's *American Encounters* is a superb exploration not only of Mexican–U.S. "border culture" but also of the often surprisingly subtle roles that Mexico and the United States have played in one another's literary and cultural imaginations, sometimes in locations that seem remote from the geographical border. Scholarship on Anglo-American literature that focuses on the relationship between literary whiteness and literary Mexicanism remains in short supply, however, especially when one thinks of the large body of recent critical work that seeks to answer Morrison's question about whiteness and Africanism in such literature. Two important manuscripts in progress make significant contributions. Both are currently available as unpublished dissertations. See Juan Alonzo, "Derision and Desire: The Ambivalence of Mexican Identity in American Literature and Film" (PhD diss., University of Texas, 2003), and John-Michael Rivera, "The Rise of Mexican America in U.S. Literary and Legal Culture" (PhD diss., University of Texas, 2000).

4. Ammons, *Conflicting Stories,* 74–75.

5. Birnbaum, "'Alien Hands,'" 324–25, and Spillers, "Tragic Mulatta," 168 (quoted in Birnbaum, "Alien Hands," 325).

6. Birnbaum does devote a few sentences to Mariequita, but she essentially takes her as just one more example of the way in which "women of color" "become representative of alternative sexual experience" (Birnbaum, "'Alien Hands,'" 333). Rebecca Aanerud gives somewhat more attention both to Mariequita as a "Spanish girl" and to the role of Mexico in Edna's development. She never notes, however, that Mariequita and Mexico play roles in Edna's "awakening" different from those played by the novel's Africanist elements, and hence Aanerud never attempts to explore the significance of such differences (Aenerud, "Fictions of Whiteness," 41–42). It is quite possible that in Chopin's mind Mariequita was not of Mexican descent. Another "Spanish" girl in Chopin's fiction, Calixta of "At the 'Cadian Ball," is explicitly identified as of Cuban descent. Longtime Spanish-speaking communities existed relatively close to Grand Isle, in and around St. Bernard and Iberville parishes, but the Hispanic settlers of these communities came either from the Canary Islands or straight from Spain. Louisiana's only long-standing communities of Mexican descent are located in the state's northwestern area, closer to the border with Texas. Chopin did live from 1879–1884 in this area, in fact in Natchitoches Parish, whose Hispanic *Adaeseños* community is mestizo and originated in Mexico. For an overview of Louisiana's Hispanic communities, see Armistead and Katz, *The Spanish Tradition in Louisiana,* 2–7. I am nonetheless considering Mariequita as part of the novel's shaping "Mexicanist" presence, how-

ever, for two reasons. First, we are explicitly told that she has "brown" skin. Second, during the section of Chopin's novel set in Grand Isle, which is where Mariequita appears, the many allusions to Mexico and Mexicans establish a textual context in which a brown-skinned, subaltern "Spanish girl" will function textually, at least for many readers, as "Mexicanist." In a broader cultural context, Mariequita clearly alludes to the stereotype so prevalent in nineteenth-century dime novels and in early American film of the Mexican "harlot, with her low-cut blouse, rose behind her ear, her hot temper, and her sexual promiscuity" (Kanellos, *Thirty Million Strong*). See also Pettit and Showalter, *Images of the Mexican American in Fiction and Film*.

7. Culley, ed., *The Awakening,* 33 and 107; subsequent page references appear parenthetically within the text.

8. Birnbaum, "Alien Hands," 326.

9. In the collections of Cornell University's Olin Library; cited by Shirley Samuels in personal conversation, November 11, 2002.

10. Larry McMurty's *The Last Picture Show* takes an at least partly parodic view of this idea of the Mexican sojourn as a passage into manhood for U.S. boys (two Texas high school boys cross the border, watch some grainy pornography and get drugged and robbed, then stagger back home), and Cormac McCarthy's *All the Pretty Horses* develops a richly layered, complexly ambivalent version of it.

11. William Dean Howells, "The Editor's Study," *Harper's Monthly,* December 1897, 155.

Chapter 4

1. Lakoff, *Moral Politics,* 108. Other than the one casual sentence quoted above, Lakoff says nothing about the asymmetrical gendering and non-gendering of the two models that he invokes: the strict *father* vs. the nurturant *parent.* The putative androgyny of the latter figure, however, belies the fact that the nurturant parent can only become available for Lakoff's argument—indeed the figure can only politically *matter* in the terms that Lakoff sets up—once it is construable as male. It is fair to say that Lakoff's argument already presumes the trajectory depicted by *Traffic,* in which a male adopts the role of nurturing parent and thereby moves to the center of a new national vision for a more liberal polity.

2. Lakoff, *Moral Politics,* 153, 12.

3. For the one location where he does not appear, the San Diego–La Jolla area inhabited by the Ayalas, Wakefield is represented by his handpicked surrogate, prosecutor Ben Williams.

4. Reviewers complained that Helena's overnight transition from naïve, pampered wife (with no idea of her husband's business) to ruthless drug operative is not believable. See James S. Torrens, "A Harsh Light," review of *Traffic, America,* April 2, 2001, 21–23; and Scott Heller, "Up in the Air," review of *Traffic* and *Cast Away, American Prospect,* January 29, 2001, 30–31. Writing in *The Nation,* Michael Massing agrees that "the movie strongly implies that it is suburban whites like Wakefield's daughter who make up the heart of the nation's drug problem" and he further points out that "every drug user depicted in *Traffic* is white and well-off. . . . It's as if Soderbergh can't trust us to sympathize with drug-using minorities." Michael Massing, "The Reel Drug War," *The Nation,* February 5, 2001, 5–9.

5. Lakoff, *Moral Politics,* 4.

6. Dyer, "Colour of Virtue," 2.

7. Williams, *Playing the Race Card,* 42.

8. Williams traces this scene from Stowe's *Uncle Tom's Cabin* and its ubiquitous late-nineteenth-century theatrical performances, through televised scenes of non-violent black protesters being attacked by white police in the 1950s and 60s, up to and beyond the nation-riveting videotape of Rodney King's beating by white LAPD officers in 1992.

9. Gwendolyn Brooks, "A Bronzeville Mother Loiters in Mississippi. Meanwhile, A Mississippi Mother Burns Bacon," lines 2, 6–9.

10. Gaghan, *Traffic,* 31.

11. Chandler, *Trouble Is My Business,* vii–viii.

12. I owe this connection with *The Searchers* to Sabrina Barton.

13. Seth is an interesting character. Reviewers almost uniformly dislike him, but despite (or maybe in conjunction with) his portrayal as a selfish shallow smart-ass, he articulates the only critique of Robert Wakefield's and the movie's own "other-ing" of the black ghetto. "What do you mean 'this place'?" he demands of Wakefield in the car as Wakefield looks out with disgust at ghetto street corners clustered with young men offering drugs. In a speech peppered with transgressive but also show-offy "fucks" and "shits," Seth urges Wakefield to "*Think* about the effect that [whites' offering easy drug money] has on the psyche of a black person, on their possibilities." As Seth becomes more and more animated and ready to argue the topic, however, Wakefield fixes him with an expressionless stare. Seth slowly stops talking and his own face loses its excited debate-team look. Nervously, he hastens to resume an expression of seriousness and concern. Staring Seth down, Wakefield's look says something like, "you are mouthing progressive pieties while my daughter, goddammit my daughter, is lost in this place." *Traffic* thus renders Seth's desire to discuss the socioeconomics of racial geography beside the point, irrelevant, a sophomoric luxury. Writing in the *Chicago Sun-Times,* Roger Ebert tellingly misremembers Seth's words as spoken by "a black man" in "one of the most heartfelt" speeches in the film. Roger Ebert, "Heavy Dose of Reality. *Traffic* Wages Screen War on Flawed, Futile Drug Laws," *Chicago Sun-Tribune,* January 5, 2001, 25.

14. Fregoso, "Recycling Colonialist Fantasy," 83. José Limón cogently critiques several aspects of Fregoso's indictment of *Lone Star* (*American Encounters,* 156–59, 236 n. 43). While Limón may be correct that, in *Lone Star,* a subtle portrayal of Sheriff Sam Deeds (Chris Cooper) as "less white than 'off-white'" works against Fregoso's presumption of a unitary and still hegemonic whiteness in that film, my reading of *Traffic* suggests that, in the context of representing a multicultural social order, "off-white" can also serve as a means for realigning whiteness with universality. Among the crucial differences between Sayles' and Soderbergh's films, however, is that *Lone Star* culminates in a historically aware, self-consciously cho-sen relationship between an Anglo man, Deeds, and a Mexican-American woman, Pilar Cruz (Elizabeth Peña), who also discover that they are related by blood. Moreover, *Lone Star* depicts a context in which Mexican Americans are about to take real political power.

15. In their study of the rhetorical structures popularized by Alcoholics Anonymous, Helena Michie and Robyn Warhol suggest that reiterated "recovery nar-

ratives"—narratives that portray recovery from addiction as an unending process dependent on regular attendance at twelve-step meetings—are designed to give the impression of "cutting across lines of gender, sexual preference, ethnicity, race, social class, religion, and nationality." The repetition of similar recovery narratives provides group members with an "autobiography-in-common." The recovery group assumes a "collective identity." (Michie and Warhol, "Twelve-Step Teleology," 328). In *Traffic,* that autobiography-in-common and collective identity are both implicitly white.

Chapter 5

1. Within Americanist literary and cultural studies it is difficult to cite sources pertinent to American exceptionalism because it has been such a ubiquitous framework. In a sense, American Studies as a discipline is founded on exceptionalist thinking, which is only most obviously evident in scholarship from the 1950s and 1960s. Perry Miller is probably most responsible for elucidating the Puritans' sense of their exceptional mission and status. See Miller, *Errand into the Wilderness* and *Nature's Nation.* See also Bercovitch, *Puritan Origins of the American Self* and *American Jeremiad.* For treatment focused on the *feelings* surrounding (and constituting) the Puritans' exceptionalist beliefs, see Leverenz, *Language of Puritan Feeling;* and Delbanco, *Puritan Ordeal,* 81–117. For differing overviews on American exceptionalism, see Madsen, *American Exceptionalism;* and Kammen, "Problem of American Exceptionalism."

2. Catherine Beecher, *A Plea for the West* (Cincinnati, 1835), 10. Quoted in Bercovitch, *Rites of Assent,* 189.

3. To sample recent treatments of American exceptionalism from outside the field of literary history, see Schafer, ed., *Is America Different?;* Adams and Van Minnen, eds., *Reflections on American Exceptionalism;* and Lipset, *American Exceptionalism.*

4. Jesse Helms, "Address by Senator Jesse Helms, Chairman, U.S. Senate Committee on Foreign Relations, before the United Nations Security Council," delivered in New York City, July 20, 2000. I downloaded Helms's address on March 12, 2002 from http://www.senate.gov/~helms/UN_Speech/un_ speech.html. This URL has been unavailable since Helms's retirement from the Senate. The speech remains posted on a number of other websites, however.

5. James, *The American,* 281. Subsequent page references appear within the text.

6. On Newman's masculinity, homophobia, and homoeroticism, see Derrick, *Monumental Anxieties,* 83–155.

7. Compare the anxiety that is inseparable from John Winthrop's classic image of the "city upon a hill," with "the eyes of all people" focused on it: "If we shall deal falsely with our God in this work we have undertaken, and so cause Him to withdraw His present help from us, we shall be made a story and a by-word through the world." Winthrop, "A Model Christian Charity," in Nina Baym, ed., *Norton Anthology of American Literature,* 105.

8. Haralson, "James's *The American,*" 484–85.

9. Henry James to William Dean Howells, October 24, 1876, in James, *The American,* 343.

10. See, for example, Delbanco, *Puritan Ordeal*, 59–80, 97–118.

11. John Carlos Rowe makes the intriguingly converse argument that Newman's intense desire to differentiate himself from Europe derives from the ways in which his "Europe" is constituted through an unconscious projection of his own characteristics and history onto it, so that "Europe" becomes an uncanny double of "America." Rowe, "Politics of the Uncanny," 79–90. See also Rowe, "Politics of Innocence in Henry James's *The American*."

12. See Jeffords, *Hard Bodies*.

13. See, for example, Prince Hall, "Petition to the Honorable Counsel & House of Representatives for the State of Massachusetts Bay," presented January 13, 1777. This document is accessible online at http://www.pbs.org/wgbh/aia/part2/2h32t.html

14. I owe the connection with Scorsese's film to the insight of my colleague Brian Bremen.

15. Christopher Marquis, "Satisfied with U.N. Reforms, Helms Relents on Dues," *New York Times,* January 10 2001, A1.

16. For a rich exploration of this notion of romance in the context of eighteenth- and nineteenth-century American literature, see Bell, *Development of American Romance.*

17. Consider the immense importance of preserving the term "innocence" for the United States and its citizens in relation to the "war on terror." Recognizing the term's powerful resonance in the wake of 9/11, even high-ranking U.S. officials sought discursive control over "innocence." As just one example, Secretary of Defense Donald Rumsfeld called it "unfortunate" that United States soldiers mistakenly killed sixteen U.S.–friendly Afghans because the soldiers mistook them for Al Qaeda or Taliban fighters. Regarding the dead Afghans, however, Rumsfeld nonetheless insisted to reporters, "Let's not call them 'innocents.' We don't know quite what they were." Thom Shanker, "U.S. Says 16 Killed in Raids Weren't Taliban or Al Qaeda," *New York Times,* February 22, 2002, A1.

18. Ellison, *Cato's Tears*, 7.

Chapter 6

1. Berlant, "'68, or Something," 125–26.

2. Rorty, *Achieving Our Country,* 7.

3. Ibid., 33.

4. Rorty's and Berlant's political visions are, it should be stressed, incompatible in several important respects. In *Achieving Our Country,* Rorty argues that "the Left should get back into the business of piecemeal reform within the framework of a market economy" (105). He has no use for (and misunderstands) "identity politics" as it has developed since the 1960s. Berlant, by contrast, vigorously pursues "the new cultural politics of difference" ("'68, or Something," 127). Rorty complains that academic leftists today seem uninterested in such political activities as formulating legislative programs and constructing electoral majorities. Berlant believes it is important not to succumb to "pressures to remain intelligible to the norms that designate what a legitimate public interest is" (127). Rorty contends that "we should abandon the leftist-liberal distinction," which he sees as

a residue of discarded Marxism. By contrast, the distinction between liberalism and radicalism is a key underpinning of Berlant's essay; she worries, for instance, that liberal feminism has lost its access to "horizons of radical possibility" (129).

5. Brown, "Resisting Left Melancholy," 26.

6. Ellison, "Short History of Liberal Guilt," 349.

7. Berlant, "'68, or Something," 128.

8. Ellison, "Short History of Liberal Guilt," 370.

9. Ibid., 358.

10. The first and last chapters of Ellison's book-length study, *Cato's Tears and the Making of Anglo-American Emotion,* draw heavily from her earlier article on liberal guilt, cited above. Quotation from *Cato's Tears,* 7.

11. Packer, *Blood of the Liberals,* 399, 402.

12. By contrast, Daniel Born insists that "persistent interrogation of oneself, often berated by critics on left and right as a sign of bad faith, is in fact the primary trait which makes the liberal sensitivity worth saving" (*Birth of Liberal Guilt,* 171).

13 Ellison, *Cato's Tears,* 173.

14. Robbins, "Sweatshop Sublime," 96.

15. Berlant, "'68, or Something," 130.

16. Born, *Birth of Liberal Guilt,* 28, 34.

17. Robbins, "Sweatshop Sublime," 87.

18 Rorty, *Achieving Our Country,* 18.

19. Rorty, *Hope in Place of Knowledge,* 20.

20. Rorty develops his model for private irony and civic faith most systematically in *Contingency, Irony, and Solidarity.*

21. Jampolsky, *Good-Bye to Guilt.*

22. Shulman, "Hope and American Politics," 15.

23. Rorty, "Achieving Our Country," 23.

24. See Bentley, *Ethnography of Manners;* Gibson, "Edith Wharton and the Ethnography of Old New York"; Trumpener and Nyce, "Recovered Fragments."

25. The artificiality of "innocence" is well illustrated for Newland by his unmarried or "old maid" sister, Janey. She is described as possessing "a kind of drooping distinction like that in certain faded Reynolds portraits" (82). Given that here appears the book's only mention of Reynolds, painter of the 1788 portrait ("The Age of Innocence") from which Wharton borrows her novel's title, one perhaps might take the description of Janey as a signal that *she* should be seen as the character who most personifies "the age of innocence." Yet her innocence is an open pretense. Although "Janey knew every fold of the Beaufort mystery," including the "other establishment" maintained by the corrupt banker for his mistress, "in public Mrs. Archer continued to assume that the subject was not one for the unmarried" (83).

26. Rorty, *Achieving Our Country,* 37.

27. Berlant, "'68 or Something," 128.

28. The presidential portrait is probably of Ulysses S. Grant, who served as United States president from 1869–1877, the time during which Wharton's novel is set. His administration is still regarded as among the most corrupt in U.S. history, although apparently Grant himself did not profit from the widespread bribery, fraud, and looting perpetuated under his "rule." Writing forty-five years

later, Wharton presumes that her readers will recognize the irony in Newland's pointing towards President Grant as a signifier of American innocence. His doing so serves to underline the artificial lacunae of knowledge necessary to maintain the category itself (here, the artificial innocence is both Grant's and Newland's own).

29. Rorty, *Achieving Our Country,* 18.

30. Poirier, *A World Elsewhere.* Gerald Graff points out how pervasive the theme of escape from the social has been across a wide range of Americanist literary scholarship: "In one way or another, all these theories tend to see American literature in terms of some form of escape from social categories" (Graff, "American Criticism Left and Right," 106).

31. Berlant, "'68, or Something," 127.

32. Walzer, "Political Action," 63.

33. James, *Art of the Novel,* 143.

34. Berlant, "'68, or Something," 127.

35. Rorty, *Achieving Our Country,* 117.

36. Salecl, *(Per)Versions of Love and Hate,* 15.

37. Bracher, *Lacan, Discourse, and Social Change,* 72

38. Born, *Birth of Liberal Guilt,* 6.

39. Limerick, *Legacy of Conquest,* 3.

40. Lewis, *American Adam.*

41. Berlant, "'68, or Something," 125.

42. Wharton, *Backward Glance,* 369–70.

43. De Man, *Blindness and Insight,* 142. The quoted passage continues, "It is not at all certain that literature and modernity are in any way compatible concepts. Yet we all speak readily about modern literature and even use this term as a device for historical periodization, with the same apparent unawareness that history and modernity may well be even more incompatible than literature and modernity." With Wharton's novel and the very notion of an "age of innocence" in mind, we can again substitute "innocence" for "modernity": "It is not at all certain that literature and innocence are in any way compatible concepts. Yet we all speak readily about innocence and even use this term as a device for historical periodization, with the same apparent unawareness that history and innocence may well be even more incompatible than literature and innocence."

44. Wharton, *Backward Glance,* 6.

45. In reviewing a book on contemporary utopian thought, Terry Eagleton writes, "It is the hard-nosed pragmatists who behave as though the World Bank and caffe latte will be with us for the next two millennia who are the real dreamers, and those who are open to the as yet unfigurable future who are the true realists." Eagleton, "Just My Imagination."

Coda

1. Trilling, *Liberal Imagination,* 5–6.

2. Ibid., 10.

3. This is not to say that conservative political beliefs, and the versions of political subjectivity associated with those beliefs, are not also self-contradictory in numerous respects. They are.

BIBLIOGRAPHY

Adams, David Keith, and Cornelis A. van Minnen, eds. *Reflections on American Exceptionalism.* Staffordshire, England: Keene University Press, 1994.

Aenerud, Rebecca. "Fictions of Whiteness: Speaking the Names of Whiteness in U.S. Literature." In Frankenberg, *Displacing Whiteness: Essays in Social and Cultural Criticism,* 35–39.

Alonzo, Juan. "Derision and Desire: The Ambivalence of Mexican Identity in American Literature and Film." PhD diss., University of Texas at Austin, 2003.

Ammons, Elizabeth. *Conflicting Stories: American Women Writers at the Turn into the Twentieth Century.* New York: Oxford University Press, 1991.

———. "Edith Wharton and Race." In *The Cambridge Companion to Edith Wharton,* edited by Millicent Bell, 68–86. New York: Cambridge University Press, 1995.

Arac, Jonathan. *Huckleberry Finn as Idol and Target: The Functions of Criticism in Our Time.* Madison: University of Wisconsin Press, 1997.

Aranda, Jose F., Jr. "Contradictory Impulses: Maria Ampara Ruiz De Burton, Resistance Theory, and the Politics of Chicano/a Studies." *American Literature* 70, no. 3 (1998): 551–79.

Aravamudan, Srinivas. "The Return of Anachronism." *Modern Language Quarterly* 62, no. 4 (2001): 331–54.

Armistead, Samuel G., and Israel J. Katz. *The Spanish Tradition in Louisiana: Isleño Folkliterature, Juan De La Cuesta Hispanic Monographs.* Newark, Del.: Juan de la Cuesta, 1992.

Babb, Valerie Melissa. *Whiteness Visible: The Meaning of Whiteness in American Literature and Culture.* New York: New York University Press, 1998.

Banta, Martha, ed. *New Essays on the American.* Cambridge: Cambridge University Press, 1987.

———. *Taylored Lives: Narrative Productions in the Age of Taylor, Veblen, and Ford.* Chicago: University of Chicago Press, 1993.

Barrish, Phillip. *American Literary Realism, Critical Theory, and Intellectual Prestige, 1880–1995.* Cambridge: Cambridge University Press, 2001.

Bauer, Dale M. *Edith Wharton's Brave New Politics.* Madison: University of Wisconsin Press, 1994.

Benjamin, Walter. "Theses on the Philosophy of History." In *Illuminations,* edited by Hannah Arendt, 257–58. New York: Schocken, 1969.

Bell, Michael Davitt. *The Development of American Romance: The Sacrifice of Relation.* Chicago: The University of Chicago Press, 1980.

Bentley, Nancy. *The Ethnography of Manners: Hawthorne, James, Wharton.* Cambridge: Cambridge University Press, 1995.

Bercovitch, Sacvan. *The American Jeremiad.* Madison: University of Wisconsin Press, 1978.

———. *The Puritan Origins of the American Self.* New Haven: Yale University Press, 1975.

———. *The Rites of Assent: Transformations in the Symbolic Construction of America.* New York: Routledge, 1993.

Berlant, Lauren. "'68, or Something." *Critical Inquiry* 21, no. 1 (1994): 124–55.

Berman, Russell. "Politics: Divide and Rule." *Modern Language Quarterly (Special Issue on Periodization: Cutting Up the Past)* 62, no. 4 (2001): 317–30.

Birnbaum, Michele. "'Alien Hands': Kate Chopin and the Colonization of Race." In *Subjects and Citizens: Nation, Race and Gender from Oroonoko to Anita Hill,* edited by Michael Moon and Cathy Davidson, 319–41. Durham. N.C.: Duke University Press, 1995.

Bloch, Ruth H. "Utopianism, Sentimentalism, and Liberal Culture in America." *Intellectual History Newsletter* 24 (2002): 47–59.

Boothby, Richard. *Freud as Philosopher: Metapsychology after Lacan.* New York: Routledge, 2001.

Born, Daniel. *The Birth of Liberal Guilt in the English Novel: Charles Dickens to H. G. Wells.* Chapel Hill: University of North Carolina Press, 1995.

Bracher, Mark. *Lacan, Discourse, and Social Change: A Psychoanalytic Cultural Criticism.* Ithaca. N.Y.: Cornell University Press, 1993.

Brodkin, Karen. *How Jews Became White Folks and What That Says about Race in America.* New Brunswick: Rutgers University Press, 1998.

Brooks, Gwendolyn. "A Bronzeville Mother loiters in Mississippi. Meanwhile in Mississippi a Mother Burns Bacon." In *The Lynching of Emmett Till. A Documentary History,* edited by Paul Mettress, 313–17. Charlottesville: University of Virginia Press, 2002. The poem was originally published in 1960.

Brooks, Joanna. *American Lazarus: Religion and the Rise of African American and American Literature.* New York: Oxford University Press, 2003.

Brooks, Peter. "The Turn of *the American.*" In *New Essays on the American,* edited by Martha Banta, 43–68. Cambridge: Cambridge University Press, 1987.

Brown, Wendy. "Resisting Left Melancholy." *Boundary 2: An International Journal of Literature and Culture* 26, no. 3 (1999): 19–27.

Bryan, Violet Harrington. *The Myth of New Orleans in Literature: Dialogues of Race and Gender.* Knoxville: University of Tennessee Press, 1993.

Burgett, Bruce. "Masochism and Male Sentimentalism: Charles Brockden Brown's *Clara Howard.*" In *Sentimental Men: Masculinity and the Politics of Affect in American Culture,* edited by Mary Chapman and Glenn Hendler, 205–25. Berkeley: University of California Press, 1999.

Burke, Kenneth. *Permanence and Change: An Anatomy of Purpose.* 3rd ed. Berkeley and Los Angeles: University of California Press, 1984.

Burton, M. Garlinda. *Never Say Nigger Again!: An Antiracism Guide for White Liberals.* [Nashville, TN]: Winston-Derek Publishers, 1994.

Butler, Judith. *Bodies That Matter: On the Discursive Limits of "Sex."* New York: Routledge, 1993.

———. *Excitable Speech: A Politics of the Performative.* New York: Routledge, 1997.

Chadwick-Joshua, Jocelyn. *The Jim Dilemma: Reading Race in Huckleberry Finn.* Jackson: University Press of Mississippi, 1998.

Chambers, Ross. "The Unexamined." In Hill, *Whiteness: A Critical Reader,* 187–203.

Chandler, James K. *England in 1819: The Politics of Literary Culture and the Case of Romantic Historicism.* Chicago: University of Chicago Press, 1998.

Chandler, Raymond. *Trouble Is My Business.* New York: Vintage Books Edition, 1988.

Chopin, Kate. *The Awakening: An Authoritative Text, Biographical and Historical Contexts, Criticism.* Edited by Margo Culley. 2nd ed. New York: W.W. Norton, 1994.

Cochran, David Carroll. *The Color of Freedom: Race and Contemporary American Liberalism.* Albany: State University of New York Press, 1999.

Copjec, Joan. *Read My Desire: Lacan against the Historicists.* Cambridge: MIT Press, 1994.

Corkin, Stanley. *Realism and the Birth of the Modern United States: Cinema, Literature, and Culture.* Athens: University of Georgia Press, 1996.

Coulombe, Joseph. "Mark Twain's Native Americans and the Repeated Racial Pattern in Adventures of Huckleberry Finn." *American Literary Realism* 33, no. 3 (2001): 261–79.

Crenshaw, Kimberlé. *Critical Race Theory: The Key Writings That Formed the Movement.* New York: New Press, dist. by W.W. Norton, 1995.

Curry, Renée R. *White Women Writing White: H. D., Elizabeth Bishop, Sylvia Plath, and Whiteness.* Westport, Conn.: Greenwood Press, 2000.

De Man, Paul. *Blindness and Insight: Essays in the Rhetoric of Contemporary Criticism.* 2nd ed. Minneapolis: University of Minnesota Press, 1983.

———. *The Rhetoric of Romanticism.* New York: Columbia University Press, 1984.

Delbanco, Andrew. *The Puritan Ordeal.* Cambridge, Mass.: Harvard University Press, 1989.

Derrick, Scott S. *Monumental Anxieties: Homoerotic Desire and Feminine Influence in 19th Century U.S. Literature.* New Brunswick, N.J.: Rutgers University Press, 1997.

Desmet, Christy, and Robert Sawyer. *Shakespeare and Appropriation.* New York: Routledge, 1999.

Dimock, Wai Chee. "Non-Newtonian Time: Robert Lowell, Roman History, Vietnam War." *American Literature* 74, no. 4 (2002): 911–31.

Dinshaw, Carolyn. *Getting Medieval: Sexualities and Communities, Pre- and Postmodern.* Durham, N.C.: Duke University Press, 1999.

DiPiero, Thomas. *White Men Aren't.* Durham, N.C.: Duke University Press, 2002.

Du Bois, W. E. B. *The Souls of Black Folk: Authoritative Text, Contexts, Criticism.* edited by Henry Louis Gates Jr. and Terri Hume Oliver. New York: W. W. Norton, 1999.

Dyer, Richard. "The Colour of Virtue: Lillian Gish, Whiteness, and Femininity." In *Women and Film: A Sight and Sound Reader,* edited by Pam Cook and Philip Dodd, 1–9. Philadelphia: Temple University Press, 1993.

———. *White.* London and New York: Routledge, 1997.

Eagleton, Terry. "Just My Imagination." Review of *Picture Imperfect: Utopian Thought for a Non-Violent Age,* by Russel Jacoby. *The Nation* (online edition), posted May 26, 2005 (June 13, 2005 issue). http://www.thenation.com/doc.mhtml?i=20050613&s=eagleton.

Ellison, Julie. *Cato's Tears and the Making of Anglo-American Emotion.* Chicago: University of Chicago Press, 1999.

———. "A Short History of Liberal Guilt." *Critical Inquiry* 22, no. 2 (1996): 344–71.

Elsom, John, ed. *Is Shakespeare Still Our Contemporary?* Proceedings of a Public Seminar staged at the Young Vic Theater, London, by the International Association of Theater Critics (date not given). London: Routledge, in association with the International Association of Theatre Critics, 1989.

Entman, Robert M., and Andrew Rojecki. *The Black Image in the White Mind: Media and Race in America.* Chicago: University of Chicago Press, 2000.

Eze, Emmanuel Chukwudi. *Race and the Enlightenment: A Reader.* Cambridge, Mass.: Blackwell Publishers, 1997.

Fisher, Philip. *Still the New World: American Literature in a Culture of Creative Destruction.* Cambridge, Mass: Harvard University Press, 1999.

Fishkin, Shelley Fisher. "Interrogating 'Whiteness,' Complicating 'Blackness': Remapping American Culture." *American Quarterly* 47, no. 3 (1995): 428–66.

———. *Lighting Out for the Territory: Reflections on Mark Twain and American Culture.* New York: Oxford University Press, 1996.

———. *Was Huck Black?: Mark Twain and African-American Voices.* New York: Oxford University Press, 1993.

Flagg, Barbara. *Was Blind but Now I See: White Race Consciousness and the Law.* New York: New York University Press, 1998.

Foley, Neil. *The White Scourge: Mexicans, Blacks, and Poor Whites in Texas Cotton Culture.* Berkeley and Los Angeles: University of California Press, 1997.

Foster, Dennis. *Sublime Enjoyment: On the Perverse Motive in American Literature.* Cambridge: Cambridge University Press, 1997.

Frankenberg, Ruth. *Displacing Whiteness: Essays in Social and Cultural Criticism.* Durham, N.C.: Duke University Press, 1997.

Fredrickson, George M. *The Black Image in the White Mind: The Debate on Afro-American Character and Destiny, 1817–1914.* New York: Harper & Row, 1972.

Fregoso, Rosa Linda. "Recycling Colonialist Fantasy on the Texas Borderlands." In *Home, Exile, Homeland: Film, Media, and the Politics of Place,* edited by Hamid Naficy, 169–92. New York and London: Routledge, 1999.

Freud, Sigmund. "The Economic Problem in Masochism." Orig. pub. in 1924. *General Psychological Theory* (1963).

Gaghan, Stephen. *Traffic: The Shooting Script.* New York: Newmarket Press, 2000.

Gallagher, Catherine. "Undoing." In Newman, Clayton, and Hirsch, eds., *Time and the Literary,* 11–29.

Garland, Hamlin. *Main-Travelled Roads.* Originally published 1891. Lincoln: University of Nebraska Press, 1995.

Gibson, Mary Ellis. "Edith Wharton and the Ethnography of Old New York." *Studies in American Fiction* 13, no. 1 (1985): 57–69.

Giroux, Henry A. "Pedagogy of the Depressed: Beyond the New Politics of Cynicism." *College Literature* 28, no. 3 (2001): 1–32.

Glavin, John. *After Dickens: Reading, Adaptation, and Performance.* Cambridge: Cambridge University Press, 1999.

Glazer, Nathan. *We Are All Multiculturalists Now.* Cambridge, Mass.: Harvard University Press, 1997.

Goldberg, David Theo. *Racist Culture: Philosophy and the Politics of Meaning.* Cambridge, Mass.: Blackwell Publishers, 1993.

Gould, Stephen Jay. *The Mismeasure of Man.* Rev. and expand ed. New York: W. W. Norton, 1996.

Graff, Gerald. "American Criticism Left and Right." In *Ideology and Classic American Literature,* edited by Sacvan Bercovitch and Myra Jehlen, 91–121. Cambridge: Cambridge University Press, 1986.

Grillo, Trina, and Stephanie Wildman. "Obscuring the Importance of Race: The Implications of Making Comparisons between Racism and Sexism (or Other Isms)." In *Critical Race Feminism: A Reader,* edited by Adrienne Katherine Wing, 44–50. New York: New York University Press, 1997.

Gutiérrez-Jones, Carl Scott. *Critical Race Narratives: A Study of Race, Rhetoric, and Injury.* New York: New York University Press, 2001.

Haralson, Eric. "James's *The American:* A (New)Man Is Being Beaten." *American Literature* 64, no. 3 (1992): 475–95.

Hartz, Louis. *The Liberal Tradition in America: An Interpretation of American Political Thought since the Revolution.* New York: Harcourt, Brace, 1955.

Henry, Peaches. "The Struggle for Tolerance: Race and Censorship in *Huckleberry Finn.* In Leonard, Tenney, and Davis, *Satire or Evasion,* 25–48.

Hill, Mike. *Whiteness: A Critical Reader.* New York: New York University Press, 1997.

Hopwood v. State of Texas Reserve Collection. Tarlton Law Library. Austin, Texas.

Howard, June. *Form and History in American Literary Naturalism.* Chapel Hill: University of North Carolina Press, 1985.

Ignatiev, Noel. *How the Irish Became White.* New York: Routledge, 1995.

Jacobson, Matthew Frye. *Whiteness of a Different Color: European Immigrants and the Alchemy of Race.* Cambridge, Mass.: Harvard University Press, 1998.

James, Henry. *The American: An Authoritative Text, Backgrounds, and Sources, Criticism.* Edited by James W. Tuttleton. New York: W. W. Norton, 1978.

———. *The Art of the Novel.* New York: Charles Scribner's Sons, 1984.

Jampolsky, Gerald G. *Good-Bye to Guilt: Releasing Fear through Forgiveness.* Foreword by John Denver. New York: Bantam Books, 1985.

Jarratt, Susan C. "Feminism and Composition: The Case for Conflict." In *Contending with Words: Composition and Rhetoric in the Postmodern Age,* edited by Patricia Harkin and John Schilb, 105–23. New York: Modern Language Association, 1991.

Jeffords, Susan. *Hard Bodies: Hollywood Masculinity in the Reagan Era.* New Brunswick: Rutgers University Press, 1994.

Johnson, Peter. *Politics, Innocence, and the Limits of Goodness.* London: Routledge, 1988.

Kammen, Michael. "The Problem of American Exceptionalism: A Reconsideration." *American Quarterly* 45, no. 1 (1993): 1–43.

Kanellos, Nicolás. *Thirty Million Strong: Reclaiming the Hispanic Image in American Culture.* Golden, Colo.: Fulcrum Pub., 1998.

Kaplan, Amy. *The Social Construction of American Realism.* Chicago: University of Chicago Press, 1988.

Kaplan, Justin. "Born to Trouble: One Hundred Years of Huckleberry Finn." In *Adventures of Huckleberry Finn: A Case Study in Critical Controversy,* edited by Gerald Graff and James Phelan, 348–59. Boston: Bedford St. Martins, 1995.

Kassanoff, Jennie. "Extinction, Taxidermy, Tableaux Vivants: Staging Race and Class in *the House of Mirth*." *PMLA* 115, no. 1 (2000): 60–74.

Kelley, Theresa. *Reinventing Allegory*. Cambridge: Cambridge University Press, 1997.

Kennedy, Randall. *Nigger: The Strange Career of a Troublesome Word*. New York: Pantheon Books, 2002.

Knapp, Steven. *Literary Interest: The Limits of Anti-Formalism*. Cambridge, Mass.: Harvard University Press, 1993.

Kott, Jan. *Shakespeare, Our Contemporary*. Garden City, N. Y.: Doubleday, 1964.

Kucich, John, and Dianne F. Sadoff. *Victorian Afterlife: Postmodern Culture Rewrites the Nineteenth Century*. Minneapolis: University of Minnesota Press, 2000.

LaCapra, Dominick. *Soundings in Critical Theory*. Ithaca: Cornell University Press, 1989.

Lakoff, George. *Moral Politics: What Conservatives Know That Liberals Don't*. Chicago: University of Chicago Press, 1996.

Lane, Christopher. "The Poverty of Context: Historicism and Nonmimetic Fiction." *PMLA* 118, no. 3 (2003): 450–69.

———, ed. *The Psychoanalysis of Race*. New York: Columbia University Press, 1998.

Lemann, Nicholas. *The Big Test: The Secret History of the American Meritocracy*. New York: Farrar Straus and Giroux, 1999.

Leonard, J. S. *Making Mark Twain Work in the Classroom*. Durham, N.C.: Duke University Press, 1999.

Leonard, J. S., Thomas Asa Tenney, and Thadious M. Davis, eds. *Satire or Evasion?: Black Perspectives on Huckleberry Finn*. Durham, N.C.: Duke University Press, 1992.

Lester, Julius. "Morality and *Huckleberry Finn*." In Leonard, Tenney, and Davis, *Satire or Evasion*, 199–207.

Leverenz, David. *The Language of Puritan Feeling: An Exploration in Literature, Psychology, and Social History*. New Brunswick, N.J.: Rutgers University Press, 1980.

———. *Manhood and the American Renaissance*. Ithaca, N.Y.: Cornell University Press, 1989.

Levinson, Sanford. *Written in Stone: Public Monuments in Changing Societies*. Durham, N.C.: Duke University Press, 1998.

Lewis, R. W. B. *The American Adam: Innocence, Tragedy, and Tradition in the Nineteenth Century*. Chicago: University of Chicago Press, 1966.

———. *Edith Wharton: A Biography*. New York: Harper & Row, 1975.

Limerick, Patricia Nelson. *The Legacy of Conquest: The Unbroken Past of the American West*. New York: W.W. Norton, 1987.

Limón, José. *American Encounters: Greater Mexico, the United States, and the Erotics of Culture*. Boston: Beacon Press, 1998.

Lipset, Seymour Martin. *American Exceptionalism: A Double-Edged Sword*. New York: W.W. Norton, 1996.

Lipsitz, George. *The Possessive Investment in Whiteness: How White People Profit from Identity Politics*. Philadelphia: Temple University Press, 1998.

Lloyd, Brian. *Left Out: Pragmatism, Exceptionalism, and the Poverty of American*

Marxism, 1890–1922. Baltimore, Md.: Johns Hopkins University Press, 1997.

Loehlin, James. "'Top of the World, Ma': *Richard III* and Cinematic Convention." In *Shakespeare, the Movie: Popularizing the Plays on Film, TV, and Video*, edited by Lynda E. Boose and Richard Burt, 67–79. London: Routledge, 1997.

Madsen, Deborah L. *American Exceptionalism*. Jackson: University Press of Mississippi, 1998.

McCann, Sean. *Gumshoe America: Hard-Boiled Crime Fiction and the Rise and Fall of New Deal Liberalism*. Durham, N.C.: Duke University Press, 2001.

McEvoy-Levy, Siobhan. *American Exceptionalism and U.S. Foreign Policy: Public Diplomacy at the End of the Cold War*. New York: Palgrave, 2001.

Mensh, Elaine, and Harry Mensh. *Black, White, and Huckleberry Finn: Re-Imagining the American Dream*. Tuscaloosa: University of Alabama Press, 2000.

Michie, Helena, and Robyn R. Warhol. "Twelve-Step Teleology: Narratives of Recovery/ Recovery as Narrative." In *Getting a Life: Everyday Uses of Autobiography*, edited by Sidonie and Julia Watson Smith, 327–50. Minneapolis: University of Minnesota Press, 1996.

Miller, Jonathan. *The Afterlife of Plays*. San Diego, Calif.: San Diego State University Press, 1992.

———. *Subsequent Performances*. 1st American ed. New York: E. Sifton Books/ Viking, 1986.

Miller, Perry. *Errand into the Wilderness*. New York: Harper & Row, 1964.

———. *Nature's Nation*. Cambridge, Mass.: Harvard University Press, 1967.

Montag, Warren. "The Universalization of Whiteness: Racism and Enlightenment." In Hill, *Whiteness: A Critical Reader*, 281–93.

Moreland, Richard C. *Learning from Difference: Teaching Morrison, Twain, Ellison, and Eliot*. Columbus: Ohio State University Press, 1999.

Morrison, Toni. *Playing in the Dark: Whiteness and the Literary Imagination*. New York: Vintage Books, 1993.

———. "This Amazing, Troubling Book." In *Adventures of Huckleberry Finn: An Authoritative Text, Contexts and Sources, Criticism*, edited by Thomas Cooley, 385–92. New York: Norton, 1999.

Murfin, Ross, and Supriyia M. Ray. *The Bedford Glossary of Critical and Literary Terms*. Boston: Bedford Books, 1997.

Naylor, Gloria. "Mommy, What Does 'Nigger' Mean?" In *Between Worlds: A Reader, Rhetoric, and Handbook*, edited by Susan and Melinda Barth Bachmann, 234–37. New York: HarperCollins College Publishers, 1995.

Nelson, Dana D. *National Manhood: Capitalist Citizenship and the Imagined Fraternity of White Men*. Durham, N.C.: Duke University Press, 1998.

———. *The Word in Black and White: Reading "Race" in American Literature, 1638–1867*. New York: Oxford University Press, 1992.

Newfield, Christopher. *The Emerson Effect: Individualism and Submission in America*. Chicago: University of Chicago Press, 1996.

———. *Ivy and Industry: Business and the Making of the American University, 1880–1980*. Durham, N.C.: Duke University Press, 2003.

Newman, Karen, Jay Clayton, and Marianne Hirsch, eds. *Time and the Literary: Essays from the English Institute*. New York: Routledge, 2002.

O'Farrell, Mary Ann. *Telling Complexions: The Nineteenth-Century English Novel and the Blush.* Durham, N.C.: Duke University Press, 1997.

Packer, George. *Blood of the Liberals.* New York: Farrar Straus and Giroux, 2000.

Patell, Cyrus R. K. *Negative Liberties: Morrison, Pynchon, and the Problem of Liberal Ideology.* Durham N.C.: Duke University Press, 2001.

Peller, Gary. "Toward a Critical Cultural Pluralism: Progressive Alternatives to Mainstream Civil Rights Ideology." In *Critical Race Theory: The Key Writings That Formed the Movement,* edited by Kimberlé Crenshaw, 127–58. New York: New Press, 1995.

Perea, Juan F. "The Black/White Binary Paradigm of Race." In *Critical Race Theory: The Cutting Edge.* 2nd ed., edited by Richard Delgado and Jean Stefancic, 344–53. Philadelphia: Temple University Press, 2000.

Person, Leland. *Henry James and the Suspense of Masculinity.* Philadelphia: University of Pennsylvania Press, 2003.

Pettit, Arthur G., and Dennis E. Showalter. *Images of the Mexican American in Fiction and Film.* College Station: Texas A&M University Press, 1980.

Poirier, Richard. *A World Elsewhere: The Place of Style in American Literature.* New York: Oxford University Press, 1966.

Poovey, Mary. "Creative Criticism and the Problem of Objectivity." *Narrative* 8, no. 2 (2000): 109–33.

Price, Alan. *The End of the Age of Innocence: Edith Wharton and the First World War.* New York: St. Martin's, 1996.

Quirk, Tom. *Coming to Grips with Huckleberry Finn: Essays on a Book, a Boy, and a Man.* Columbia: University of Missouri Press, 1993.

Richard, Alfred Charles. *The Hispanic Image on the Silver Screen: An Interpretive Filmography from Silents into Sound, 1898–1935.* New York: Greenwood Press, 1992.

Rivera, John-Michael. "Embodying the Public Sphere: The Mexican Question and Elite Mexican American Literary and Political Culture at the Turn of the Century." PhD dissertation, University of Texas at Austin, 2000.

Robbins, Bruce. "The Sweatshop Sublime." *PMLA* 117, no. 1 (2002): 84–97.

Robinson, Cecil. *Mexico and the Hispanic Southwest in American Literature: Revised from With the Ears of Strangers.* Tucson: University of Arizona Press, 1977.

Robinson, Sally. *Marked Men: White Masculinity in Crisis.* New York: Columbia University Press, 2000.

Roediger, David R. *The Wages of Whiteness: Race and the Making of the American Working Class.* London: Verso, 1991.

Rorty, Richard. *Achieving Our Country: Leftist Thought in Twentieth-Century America.* Cambridge, Mass.: Harvard University Press, 1998.

———. *Contingency, Irony, and Solidarity.* Cambridge: Cambridge University Press, 1989.

———. *Hope in Place of Knowledge: The Pragmatics Tradition in Philosophy.* Taipei, Taiwan: Academia Sinica, 1999.

Ross, Dorothy. "Liberalism and American Exceptionalism." *Intellectual History Newsletter* 24 (2002): 72–83.

Rowe, John Carlos. *The Other Henry James.* Durham, N.C.: Duke University Press, 1998.

———. The Politics of Innocence in Henry James's *The American.*" In *New Essays on the American,* edited by Martha Banta, 69–98. Cambridge: Cambridge University Press, 1987.

———. "The Politics of the Uncanny: Newman's Fate in *The American.*" *Henry James Review* 8, no. 2 (1987): 79–90.

Ryan, Alan. "Liberal Political Theory: Always Unpopular." *Intellectual History Newsletter* 24 (2002): 4–13.

Said, Edward W. "Opponents, Audiences, Constituencies, and Community." In *The Politics of Interpretation,* edited by W. J. T. Mitchell, 7–32. Chicago: University of Chicago Press, 1982.

Salecl, Renata. *(Per)Versions of Love and Hate.* London: Verso, 1998.

Samuels, Robert. *Writing Prejudices: The Psychoanalysis and Pedagogy of Discrimination from Shakespeare to Toni Morrison.* Albany: State University of New York Press, 2000.

Sánchez-Eppler, Karen. *Touching Liberty: Abolition, Feminism, and the Politics of the Body.* Berkeley: University of California Press, 1993.

Savran, David. *Taking It like a Man: White Masculinity, Masochism, and Contemporary American Culture.* Princeton, N.J.: Princeton University Press, 1998.

Schafer, Byron E., ed. *Is America Different?: A New Look at American Exceptionalism.* Oxford: Oxford University Press, 1991.

Sedgwick, Eve Kosofsy. *Epistemology of the Closet.* Berkeley: University of California Press, 1990.

Seltzer, Mark. *Bodies and Machines.* New York: Routledge, 1992.

———. *Henry James and the Art of Power.* Ithaca, N.Y.: Cornell University Press, 1984.

Seshadri-Crooks, Kalpana. *Desiring Whiteness: A Lacanian Analysis of Race.* London: Routledge, 2000.

Shulman, George. "Hope and American Politics." *Raritan* 21, no. 3 (2002): 1–19.

Silverman, Kaja. *Male Subjectivity at the Margins.* New York: Routledge, 1992.

Simon, Richard Keller. *Trash Culture: Popular Culture and the Great Tradition.* Berkeley and Los Angeles: University of California Press, 1999.

Simpson, David. "The Case for 'Antiquarian History.'" *SubStance* 28, no. 1 (1999): 5–15.

Smiley, Jane. "Say It Ain't So, Huck: Second Thoughts on Twain's 'Masterpiece.'" *Harper's Magazine.* January 1996, 61–67.

Smith, David L. "Huck, Jim, and American Racial Discourse." In Leonard, Tenney, and Davis, eds., *Satire or Evasion,* 103–20.

Smith, Robert Charles. *Racism in the Post–Civil Rights Era: Now You See It, Now You Don't.* Albany: State University of New York Press, 1995.

Spillers, Hortense. "'All the Things You Could Be by Now, If Sigmund Freud's Wife Was Your Mother': Psychoanalysis and Race." In *Female Subjects in Black and White: Race, Psychoanalysis, Feminism,* edited by Elizabeth Abel, Barbara Christian, and Helene Moglen, 135–58. Berkeley and Los Angeles: University of California Press, 1997.

———. "The Tragic Mulatta: Neither/nor—Toward an Alternative Model." In *The Difference Within: Feminism and Critical Theory,* edited by Elizabeth Meese and Alice Parker, 147–59. Philadelphia: J. Benjamins, 1989.

Stewart, Suzanne R. *Sublime Surrender: Male Masochism at the Fin-de-Siècle.* Ithaca, N.Y.: Cornell University Press, 1998.

Stokes, Mason Boyd. *The Color of Sex: Whiteness, Heterosexuality, and the Fictions of White Supremacy.* Durham, N.C.: Duke University Press, 2001.

Sundquist, Eric J. *To Wake the Nations: Race in the Making of American Literature.* Cambridge, Mass.: Harvard University Press, 1993.

Szalay, Michael. *New Deal Modernism: American Literature and the Invention of the Welfare State.* Durham, N.C.: Duke University Press, 2000.

Trilling, Lionel. *The Liberal Imagination.* New York: Doubleday & Company, 1950.

Trumpener, Katie, and James M. Nyce. "The Recovered Fragments: Archeological and Anthropological Perspectives in Edith Wharton's *The Age of Innocence.*" In *Literary Anthropology,* edited by Fernando Poyatos, 161–69. Philadelphia: John Benjamin, 1988.

Turner, Frederick Jackson. *The Frontier in American History.* New York: Henry Holt and Company, 1921. Accessed in electronic format at http://xroadvirginia.edu/~HYPE/TURNER..

Twain, Mark. *Adventures of Huckleberry Finn: An Authoritative Text, Contexts and Sources, Criticism.* 3rd ed., edited by Thomas Cooley. New York: Norton, 1999.

———. *Adventures of Huckleberry Finn: A Case Study in Critical Controversy.* Edited by Gerald Graff and James Phelan. Boston: Bedford St. Martins, 1995.

Wagner-Martin, Linda. *The Age of Innocence: A Novel of Ironic Nostalgia.* New York: Twayne Publishers, 1996.

Walzer, Michael. "Political Action: The Problem of Dirty Hands." In *War and Moral Responsibility,* edited by Marshall Cohen, Thomas Nagel, and Thomas Scanlon, 62–82. Princeton, N.J.: Princeton University Press, 1974,

Wallace, John H. "The Case against *Huck Finn.*" In Leonard, Tenney, and Davis, eds., *Satire or Evasion,* 16–24.

Warren, Kenneth W. *Black and White Strangers: Race and American Literary Realism.* Chicago: University of Chicago Press, 1993.

Wharton, Edith. *The Age of Innocence.* Orig. published 1921. Ontario, Canada: Broadview Press, 2002.

———. "*Autre Temps . . .* " In *Edith Wharton, Roman Fever and Other Stories.* Edited by Cynthia Griffin Wolff. New York: Collier Books, 1987.

———. *A Backward Glance.* Orig. published 1935. New York: Charles Scribner's Sons, 1964.

———. *The Mother's Recompense.* Orig. published 1925. New York: Simon & Schuster, 1986.

Wiegman, Robyn. *American Anatomies: Theorizing Race and Gender.* Durham, N.C.: Duke University Press, 1995.

———. "Whiteness Studies and the Paradox of Particularity." *Boundary 2: An International Journal of Literature and Culture* 26, no. 3 (1999): 115–49.

Williams, Kenny. "*Adventures of Huckleberry Finn,* or, Mark Twain's Racial Ambiguity." In Leonard, Tenney, and Davis, eds., *Satire or Evasion,* 228–38.

Williams, Linda. *Playing the Race Card: Melodramas of Black and White from Uncle Tom to O. J. Simpson.* Princeton, N.J.: Princeton University Press, 2001.

Williams, Patricia J. "Diary of a Mad Law Professor." *The Nation* (online edition), posted April 18, 2002 (May 6, 2002 issue).http://www.thenation.com/doc.rem.mhtml?; =2002050685=williams.

———. *The Rooster's Egg.* Cambridge, Mass.: Harvard University Press, 1995.

Williams, Raymond. *Marxism and Literature.* Oxford: Oxford University Press, 1977.

Winthrop, John. "A Model of Christian Charity." In *The Norton Anthology of American Literature,* edited by Nina Baym, 95–106. New York: W.W. Norton & Company, 2003.

Woodard, Helena. *African-British Writings in the Eighteenth Century: The Politics of Race and Reason.* Westport, Conn.: Greenwood Press, 1999.

Zizek, Slavoj. "Love Thy Neighbor? No, Thanks." In *The Psychoanalysis of Race,* edited by Christopher Lane, 154–75. New York: Columbia University Press, 1998.

INDEX

Aanerud, Rebecca, 144n6
Adams, David Keith, 147n3
Adventures of Huckleberry Finn
(Twain), 9, 41, 48–50, 53, 120. *See*
also under "nigger"; pedagogy
affirmative action: and diversity, 22,
27–28, 42, 50; and higher education, 18; and law, 1, 14–16; and
rationality, 26; and temporality,
14–16. See also *Hopwood v. Texas*
African-Americans, 58, 61. See also
under *Awakening, The; Traffic*
Age of Innocence, The (Wharton), 10,
11, 113, 116; and ethnography,
114, 115; fantasy in, 118–20,
122–25, 126, 129, 130–31 (*see also*
utopian thought); and First World
War, 128–29, 130; gender and sex
in, 114–15, 117–18, 119; as historical fiction, 126–30. *See also*
innocence
Alonzo, Juan, 144n3
American, The (James), 10, 98; "good
fellow wronged" in, 95, 97–98,
99–100, 102, 105–6; freedom the-
matized in, 103; masculinity in,
97, 103, 104; preface to, 105, 107;
race in, 104, 105
American exceptionalism, 94, 95, 97,
102, 105, 107, 112, 120, 147n1,
147n3
American Renaissance, 4
Ammons, Elizabeth, 62, 63
anachronism, 3. *See also* critical presentism
Arac, Jonathan, 49
Armistead, Samuel G., 144n6
Atkinson, Richard C., 32, 33, 34
Atlanta Constitution, 45
"*Autre Temps . . .*" (Wharton), 1, 7, 9,

22, 32, 96, 123; blushing in, 27,
39–40; "cutting" in, 25, 41; fixation on the past in, 24; liberalism
in, 23; and pedagogy, 2–3; social
exclusion in, 7, 39
Awakening, The (Chopin), 58, 60, 83,
89; African Americans in, 62–63,
65; Creole culture in, 68; female
sexuality in, 62–63, 64–65, 68;
and feminism, 60, 68; masculinity
in, 64, 67, 68; Mexico and
Mexicanism in, 63, 64–67, 68;
narrative voice in, 69; New Orleans
in, 65, 66; "old world" whiteness
in, 69–70, 87; suicide in, 68

Back to the Future, 139n4
Backward Glance, A (Wharton), 129
Bakke v. University of California,
138n3
Banta, Martha, 5
Barrish, Phillip, 137n4
Barton, Sabrina, 146n12
"Beatrice Palmato" (Wharton), 40
Beecher, Catherine, 94
Bell, Michael Davitt, 148n16
Benjamin, Walter, 19, 109
Bentley, Nancy, 149n24
Bercovitch, Sacvan, 137n2, 147n1
Berlant, Lauren, 11, 108–9, 110, 111,
113, 120, 121, 126, 148n4
Berman, Russel, 19
Birnbaum, Michelle, 63, 144n6
Birth of a Nation, 79, 80, 82, 83
Bloch, Ruth H., 14
Bogdanov, Michael, 21
Bond, Julian, 45
Born, Daniel, 111, 125, 149n12
Boston Globe, 45
Bremen, Brian, 148n14